In the Shadow of the Big Top

In the Shadow of the Big Top

The Life of Ringling's Unlikely Circus Savior

Maureen Brunsdale

ROWMAN & LITTLEFIELD
Lanham • Boulder • New York • London

Published by Rowman & Littlefield
An imprint of The Rowman & Littlefield Publishing Group, Inc.
4501 Forbes Boulevard, Suite 200, Lanham, Maryland 20706
www.rowman.com

86-90 Paul Street, London EC2A 4NE, United Kingdom

British Library Cataloguing in Publication Information Available

Library of Congress Cataloging-in-Publication Data

Names: Brunsdale, Maureen, author.
Title: In the shadow of the big top : the life of Ringling's unlikely circus savior / Maureen Brunsdale.
Description: Lanham, Maryland : Rowman & Littlefield, 2023. | Includes bibliographical references and index. | Summary: "The first-ever biography of Art Concello, one of the world's greatest trapeze artists and circus businessmen, this book goes beyond the showmanship displayed in the ring to reveal the inner workings of the circus that could both thrill a crowd and make incredible money"—Provided by publisher.
Identifiers: LCCN 2022035777 (print) | LCCN 2022035778 (ebook) | ISBN 9781538172100 (cloth) | ISBN 9781538172117 (epub)
Subjects: LCSH: Concello, Art (Arthur M.), 1911–2001. | Ringling Brothers Barnum and Bailey Combined Shows—History. | Circus—United States—History. | Circus—Economic aspects. | Aerialists—United States—Biography.
Classification: LCC GV1811.C59 B78 2023 (print) | LCC GV1811.C59 (ebook) | DDC 791.3092 [B] —dc23/eng/20221013
LC record available at https://lccn.loc.gov/2022035777
LC ebook record available at https://lccn.loc.gov/2022035778

This book is dedicated to my father and twin sister:
the J.E.B.s in my life who inspire, provoke,
and encourage improvement and who, by doing so,
make the world a better place.

Contents

Acknowledgments

Books are rarely written alone, and this one is no exception. Steve Gossard first told me about Bloomington's truant turned executive, Arthur M. Concello, in 2008. Fred Dahlinger stoked my curiosity, Don Raycraft fanned the flames, and Mort Gamble brought the words. Fred D. Pfening III questioned everything and, in doing so, taught me more than I thought possible.

Mort died. Then COVID-19 hit. Grounded by my colleague/friend/investigator extraordinaire Mark Schmitt as well as a core of friends who put up with lots of conversations skirting the perimeter of circus rings, I wrote. Encouraged by Jim Dexheimer, the North and Ringling family historian, as well as assisted by Pete Shrake, Circus World's librarian and archivist, and Kathleen Messier, assistant archivist of the Roman Catholic Diocese of Burlington, Vermont, the manuscript grew.

Members of the Circus Historical Society and Circus Fans Association of America gave interviews and guided me to others, who helped me gain a clearer understanding of the enigmatic man and his wife Antoinette. Expert flyers, show girls, clowns, caretakers, workingmen, and show owners—too many to name, but they're all in my heart—shared perspectives and insights. The flyers, starting with Tony Steele and Al Light and, later, with Richie Gaona and so many, many others, welcomed and instructed me, never seeming to tire of my questions.

Many times, I wanted to quit. Friends and family urged me to continue polishing the manuscript. Help for that came from Paul Slansky, whose daughter Grace flies on the trapeze. That seemed a sign.

The relentless pandemic turned my home into my office and space filled with boxes of photocopies of articles and other primary source materials. Charts, photographs, and a color-coded timeline decorated the walls. A growling, Concello-esque "Get it right, kid!" invaded my dreams. I have tried my best to do so.

To all these people and the fabulous folks at Rowman & Littlefield, I give my thanks. Most especially, gratitude goes to my family for their support and love.

Introduction

> "This fellow Concello is a shrewd conniving little fellow and has made quite a bit of money, I understand."[1]
>
> —Zack Terrell

John Ricketts presented the first circus in America in 1793. Humble in its origins and heavy in equestrian feats, this entertaining spectacle evolved in thousands of ways over the coming centuries. Starting in 1825, tents were introduced. By 1872 railroads made it possible for larger aggregations to skip small towns to play in bigger markets, increasing revenue. Competition led to larger circuses as show owners jockeyed to give the audience as much as (if not more than) they wanted. Two-ring circuses appeared in 1873; three ringers debuted in 1881. Shows brought exotic animals, sideshows, technological innovations, acrobats, clowns, riders, jugglers, wire walkers, and scores of other types of performers. Thousands of circuses were conceived, born, and often died—in quick succession—along the tanbark trail, due to a weak economy, poor business plans, lack of experience, and the weather.

Ringling Bros. and Barnum & Bailey Circus was The Greatest Show on Earth for the millions who went to see their productions. It was a circus with small-town roots. Five brothers named Ringling took out a little wagon show that was organized in 1884 in Baraboo, Wisconsin, a backwater town. Reinvesting profits annually, they made the leap to rail in 1890, which raised both their costs and income. In the first decade of the twentieth century, the number of tented entertainment shows was around one hundred, an indication of their tremendous popularity. Barnum & Bailey had been Ringling's major competitor. During the Panic of 1907, the Ringlings purchased their rival to become kings of the circus world. They ran their circuses as separate entities until 1919, when they combined to become Ringling Bros. and Barnum & Bailey Circus.

John Ringling outlived all his brothers. After making lots of money in the 1920s, he purchased the American Circus Corporation, his biggest rival, in September 1929. His circuses began having financial trouble starting in 1930 because of the Great Depression. Nevertheless, in 1932 The Greatest Show on Earth was still by far the biggest one operating. It moved on about ninety railcars and used a tent that held ten thousand people. The next largest show used thirty cars with thousands fewer customers under its canvas.

This is the world into which Arthur M. Concello landed. The son of a railroad foreman, he grew up in an eight-room home that once served as a boardinghouse smack-dab in the middle of corn country. For someone who entered life as a nobody, he sure turned into a somebody. He first used his muscles and then his brains, both of which he had in abundance, to make the transformation.

Art always looked forward, never back. The past didn't make him money, but the future did. There were lots of ways to make extra money in a circus. Some took up barbering. Others repaired watches or acted as the circus's mailman. Concello's side hustle was moneylending, which he started doing at the tender age of twenty. He made loans to ringmasters, circus producers, fellow performers, and workingmen. By 1943, when he was thirty-two, he told an investigator who came to interview him about missing show properties that in the last few years, he had made $50,000 annually. What he didn't tell the man was *how* he did so.

Concello had eyes everywhere. Some called his network of close contacts and confidants the Sneeze Mob. As for his own steel-gray eyes, they witnessed what happened to arguably the greatest trapeze flyer of all time, Alfredo Codona. After establishing himself as without an equal in the air, Codona tried to run a winter show in Mexico in 1929. It failed after a few weeks. Ultimately and shockingly, less than ten years later, he committed murder/suicide after an injury forced him to the ground. Concello, who could easily execute the most dangerous tricks Codona was known for, understood the risks of his chosen profession. He knew money could be made doing it, but he wanted more. The taste of control he got from having people indebted to him, a nothing from the corn capital of the Midwest, was both delicious and addictive.

Not satisfied with the money earned by flying, he moved into management. Over the course of his career, Concello brought trapeze acts and circuses to all corners of the world—from Europe to the Soviet Union, from South America to Australia. He ran the Ringling Bros. and Barnum & Bailey Circus when it was a tented titan and then transformed it into an indoor arena behemoth. As he climbed the ladder of success, he interacted with a cavalcade of characters, including the biggest names in entertainment, like Clyde Beatty and Cecil B. DeMille. He also worked with men like Jimmy Hoffa, a man who, like him, preferred to rule his world from the shadows. Besides, for Concello, most of it was for Antoinette, whom he married when they were both teenagers and relatively new to show business. Her climb to the top was every bit as interesting, dangerous, and provocative.

Chapter 1

Truant and Prodigy

1911–1929

"Jesus Christ, everything is fun when you're eighteen!"[1]

—Art Concello

Mornings started early in the Vasconcellos' house. Arthur D., "Papa Vas," was up before the roosters to make it to his job as a machinist at Bloomington's Chicago and Alton Railroad shops, located a few blocks from his westside home. His wife Mattie was up early, too, making coffee for the handful of men boarding with them and getting her children from her first marriage, Grace and Joseph, ready to go to high school. Her youngest son, Artie, never seemed to struggle in the mornings. He woke up full of spirit and ready to go anywhere—except school. He had things to do and places to go! Why should he slow down enough to sit at a desk, even if that desk was just a four-minute walk from his house at 801 W. Locust Street?

Edwards School, the institution his parents thought their youngest attended regularly, was on Market Street. Up the road a piece (another four-minute walk but, this time, to the east) was the high school on Washington Street they hoped he would attend.

In a few years, Bloomington would emerge as a center for the insurance industry, but right now, in the months leading up to America's entry into World War I, its role as the county seat made it a hub for politicians past, present, and future. Abraham Lincoln first visited Bloomington in 1837, when he was a young attorney trying cases in Illinois's eighth judicial circuit. The friends he made there, Jesse Fell and David Davis, became pivotal backers for his rise to the presidency. Adlai Stevenson attended Bloomington's Illinois Wesleyan University before being selected as the nation's twenty-third vice president under Grover Cleveland. After his service to the country, he returned to town where he could watch his grandson, who was also his namesake, grow. Little did he know that the boy, Adlai Stevenson II, would become governor of Illinois, the Democratic Party nominee for president twice, and the US Ambassador to the United Nations, all while calling Bloomington his hometown.

The Evergreen City, as Bloomington was then known—135 miles from Chicago and 160 miles from St. Louis—was surrounded by rich soil tilled and drained to produce crops that consistently made farmers more money than it cost to plant them. Merchants pulled visitors from a fifty-mile radius to its bustling downtown, which boasted thirty blocks of buildings along its twelve busiest streets.[2]

The iron horse connecting the two midwestern hubs was the Chicago and Alton Railroad, whose shops on the west side supported a corps of nearly 1,800 skilled and semi-skilled workingmen. The area surrounding the shops became its own community, with businesses designed to support the needs of railroad employees and their families. A hotel, a cigar factory, and even a library funded by an independent employees' association were situated on the west side. The library offered twenty daily newspapers and three hundred weekly or monthly magazines to its patrons, whose native tongues were German, Russian, French, Swedish, Portuguese, and English.

Along with being ethnically diverse, the city of nearly twenty-five thousand people hosted a wide range of attractions. Vaudeville theaters sprinkled the downtown district. Big name entertainers, like the Marx Brothers and Mae West, played Bloomington—often immediately before (or after) they played Peoria, a city thirty-eight miles to the northwest. Circuses often drew larger audiences than vaudeville theaters and Bloomington had been providing a practice playground for the biggest stars under the white tops for decades. Circus stars could become celebrities in their own right and, therefore, they could often command huge salaries. This was, after all, a time when Americans were fascinated with movie stars like Mary Pickford, Charlie Chaplin, Lillian and Dorothy Gish, and Douglas Fairbanks. While rural and small-town America could only dream of seeing those luminaries in person, circus celebrities traveled the nation, stopping at nearby cities, making their stars shine brighter. "There is a glamour about circus," said Texas's *Kerrville Times* in 1931, "which clothes all of its people with a tinge of romance. Perhaps it is because most of us had our first experience with the world of entertainment at the circus. At any rate, circus performers always seem, to most people, to be more interesting than mere movie actors and theatrical stars."[3]

By the turn of the twentieth century, flying trapeze acts were among the most popular and highest status acts in circuses, replacing equestrians and talking clowns, who had been the premier routines since the 1790s. Trapeze performers enjoyed some of the highest salaries and often endorsed products of the day in print advertisements. Their popularity began with Jules Leotard, who invented the flying trapeze routine. His debut performance, above the heads of spectators in Paris's Cirque Napoleon in 1859, skyrocketed its popularity and transformed it from an exercise apparatus to one used for entertaining.

By 1875, I. P. Fell, Jesse Fell's nephew, opened the first gymnasium in Bloomington at the western corner of East and Washington streets and installed a fly bar there.[4] Brothers Fred and Howard Greene demonstrated such a daring acrobatic proficiency that the local newspaper proclaimed them "doing most of the feats now in vogue among the professionals."[5] That's all they needed to hear. Within a few years, they were touring the world with their act while other Bloomington boys worked out on the riggings now sprinkled around town.

Aerial routines began with relatively simple tricks, with trade names like "bird's nest," "seat jump," and "plange." Then came the more spectacular stunts like the midair or passing leap, which never failed to impress audiences as the catcher caught one performer, exchanged him or her for another midair, and then both flyers returned to the starting platform (called a pedestal board) via the same bar. The biggest trick, which was also known as the killer trick because so few could do it and so many died trying, was the triple somersault. To do it, a flyer made three revolutions after leaving his bar and before being caught by the fellow hanging head down about twenty-five feet away, while also thirty or so feet above the ground.

Press agents like the loquacious Dexter Fellows adored visiting newsrooms to tout the aerial acts of the circus that employed them. He provided alluring verbiage like, "Desperately dangerous displays of unrivaled aerialism . . . the greatest high-air gymnasts in the world in single, double and triple flying somersaults passing each other in mid-air, catching one another by the hands or feet, playfully tossing one performer to the waiting hands of another across a yawning chasm, and numberless other astonishing and audacious feats of finished flight and reckless rarity."[6] The perceived effortlessness of human flight, along with its inherent speed and danger, tantalized the throngs who paid to see feats of strength and grace performed under canvas tops. Circus owners knew trapeze acts drew audiences to their shows and often placed the aerial acts at the end of the performance, so that all other acts built excitement for them.

Learning to fly took physical discipline and raw courage. For some, climbing up a rope ladder to a board thirty feet above the ground ended their careers before they started. Once up there, they found grabbing the fly bar in front and looking down to a net filled with holes sometimes instilled a catatonic state. If the bar was grasped, then there was the act of letting go, of falling into that net. While it looked to be as easy as falling into a feather bed, in reality, it could mean a broken neck or even death if not done correctly. If the courage to do all that could be called upon repeatedly, there were yet more challenges to deal with—namely, the legendary physical demands of flying, which produced pulled or dislocated shoulders, torn muscles, net burns, and abrasions.

By the dawn of the twentieth century, Bloomington was known as the Trapeze Capital of the World because so many of its stars trained there. Less than two decades later, there were two main trapeze schools in town: the Young Men's Christian Association (YMCA or Y), across the street from where the first gymnasium was located, and the Eddie Ward barn. These facilities and the men who operated them shaped young Artie's character.

Shortly after the turn of the century, years before Artie came into the world, Artie's father followed his brother Martin to work for the railroad in Bloomington, just over one hundred miles from their birthplace in Jacksonville, Illinois. These young men of Portuguese descent roomed not far from the railroad shops and one block away from John and Mattie Killian's eight-room boardinghouse. Within months of John Killian's death in 1909—a plasterer, he struggled with illness for years—Mattie wed Arthur and welcomed him into her house. Following the machinist apprenticeship path, Arthur D. and his pregnant wife moved to Washington state. There he joined his brother Howard in working for the Great Northern Railway in Spokane. When his stint with Great Northern was completed, he went to work for the Oregon Railroad and Navigation Company in Starbuck, Washington. On March 25, 1911, Arthur Marshall Vasconcellos was born there to Papa Vas and Mattie. By November, the family moved back to their central Illinois home, where Arthur resumed working for the Chicago & Alton Railroad Shops as a journeyman machinist.[7]

In 1916, they enrolled five-year-old Artie in Edwards School. A couple of years later, in early November 1919, new truancy laws took effect in the county, demanding that children between the ages of seven and sixteen attend school. Photographs of Artie from the time he was eight weeks old to his high school yearbooks show a youngster of exceptional energy—always looking elsewhere, pondering something other than the camera perched in front of him—and with phenomenal academic disinterest. "He was quick, but unprepared, impatient with an educational system so ceremoniously devoted to the ghosts of departed foreign generals."[8] Yet he did make the honor roll, albeit in the Sunday school lessons taught in his father's church.[9]

As ten-year-old Artie perfected truancy on the streets of Bloomington, smoking cigars likely procured from the factory nearest his house, he came to the attention of C. D. Curtis, one of Bloomington's most influential athletic trainers. Curtis came to town in 1922 to work at the local Young Men's Christian Association as a coach and physical director. He was assisted by Chuck Holloway. One of the largest events they oversaw was the annual Y Circus, produced in the winter when professional circus performers were off the road. In exchange for using the facility during the off-season, these performers provided the bulk of entertainment pro bono for the Y's circus, which served as a fundraiser. While the Y Circus was their largest event, their greatest responsibility was rehabilitating boys on their way to nowhere good.

One day (it's easy to suppose it was a school day) when he was eleven, Artie visited the Y and watched Curtis working out on the rigging. Slight of build but insatiably curious, the boy stuck around long enough to ask if there was any money to be had in doing such a thing. Knowing Bloomington's record for producing high-profile and prosperous trapeze troupes, Curtis replied by first telling the boy with the ever-present cigar about the dangers of smoking. About the trapeze, he told him if he were good enough, "it's a gold mine."[10] Artie forgot everything Curtis said except for the part about gold.

From that point forward, he applied himself to the fun of flying. He wasn't alone in this endeavor. Boys like Harold "Tuffy" Genders, Elden Day, Eldred "Red" Sleeter, and Wayne Larey also worked out on the Y's rigging. All were in the right place at the right time for their aspiring careers. The town had been the cradle for trapeze acts for decades, and riggings could be found scattered throughout it—in theaters, in backyards, at the Y, and in a barn on the eastern outskirts of town owned by the Flying Wards, a well-known aerial troupe from Bloomington.

Eddie Ward, the catcher and manager for that troupe, furnished flying acts for the big railroad shows owned by the American Circus Corporation, the main competitor in the 1920s to the Ringling Bros. and Barnum & Bailey Circus. Constructed in 1915 on a ten-acre lot, the barn was seventy-seven feet long and more importantly, with a lowered floor, the building achieved a height of nearly forty feet—approximately the same distance from the ground to the top of a circus tent. Outfitted with ropes and rigging, a handmade net almost as wide as the building itself, and a ring that permitted rehearsals, the barn was a fully equipped school for many acts originating in Bloomington. Known commonly as the Farm, the barn became important as a trapeze landmark, putting performers in the air and Bloomington on the show-business map. The town's newspaper commented that Bloomington hosted more circus and theatrical performers than any other city of its size in the country.[11] The fact that Artie grew up in this town, this trapeze capital, was not the first or only time fate smiled on the rascally youth.

The Farm was built by Eddie Ward, who started working two jobs—one as a butcher boy in a meat market, the other as a newspaper boy—at the age of seven to help support his family. His major career break came in 1903, when he and his sister Jennie were working their double trapeze act at an Atlanta, Illinois, fair. Unlike a flying-return act where the flyer left a pedestal board via the fly bar, a double trapeze employed two parallel vertical ropes on which two horizontal bars were placed, one about ten feet below the other, with no safety net below. The appeal was the speed with which they performed. Often enough, they fell.

Eddie, who performed as the catcher on the lower bar for his sister on the upper one, explained the transition for their troupe from double trapeze to flying trapeze: "I got to studying these falls, generally from a hospital cot, and made up my mind there was no future in the straight [double] trapeze business. The salary was limited, the act was old."[12] With the addition of Jennie's husband, Alec Todd, and Eddie's wife, Mayme, they had the personnel necessary to build a flying-return trapeze act, which also used two bars, but they were widely separated. One was positioned about sixteen feet away from the pedestal board for a flyer—or a leaper as they were known in those days—to grab hold of while leaving that pedestal board. The other bar, about twenty-five feet away from the flyer's bar, was for the catcher to hang backward by his knees while preparing to lock wrists with the leaper coming toward him.

Eddie's barn was a training space for more than fifty boys and girls who wanted to learn the trapeze arts. He used a safety belt known as a "mechanic" to give students confidence once they graduated from handsprings on the ground to the fly bar thirty feet in the air. After learning to fall into the net correctly—always on the back or shoulders, not feet first, and never on the head—Ward worked on his pupils' timing. He taught his catchers to "go to the flyers"—yelling "hup" to the flyer when it was time for them to release the bar and reach for the wrists of the catcher.[13]

Word spread through Bloomington that C. D. Curtis had a natural talent working out on the Y's rigging. When Ward heard this, he made the short trip to see for himself. There Artie was, up on the pedestal board, taking the trapeze in his hands, flying off, and doing simple tricks with an unparalleled ease. Ward knew he wanted the youngster as one of his own, even though the kid had a reputation for getting into trouble. He believed he could train Artie and use him in one of the many Ward flying acts he booked with the American Circus Corporation. Soon, Artie transferred from working out primarily downtown to training with other flyers in Ward's gymnasium.

By the mid-1920s, Ward had twenty-six pupils flying professionally in one of three troupes. Some of the performers in Flying Ward troupes one and two and the Ward-Kimball troupe were Harold Voise, Eileen Sullivan, the Hubbell sisters, Mickey Comeau, Lester Thomas, Herb Fleming, Paul and Irene Sullivan, and Eddie's wife, Mayme Ward. Dozens more were learning back in Bloomington, with some striving to become circus stars on the flying trapeze; others were more inspired by the possibility of making really good bank.

The accumulation of money was important to Artie. His father's hourly pay was seventy-five cents.[14] His weekly pay, thirty dollars, put his family in the second-lowest income bracket for 1927.[15] Listening to performers who came in from the road at the end of the season, Artie learned that he could be paid twenty-five dollars each week for his work as a Flying Ward, and there were always little ways for circus performers to earn more money ("cherry pie," in circus jargon). Some performers supplemented their income by making slop shoes to protect slippers from getting dirty on the lots, others barbered, some fixed watches, and others became loan sharks. Sure, he had to risk his life twice each day, but flying wasn't like school or work for him. It was exhilarating; it provided a means to see the world outside Bloomington, and just maybe, if he got good enough, he could earn much, much more.

Artie tried to enjoy school. He had joined the Manual Arts Club and had gone out for baseball and basketball (as a guard) in high school, but the lure of the road—and the money it promised—proved too much for him to continue his formal schooling. One evening, returning to his house (supposedly after a day at school but definitely after a session of trapeze training), he made a surprise announcement to his parents: he needed a pair of tights from Klemm's Department Store because, in the morning, he was going to join the Flying Wards.[16] It was 1927 and Art had just turned sixteen, the age when compulsory school attendance ceased.

Art was eager to take to the road as a Ward flyer, and Eddie was ready to use him. Ward placed him as one of the seven flyers in his Ward–Kimball troupe, which he booked with the Hagenbeck-Wallace Circus. Based out of Peru, Indiana, this first-class show travelled on thirty railcars and was managed by the rough, tough Danny Odom. Newspapers of the time printed the show's press releases, exaggerating that the circus carried one thousand performers, 750 horses, seventy-five clowns, and twenty-five performing elephants, and $75,000 was spent providing wardrobe for the two spectacles presented: "The Geisha" and "Glittering Glory." Clyde Beatty, an up-and-coming big-cat trainer, was touted to "subjugate twenty-nine lions, lionesses and tigers for twenty minutes" during each performance.[17] Its nineteen displays heavily featured animal acts in its three rings and were thrilling entertainment for children of all ages.

Art presented as an eager and talented trouper, ready to learn everything he could about the world under the white tops, a world so unlike anything in central Illinois. Over the course of the season, news of his aerial feats got mentioned in *The Billboard*, a trade paper known as the performers' bible. By June, his name had appeared twice, and in September the publication noted a reunion he had with his parents in Danville, Illinois.[18] In the times between the six or so minutes spent on the pedestal board and performing tricks, he watched, listened, and learned from those Wards who flew with him: Jessie, Irene, Elsie, Rose, Billy, and Jimmy, as well as, from a distance, Eddie Ward.

Jimmy Arbaugh was the manager of the act.[19] As such, it was Arbaugh who paid Artie the twenty-five dollars he earned each week as a member of the Ward–Kimball Troupe. Ward himself traveled with the Flying Wards on the corporation's flagship show, the Sells-Floto Circus.

Ward instilled in his flyers a respect for both gravity and catchers, saying that a flyer had to have the daring to take the leap but then, simply, had to obey the orders given to them by the catcher. It was the catcher who completed the trick. The catcher had to make decisions almost automatically.[20] As a catcher himself, he saw the advantage of training his students to catch first in order to understand the importance of timing tricks. As an entrepreneur, he anticipated the consequences of injuries. Training his students in both skills kept his acts operating.

Ward's prosperity grew from his years of commitment to his craft. He didn't tolerate students calling in sick or imbibing alcohol. Dating between the performers was also forbidden.[21] After he incorporated the Flying Ward troupe in 1923,[22] a national publication profiled him for readers clamoring for more information about the stars of the Tanbark Trail, noting that Ward's net worth was in the range of $150,000 (over $2.26 million in today's dollars)—a fact not lost on Artie.[23] Unlike his young protégé, Eddie's inspiration was not based on money. In 1927 he described what propelled him—and others—day after day: "I don't have to dress in tights and do stunts for the towners twice a day in all kinds of weather. But a fellow gets a kick out of doing any star act, in a circus or out of it. It's great stuff while it lasts."[24]

Now a young man of chiseled and rock-solid muscles, Art stood five feet, four inches tall, the perfect physique for a flyer. Ward knew his young employee was hooked on circus life after just his first summer trouping. "Once a flyer has had a season on the road, he generally becomes a confirmed trouper," Eddie told a journalist, adding that he rarely had a "first-of-May" (an industry phrase describing a trouper's inaugural tour) performer quit, "even after a long spell of rain and mud."[25] As for Art, he knew that he would go wherever Eddie sent him, wherever he was needed. He finished the season and planned to go back home to

Bloomington while the circus went back to its winter quarters in Peru, Indiana.

Upon his return, Artie surprisingly went back to school, likely at the behest of his mother. Meanwhile, Eddie booked two of his acts out with indoor circuses that performed during the winter mostly for Shrine Temples. As the Ward flyers worked where the Shriners and other service clubs booked them, Eddie's youngest flyer, still sixteen, fooled around in the Y's gym, playing with his boyhood friends Elden Day, Tuffy Genders, and Wayne Larey.

Artie, in his lavender-and-white-striped trunks over white tights, was easy to spot up in the rigging. Tuffy in all white, Elden in dark blue tights with green trunks over them, and Wayne all in yellow were up there with him. Serving as their catcher, Elden hung upside down on his catch trap, timing his swings to meet the flyers. On the ground were coaches C. D. Curtis, Montgomery Thorp, and Charles Holloway, men who worked with the boys several seasons at the YMCA. They had been watching Art since he was eleven, and they were awed when he turned a backward somersault the first time he attempted it.

It hardly seemed like work for the slenderly built, light-complexioned young man. It appeared that the sensation of flying itself, not the praise or applause earned, made flying interesting to him. "Art, there, has never been hurt," Coach Curtis told a newspaperman who had come to watch the youngsters spend their Tuesday and Friday nights in the downtown gym. "He's never had an accident, done everything, and doesn't know what fear is." Other spectators seemed incredulous, asking if incorrect falls to the net ever hurt the youngsters. Curtis responded, "Oh, it puts a few 'waffles' [referring to the wide weave of the net] in the backs occasionally, but never anything serious. There is, though, always the possibility of danger. For that reason aerial performances must be fearless. Art, there, is one of the best. He doesn't know what the word means."[26]

Failing a trick and landing in the net, Artie picked his way gingerly to the rope ladder so that he could climb back up to the pedestal board. "A little too early, Artie," called his coach from below. "Better try it again!" Another bystander chimed in with, "Pretty dangerous, isn't it?" Artie responded to that quip quickly, "Huh. Aw, that's nothing," before trying it once more, this time with the flair of success that inspired him to try yet another trick. As he swung out from the board, he dropped from the bar when he was squarely over the net. Hitting the net on his back, he bounced up to do a backward somersault and caught the fly bar with his toes. He hung there for a short while before releasing his toe hold and dropped head first to the net, only taking a fraction of the last second to tuck his head in so that he could land on his still developing broad shoulders.[27]

Curtis was seldom surprised by Artie's antics. By turning him over to Ward, Curtis believed he helped turn Artie from a devil on the path to St. Charles' State Home for Delinquent Boys, to a budding trapeze star. Mayme protested that the kid still had a reputation for getting into mischief, but the raw and eager talent Eddie saw quieted her concerns.

One thousand miles away, a girl was growing up who would forever influence Arthur. Named after the French queen, Marie Antoinette, her early life story was anything but regal.

The origins of a person's character, it could be argued, reach back at least two generations. Benjamin Comeau, a native of Sutton, Quebec, Canada, brought two hundred pounds of uncombed wool and six sheep pelts over the border (without paying duty) to sell in the United States for more money than he could get for them in Canada. He was caught and arrested.[28] When America began Prohibition in 1920, the potential for profiting from smuggling goods went up—so, too, did the risk. Benjamin's son, Toussaint, may have begun working in the silk and cotton mill, but what he recalled most vividly near the end of his century of living was the time he spent bootlegging. Most of the booze he hustled across to the United States came from Holland. John DeKuyper gin sold for $1.25 in Canada and $5.00 in the States. "I knew all the back roads and never once was caught. The highest amount I ever carried over was a $300 load," Comeau bragged. "This was sewed into a burlap sack and I carried it on my back."[29]

The man with the family history rich with risk may have already whet his appetite for it at the poker table, where the possibility of increasing—or losing—the family's income was real. By the turn of the century, Toussaint, sometimes called Mike, was a widower looking for easier ways to support himself and his family. Why shouldn't he join a friendly game with the boys after a hard week of work, whatever that work was?

Family lore has it that Mike, in his early forties, won a pubescent bride during such a poker game.[30] That bride, Jane Hudson, was, at fourteen, the same age as one of his daughters from his deceased wife Florence when they exchanged vows in Sutton, Quebec's St. Andre Catholic Church in 1902.[31] Children Joseph, Gertrude, Alma, Marie Antoinette, and Ernest joined the family before Toussaint and Jane celebrated their tenth anniversary.

With an employment picture always brighter in the next town (or a few towns over), the family moved a lot. Later in life, one of their children remembered 1910 as the year the family came across to the United States. Thereafter, they lived in a number of small New England towns like Swanton, Richford, Shelburn Springs, Newport Farms, and St. Albans. Around 1917, Toussaint heard of well-paying jobs in mills at Holyoke,[32] so they moved yet again.

Jane's oldest girl, Gertrude, became known as "Little Mike" or "Mickey" before she was three years old because she was so much like her father.[33] Taking risks and moving frequently became the norm for her too. She took a huge chance in 1920, shortly before her mother became pregnant with her seventh child, by running away from home to live with her grandmother in Canada. She returned to the States after a friend got her a job as a nanny in Massachusetts.[34] When that job dried up, she followed the path of so many French Canadian minors in the Northeast by joining the ranks of children working in woolen mills.

Mickey ditched her factory work one day to go investigate what was up with all the posters hanging throughout town. What she found was the Sells-Floto Circus. Tantalized by everything she saw on the circus lot, she ran back to her lodging to forge a note from her mother giving consent for her seventeen-year-old to join the show. After getting to the next town where the circus was presenting, Mickey did just that.[35] While hired as one of the show girls, she caught the eye of Eddie Ward, who was also employed there with his flying act. Impressed by her fearlessness on his rigging—and always looking for girls to train for his acts—he accepted her into his Flying Ward fold and at the end of the season, brought her with his act back to Bloomington.

Mickey eventually married animal trainer Allen King, but she continued trouping as a member of the Flying Wards. Of her first employer, Mickey boasted, "Mr. Ward was the greatest catcher of flyers there ever was, now, then, or anytime. He was stern, and by cracky, you did what he said to do."[36] One of the first things he trained her to do was the iron jaw act, where she was pulled into the air, suspended by her teeth at the end of a length of rigging over the ring, with no net beneath her. Once up there, she performed a routine to music.

Meanwhile, at her family's home and sometime after giving birth to Edwin in 1922, Jane fled Comeau to be with another man. Toussaint, now sixty-two, was left in Vermont, where he faced charges of non-support for the youngest of the twenty-one children he'd fathered.[37] In court, he claimed he worked hard to provide for his children, but Jane's abandonment forced him to place his younger children in the hands of different organizations. In 1924, Marie Antoinette and Edwin became wards of the Vermont Children's Aid Society. Most female orphans were sent either to families who could use them or put in vocational programs that trained them to be nursery maids.[38]

The plump, attractive brunette's life was anything but easy. Coming into the world as a fourteen-pound baby, Marie Antoinette was born April 22, 1910, in Sutton, Quebec.[39] Her mother, with five small children under foot, had little time to interact with each child individually. They did hear this nursery rhyme fall from her lips a lot, however:

"When I was a little girl about so high,
My mama used to take a stick and whip me to make me cry.
But now I'm big, and she can't do it!
Papa takes a stick and he goes right to it!"[40]

Orphaned, Antoinette (as she was known) came under the charge of Alice Hickox Gray, a social worker who saw her intellectual potential and worked hard to get her young charge into Burlington's Mount St. Mary's Academy that helped prepare young girls for lives spent in worthy ways—either in the family home or in the house of God. Mickey had joined an active and itinerant profession. But for Antoinette, life was dreadfully strict and stagnant. She sat through her Latin and Greek classes, dreaming of an escape from her classical course of study.

As if being left by both parents weren't enough, her French Canadian ethnicity brought Antoinette no reward from the Sisters of Mercy, nor from her classmates. *The Eugenics Survey of Vermont* summarized the prevailing Vermonters' low opinion of French Canadians during the 1925–1936 time period, stating: "You cannot believe a thing they tell you . . . they are a pretty genial folk but many have a pretty low I.Q. . . . socially of course they will never be recognized . . . They are a fine people—at a distance."[41]

A fellow student at the academy remembered Antoinette as an intelligent, promising student who loved athletics.[42] Indeed, she was a fierce competitor on the basketball court,[43] made the honor roll, and was just plain miserable. There was a seriousness to her that seemed to pervade her existence. There is no doubt the trauma of having parents abandon her to the care of others fueled her determination never to be left behind again.

Antoinette didn't see any family during her time at the convent school, but the Comeau sisters remained in touch via letters. Communicating with Mickey made Antoinette realize her own life could be different. Antoinette sent letters ahead, via general delivery, to the post office of the town where the circus was set to perform. The tone of Antoinette's letters alerted Mickey to the fact that her little sister hated her life at the convent school, even though she was on the cusp of taking her first-year vows to become a nun.[44] Before her graduation ceremony and after she'd earned a scholarship to attend the College of New Rochelle, Antoinette got a letter from Mickey, along with train fare to use so the sisters could reunite in Detroit.[45] On July 24, 1927, Antoinette traveled the five hundred plus miles alone by train, got to the circus lot, and loved what she had never before seen. She begged her older sister to get her a job, pleading: "You've got to, you've got to! If you don't get me a job, I won't go back. I'll jump in the river!"[46] Mickey went sobbing to Eddie, who granted her sister's wish to travel with the show. He even allowed her to earn a stipend of fifteen dollars each week.[47]

The circus exacts from all its personnel some contribution to the welfare of the organization. In circus parlance, this is referred to as being "generally useful." Antoinette, nicknamed Tony, pitched in to mend costumes and repair props, listening and watching all the while. She also worked with her sister on building her strength. Encouraged by Eddie, she learned a simple swinging-ladder act, and then she moved on to learn an iron-jaw routine. By the end of the summer, her natural athleticism had turned her body from plump to svelte. The trapeze, in motion with the gentle breeze that stirred the great canvas tent and its rigging as well as the bar that challenged a select few to climb upward, beckoned to Tony, too. She yearned to fly. After spending his lifetime hanging upside down and training flyers, Eddie knew she could do it, but before that, he had to teach her how to catch. She was trained to reach first for the wrists of her sister.

She hated it. "I was heartbroken! I never wanted to catch!"[48] But she was driven, determined to be invaluable. During training, her five-foot-five-inch, one hundred-and-twelve-pound frame developed the sturdy shoulders and strong arms of a trapeze performer. Her palms told the real story of the months spent training. "I'd been in a convent school for four years," she recounted to a reporter, "so it was quite a change—from calluses on my knees to calluses on my hands."[49]

She worked those hands so hard that she couldn't join the Wards on their 1927–1928 winter dates. Figuring out a bar routine with Billy Ward (who was no family relation to Eddie), without taking the time to trim their calluses with razor blades, left their hands a bloody mess.[50] A raging blood infection set in and put both her and Billy's arms in slings. They stood on the platform, watching the train carrying the Flying Wards away from Bloomington and to their engagement with what they later called the "indoor and out of money circus," the London Hippodrome Circus,[51] managed by American Circus Corporation executive R. M. Harvey. The train left without her this time, but never again.

It seems likely that Art first saw the exotic (for central Illinois) beauty, Antoinette, either at the Farm or in Bloomington's old coliseum. He probably heard Mickey talking about her little sister and saw firsthand Tony's drive and determination. Perhaps he was charmed by her fearlessness and vulnerability, her smarts and ambition. A romance definitely was budding. He and his boyhood chum Tuffy, a rough and tumble Golden Gloves boxer turned acrobat, took her on as a flyer—not catcher—trainee. Tony found Art's unquenchable confidence contagious and quickly moved on to learn increasingly complex tricks. "Art knows exactly when you're ready. All you've got to do is listen," she said of learning the art of flying from him. Of falling in love with him, she said, "Arthur and I were flirting around and playing around. We had to be very careful when Edward was around because he wouldn't allow that. We had to sneaky poo . . . I was green around the ears yet. I hadn't been out of the convent very long."[52] With an instinct for knowing exactly what a person was capable of—a talent that carried over into later phases of his career—Art molded Tony's natural athletic ability into the skill of a first-class trapeze artist.

Both prepared for the 1928 season. Prior to each new season, Ward wrote the managers of the shows looking for flying acts, proposing terms and requesting that contracts be drawn up for his troupes. Months before the opening of the 1928 Sells-Floto Circus season, Ward wrote manager Zack Terrell. Ward suggested placing Bloomington's Flying Fisher and Flying Sullivan acts for $1,500 for the show's big two-week opening date starting April 14 in Chicago's Coliseum.[53] Ward was going to book Artie in this act and knew his star would shine brighter in the coming season.

The innumerable hours spent in the YMCA and in Ward's rigging back at the Farm started to pay off for the young flyer. He had learned how to correct errors that left Eddie black-and-blue at best and unconscious at worst. He bruised Eddie's face and knocked him out of his catch trap after he neglected to spread his feet when going to Eddie feet first. Afterward, Ward didn't yell or cuss him out, he simply pointed to his face and asked his young flyer to try again.[54] The lesson was learned.

Ward booked his acts with the circuses and then assigned a performer to manage each act. That manager would get a payment each week, out of which came the sums due to each individual in the act. Art was given a raise of ten dollars a week as a Ward flyer in 1928. That raise was likely because he was now completing doubles, two-and-one-half somersaults, and the passing leap consistently.[55] A photo from that season shows the young performer standing ramrod straight, arms folded behind him, eyes leveled at the camera with cool confidence and a hint of contemptuousness that's sometimes associated with veteran show-business stars. He started signing some of those photos as Art Vass; no longer did he sign himself as Art Ward. In his second season as a circus performer, Art was not yet a veteran of the big top, but he was on his way.

Art opened his 1928 tour with the Sells-Floto show but spent the bulk of the season with the John Robinson Circus, another troupe owned by the American Circus Corporation. His real employer was Ward, with him working wherever Eddie sent him.[56] The same was true for Antoinette. She now worked on the V-shaped, felt-like rope called a cloud swing in addition to her ladders and iron jaw act. Both worked wherever they were needed on corporation shows, where Eddie controlled the aerial acts.

Their relationship continued to develop, united by their growing skills as aerialists, their common employment by Ward, and the often-inevitable grip that the circus had on those who had abandoned life on the outside. Such was the fate of troupers who entrusted their existence to the circus, an enterprise of ironclad rules and traditions, but one that was more vulnerable than others to unexpected developments.

The following year, 1929, was such a season for Art and Antoinette. Eddie Ward was catching for his act on the John Robinson show. He died unexpectedly and mysteriously on May 8, in Muncie, Indiana. Earlier that year, heavily in debt and deemed by his wife Mayme and the court as a "distracted person," Eddie and his affairs came under the control of a court-appointed conservator. In March more chaos rained down on the Ward Farm as authorities investigated an unrelated shooting there. Eddie's death that spring was believed by some to be from complications of syphilis, while others speculated that he had been poisoned. Whatever the cause of his untimely death, it opened a door for Art and Antoinette to break away from the act.

The Vasconcellos-Comeau partnership was formalized by their marriage—Art and Antoinette split away at the end of May to wed. The May 30 ceremony took place at the First Congregational Church of Detroit with Ward flyers Elden Day as best man and Gladys Bunker as a bridesmaid. Mayme was furious. She fired Art, who went back to Bloomington, and let Antoinette stay with the act.[57] At the end of the season, Art went over to Peru, Indiana, to pick up his bride and after returning to Bloomington, they began practicing their own act. Come January 1930, they would be known as the Aerial Concellos.

Stepping out now from his mentor's shadow, Art Concello—he rarely used his full legal name after this point—started to find his own managerial style modeled after Eddie Ward's. He first assembled and booked his own act under his own name, and then he later lined up other acts for the profitable winter indoor dates starting in 1931. He never looked back.

Meanwhile, more drama was in store for the circus world. In September 1929, John Ringling, the surviving brother of the Ringling boys from Baraboo, Wisconsin, decided to meet his competition head-on. He bought the American Circus Corporation, including all of its titles, equipment, and winter quarters, signing a personal note for the purchase. He was now the ultimate circus king. A few years earlier, he had moved the winter quarters of the Ringling-Barnum show from Bridgeport, Connecticut, to the Florida Gulf Coast community of Sarasota. There he and his wife Mable had constructed a lavish Venetian Gothic mansion called Ca' d'Zan and maintained extensive real estate holdings, along with a huge collection of paintings and sculptures.

Ringling's timing could not have been worse. The Roaring Twenties crashed with the stock market that October. The Ringling-Barnum show passed from family control to the balance sheets of New York bankers and, ultimately, nonfamily management. The onslaught of the Great Depression brought additional changes to the circus business. The decade of the 1930s would see the closing of many famous shows, but it would also see the rise, prominence, and riches of those who seized opportunity and worked the peculiar business nature of the big top to their advantage.

Arthur Vasconcellos, now known professionally as Arthur M. Concello, was just such an entrepreneur. For now, he and his wife had more flying to do, more stardom to achieve. In the shadows of the big top, fate waited to intervene to deliver them to the center ring of the biggest show of all.

Chapter 2

The Upswing

1930–1938

"People who have nerves shouldn't do this kind of work. I've got no nerves, or maybe I've got no sense—I don't know which."[1]

—Antoinette Concello

Fred Buchanan wanted to be a showman on the scale of P. T. Barnum. Born July 23, 1872, in Cherokee, Iowa, to parents who'd emigrated from Scotland, he spent his young adulthood much like Barnum spent some of his early professional years—in a newsroom. Buchanan initially worked for his father's Sioux Falls, South Dakota, newspaper before moving to Des Moines, Iowa, to work as city editor for *The Register*.[2] By 1903, he was managing Des Moines' Ingersoll Park in the summers and looking for opportunities to own a traveling show.[3] Over the course of the next thirty years or so, he tried and failed touring at least three circuses before he found success with the Robbins Bros. Circus.[4]

In 1930, the Robbins Bros. Circus traveled on thirty railroad cars, which moved all the show's personnel and equipment. There was one advance car, seven stock cars, fifteen flats, and seven coaches, including Buchanan's private car, "Rover," long rumored to have once been used by Teddy Roosevelt.[5] Traveling on thirty cars meant that the show was not as large as the Ringling Bros. and Barnum & Bailey Circus, which used ninety cars, nor as small as the Cole and Rogers Circus, which used three. Solidly in the middle of the pack, nearly one thousand people were employed by Buchanan; almost two-thirds of them were performers, its exaggerated press release stated.[6]

On May 3, 1930, residents of Newton, Iowa, enjoyed Robbins Bros. Circus' pre-performance street parade. On the midway, sixteen colorful, double-decked sideshow banners, the flags of many nations, and fluttering pennants rustled in the breeze. By showtime, the big top, which was reported to have had six center poles, was comfortably filled by people who enjoyed fine displays of bravery in the rings by man and beast alike. *The Billboard* paid particular attention to Arthur Concello, who completed double twister somersaults while blindfolded,[7] and his wife, Antoinette, who performed double somersaults.

Flying acts were wildly popular and a good draw for circuses at the time. Aerialists could command high salaries, and the Concellos, even though they were new to booking their own act, negotiated one. Buchanan had little experience with flying acts[8] and paid them $250 each week.[9] They were required to perform and to appear in the opening spectacle, though they did not have to participate in the parade, which was both a relief and proof of their top-tier status. Few circus actors relished walking in the heat, rain, or wind of cities and towns visited. The circus furnished them a stateroom and one single-occupancy berth (not to be shared) for the third member of the troupe, George Valentine. All parties signed the contract on March 14, just forty-five days after the Concellos presented their own flying-return act for the first time in the Minneapolis Shrine Circus.[10]

Even Ringling Bros. and Barnum & Bailey Circus wasn't doing the world's greatest business in 1930. While the country was floundering in the beginning stages of the Great Depression, Buchanan, noted for flashing his confident smiles of triumph, poured money into his business. New talent for his sawdust circles, new tents, new poles, and new stakes were accompanied by a new white ticket wagon that rolled out of the paint shop.[11] His nearly all-new midway and show grounds presented a wonderful sight to all who visited. Good crowds were needed to pay for these things, yet all he really got that season were poor-to-modest ones. And sometimes, those crowds brought along unsavory characters. Less than two weeks after opening, on May 6, in Keokuk, Iowa, three armed bandits robbed the show, taking nearly $2,000 as it was being transported from that new ticket wagon to the train's safe.[12] Unfortunately, the robbery was a harbinger of things to come for Buchanan's circus.

One week later, when the Robbins Bros. Circus appeared in Circleville, Ohio, calamity struck closer to the Concellos. Antoinette's sister, Mickey King, who Buchanan also had under contract, fell out of the Roman rings during her act and landed facedown on the hardwood stage placed between the show's two rings. Her body was hurried off the platform while clowns came forward to divert the audience's attention away from what they had just seen. What to do with her became the subject of discussion. Ultimately, they put her in her berth to let nature take its course. Antoinette sat by her side the whole night as the show's train rattled to the next destination. The next morning, Mickey woke up with double vision but insisted she would work again.[13] Miraculously, she did so in a matter of days.

Nevertheless, the Flying Concellos and Mickey King stayed on Buchanan's payroll only a few weeks. The poor economy translated into small audiences, and by June, rumors were running rampant that the show would be cut by twenty cars. In the backyard of the circus, morale was buoyed by celebrations whenever possible. Art and Antoinette's first wedding anniversary was one such occasion. At the end of May, a surprise party was thrown for them in Independence, Iowa. Their friends presented the couple with gifts. General agent and traffic manager Jake Newman—a man who would change the course of Art's life about a dozen years later—may have offered them congratulations or perhaps even enjoyed the celebratory chicken dinner served in the cookhouse.[14]

Buchanan did cut his show down. The number of railcars was trimmed—from thirty to twenty cars—less than two months into the season.[15] At least three versions of how the show shrunk exist. Mickey King's version centered around the big top's center poles being literally cut down: "Art was on the make for the guy's wife, see, and he [Buchanan] found out about it. So, when they loaded the poles out, putting the tent up, they sawed off five feet of each center pole so they couldn't hang a flying act. The guy gave him a reason why he had to do that, that he was sorry, [but Art] couldn't hang the flying act!"[16]

Antoinette also stated the center poles were cut down, but possibly, she meant the number of poles was reduced, not their length.[17] Buchanan may have made the decision to downsize the big top tent, perhaps, by taking a middle section out of it, which would translate into a need for fewer poles, or by using a smaller tent—maybe one the size of the menagerie or kid show (circus vernacular for sideshow) tent. A smaller tent wouldn't provide the height necessary for hanging a flying rig.

As for Art, he remembered time spent on Buchanan's show this way: "He talked to me about cutting down the show, and I said, 'Fine, if you're going to cut down and have a little show, I can't get up in there.' I said, 'the best thing is that I get away from here and it won't cost you any monies.' He said, 'That'll be perfect.'"[18]

No matter what happened to the tent, Buchanan wanted to cut expenses by eliminating the most expensive acts. It's also possible Concello had already worked out a plan on where to go next.

Zack Terrell, manager of the Sells-Floto Circus, needed a mid-season replacement act for the Flying Thrillers.[19] On August 12, the Concellos signed a contract with him to provide a three-person flying act with two men and one lady. In addition to the flying act, the contract stipulated that Antoinette also perform in a swinging-ladder routine. As with

Buchanan, the troupe was paid $250.00 each week. They finished out the season with the Sells-Floto Circus, which included movie star Tom Mix and one of the Flying Ward troupes.

While the Concellos would never again work for a small circus like Robbins, they learned a lot—particularly, Art, who probably had never seen scams operating on the scale they did there. Shortchanging and rigged games of chance were likely some of the grifting practices on Buchanan's show.[20] Ever the student of circus management in all of its forms, Art no doubt took note of these practitioners and their contributions to the show's bottom line, meager though it was in 1930.

Generally, the under-canvas circus season lasted from April through October. Never contented with resting for long, Art pursued contracts with shows that appeared indoors during the winter season to keep money flowing his way. Art and Antoinette first reached out to winter circus producer Orrin Davenport, a pioneer in producing large indoor circuses, to inquire if their act could be placed with him. In January 1931, Art acknowledged a reply from Davenport, and the Concellos signed on for some of his winter dates, including the Detroit Shrine Circus, the biggest Shrine date in the country.

Pat Valdo, personnel director for the Ringling Bros. and Barnum & Bailey Circus, saw the young Concellos perform on Sells-Floto. Alfredo Codona, the greatest flyer of all time, reached out to Valdo to tell him that he had seen the Sells-Floto Circus and hated it—except for one act, the Concellos. Codona wrote, ". . . the Concellos have a very good Act. The Girl is Excellent, and with a good teacher, she would be An Artist" [capitalization in original].[21] Valdo, having been with circuses for decades, could spot good performers easily, and with Codona's endorsement, Valdo told John Ringling of both the Concellos' current routines and great potential. Once the last surviving Ringling brother determined he wanted them to sign on for another tour with Sells-Floto Circus, he sent Valdo to go get them—and for the same price Robbins offered them. At nineteen, Art seized the opportunity and had the guts to negotiate for more money when the nation was gripped by the Great Depression. After some dickering, he got it: an additional twenty-five dollars per week for the 1931 season.[22]

In mid-April 1931, fifty-four-year-old Charles Siegrist, long considered the best all-around circus performer, broke his neck doing the triple somersault into the net at the end of his flying act. This left John Ringling in need of a replacement. The Concellos were called up to fill the end-ring spot left vacant by the Flying Pattersons, Siegrist's troupe. While they got a taste of life on the Big Show in Madison Square Garden, they were sent back to finish the season with Sells-Floto at the end of the New York stand.[23] In October 1931, Art inked the last of three contracts to perform with the Floto show, as it was called in the business, for the 1932 season.

Art did not like being pulled from one show to work in another, so he added a stipulation to his Sells-Floto Circus contract for the 1932 season that read, "This contract positively for Sells Floto Circus only. If Mr. Ringling wants this act used on any one of the other shows then this contract shall be changed from a financial standpoint to the satisfaction of Art Concello; otherwise it is null and void."[24]

Art seemed prescient. Less than six months later, still only twenty years old, Art signed a contract with John Ringling in February to appear in the Ringling Bros. and Barnum & Bailey Circus—though he was unable to get more than $275 each week (about $4,700 in today's dollars) for the 1932 season.[25] He signed another contract later that year for the 1933 season for the same pay. That was really good pay, but not top dollar. The Flying Codonas, by comparison, earned $450 each week (about $9,000 in today's dollars) that year.[26] Their success on Ringling's shows, evidenced by their rapidly evolving and ever-improving performance in the air, ensured their continued appearance at Madison Square Garden through the 1943 season.

Every person wanted year-round employment in the 1930s, and Art and Antoinette were certainly no exception. Driven by a need for financial security that they never had growing up and after a full season on the Ringling-Barnum Circus, they sought bookings in Europe, a place with a rich circus history and permanent buildings in which to display. Perhaps they were tipped off to the fact that they could be a draw on the Continent by British impresario Cyril Mills, who signed them with his father's 1932–1933 circus.[27] With a booking in England during the winter holidays secured, they pursued other engagements before that time. They found work with the Scala nightclub in Berlin. The dimly lit venue often employed circus acts, sometimes in a dinner theater-like setup.[28] There they hobnobbed with the likes of boxer Jack Johnson, the Amadori act of flyers, and the Codonas—Vera Bruce, Lalo, and Alfredo. A photo from this time shows Art and Alfredo raising glasses to one another. A copy of this image was signed by Alfredo, wishing the younger flyer "good luck."[29] Neither could know that within a year's time, the Concellos would take the Codonas's center-ring spot on The Greatest Show on Earth.

With their Scala commitments concluded—and after torn shoulder tendons sidelined Antoinette for nine days in a Berlin hospital[30]—the Flying Concellos made their way to London. Their contract for the Bertram W. Mills' Circus mandated that the act execute a triple somersault. At the time, Art was the only member who could throw the triple, but it would be a couple of years before he would be consistent. Because that trick was not completed in either rehearsal or on opening night, December 22,

1932, Mills fired them. The next day Art, Antoinette, and their catcher, Everett White, boarded the S.S. *Albert Ballin* to sail back to America. Now they were at liberty to honor the $800 contract to perform in Detroit for its Shrine there.

Then fate intervened to send the Concellos stars into a more illustrious orbit. In Madison Square Garden, Alfredo Codona hurt his shoulder for the second time.[31] He was expected to be out for at least six weeks, but as it turned out, he never flew again. At the next stand, the indoor date in Boston Garden, The Flying Concellos walked out to see their rigging over the coveted center-ring spot.[32] By 1936, they called that spot their home.

The next time they were in Europe, in the winter of 1934–1935, they were not sent home the day after their premiere in London's Olympia Grand Hall, where the Bertram W. Mills' Circus exhibited. The Concellos began their act to the tune of "The Man on the Flying Trapeze,"[33] where, presumably, Art showcased his consistently caught triple somersault. Then Antoinette was announced doing a two-and-a-half somersault midair to be caught by her ankles.[34] Time and time again, their names appeared in favorable reviews, especially when the only daughter of King George V and Queen Mary (and aunt to Queen Elizabeth II) visited the show in January.[35] One of the last times their act was mentioned in London's *Daily Mail*, a columnist remarked how thrilled he was to meet the Concellos in a local restaurant. He asked, "'How do you feel when you are flying through the air at that giddy height?' 'Oh,' said the leader of the troupe laconically, 'it's just like going to the office.'"[36]

Art provided little of what rolled through his mind in his diary. The expected details are given—when ships sailed to and from the Continent—but noted, too, were how large the crowds were at Cirque D'Hiver when his act debuted there. Terse phrases were scribbled next to the date when they opened and closed at Bertram W. Mills' Circus—December 20, 1934 ("Fair business") and January 24, 1935 ("Very big business").[37] He recorded when his triples (Art spelled this trick "tripples") were not caught, which wasn't often.

Far more pages were dedicated to how much money Concello could make by assembling acts and placing them with various shows. Under the phrase "2 fours and one 3 people," he listed the personnel he wanted in two four-person acts and one three-person act as well as how much he could get for their placement on circuses. Next to each person's name, he listed the salary that person would make—anywhere between thirty and fifty-five dollars—and then deducted the expenses, like rigging, from the contracted price for the act. He figured the acts he put together would clear him $230 each week. Added to that was the profit for his act, $280, yielding a total "Profit per week [of] $510.00." On page after page, he made computations such as "3=3 people acts $900"; "One three people act and two fives $1100"; and "One six people act 2 three people acts, $1050."[38]

He kept meticulous notes on travel arrangements, addresses of business colleagues and friends, along with who owed him money, how much they owed, and sometimes, the repayment schedule. In his 1931 diary, for example, one page is dedicated to Fred Bradna, the equestrian director for The Greatest Show on Earth and a winter show producer for Shrine Temples. Bradna became indebted to Concello for $150, and in Miami another $175 was added to the tally. Bradna paid Concello sixty-five dollars in Cleveland, leaving a "balance due $260." Another page listed Orrin (presumably Orrin Davenport), who "owes me $660.00 (due Feb. 1935)."[39] His detailed and compulsive scribbling reveal a man with the need to control every detail of his life.

He was well aware of the dangers of his profession. He carried three twenty-year New York Life insurance policies, initially purchased in 1931, each with annual $1000 premiums. Two were for him, the other covered Antoinette. The act wouldn't be such a success without either of them, and Art knew it.

The amount of money to be made for circus acts performing in Europe and the United States steadily decreased during the 1930s due to deflation. Contracts which once topped one hundred dollars a day for twelve days' work, by the mid-1930s, brought in sixty dollars each day for ten days of work.[40] Correspondence between Concello and European agents tell a similar story.[41] Yet the prestige of appearing in Europe (and before royalty, no less) was, arguably, priceless.

Back in America, the Concellos became a fixture of the Ringling Bros. and Barnum & Bailey Circus for most of the 1930s. The press touted Arthur's consistent triples while Antoinette's two-and-a-half somersaults wowed audiences repeatedly. Indeed, Antoinette, Tony to her friends, became something of a darling to those assigned to cover her activities. *The Billboard* stated that she was ". . . a charming little lady, unaffected and unspoiled and one of the greatest female aerialists, not only of her day, but of all days, two and a half somersaults in mid-air, done possibly by no other, from her trapeze to the catcher; it is a feat unbelievable."[42] Their future was brighter than ever. They rotated appearances in the off-season between international venues. They went to Cuba in 1936–1937 and again in 1939–1940 with the Santos and Artigas Circus, directed by Fred Bradna.[43] Though tempted, getting money out of Germany at that time was prohibitive, so he canceled his plans to go there,[44] and he instead worked in various Shrine circuses in the United States.

During their extensive travels, they remained in contact with Art's parents at home in Bloomington. Art trusted his father, Papa Vas, to receive payments of money owed him by the managers of his salaried flying acts, such as Oscar Jordan and Wayne Larey. With cash accumulating, the likes of which few Bloomingtonians saw, Art made a decision in August 1935 to invest some in something he knew well.[45] At twenty-four years old, Art said, "I decided if I could get a corner on this flying act business I would make money. I raised all the money I could beg, borrow, or steal and bought his [Eddie Ward's] barn."[46] With the Ward barn secured, he continued training and then assembling acts without fear of losing the practice venue. Valdo, of Ringling-Barnum, contacted him when flying acts were needed on that show. Art recalled asking Valdo how many people were needed, getting the act together, and telling Valdo how much it would cost the circus.[47]

By 1937, Concello had six acts working for him: the Artonys, the Flying Vassars, and the Flying LaVards were with smaller circuses, while the Flying Comets, the Flying Concellos (now with Eddie A. Ward, son of Eddie W. Ward, serving as their catcher),[48] and the Flying Randolls were on the Ringling Bros. and Barnum & Bailey Circus. He set up each manager of the non-Ringling acts with a record book and told them to document how much each performer made, what the expenses were (including things like friction tape, Vaseline, train fares, and Social Security), and how much would be sent either to Papa Vas or himself. A similar book for his three acts on Ringling-Barnum was kept, though the entries appear to be in Antoinette's careful hand, not Art's scrawl. The contract he signed to supply aerial talent provided an $875 salary for the nine flyers in three acts. The salary documented in his personal ledger book was $975 for six men and five women.[49] He paid his two other acts on Ringling—the Randolls (a nod to his mother's maiden name) and the Comets—a combined $330 weekly, with a salary of around $320 for himself and Antoinette. Expenses came out of the salaries and were noted down to the penny—for example, the cost of sending telegrams for the week of April 14–20 was twenty-six cents.

In addition to helping her husband keep financial records, Antoinette continued to amaze audiences with her feats of graceful aerial acrobatics, and consumer goods companies were quick to sign her to help them market products. A spokesperson for Camel cigarettes since 1934, her likeness appeared in newspapers and magazines, touting the smokes which she could enjoy "all I want to for they never upset my nerves."[50] Wheaties cereal featured her in its 1935 and 1941 "Breakfast of Champions" campaigns, Ward Baking Company used her name and likeness in its advertisements, as did Parker pens, "the Official Pen of This Circus." Reviews frequently hyped her beauty, skill, and bravery high above the center ring.

While Antoinette got cigarettes and cereal, her husband was signed only to Pabst-ett, a "delicious, digestible cheese food," as one of its celebrity endorsers.[51]

A successful trapeze flyer must have a tremendous work ethic, a healthy respect for gravity, physical strength, and courage. Antoinette had them all; she was nothing if not driven. "The discipline learned under the Sisters was just what she needed for a background combined with a desire to succeed, a charming personality, a perfect body, and a healthy mind," reported a Canadian newspaper.[52] Her unhappy experiences with the Sisters of Mercy, along with her fear of abandonment, motivated her to prove herself in the dramatically different world of tented entertainment. Determined to succeed and resolved to stay relevant in her husband's life, Antoinette put her complete trust in him and his training regimen. As for Art, whenever possible, he turned reporters' attention toward her and her pursuit of the triple. "Yes, I think she'll get it all right in time,"[53] he told a reporter of her triple quest in 1934. The next year he told another, "She is unusually quick, mentally and physically. Flying and somersaulting comes natural to her, and she has plenty of confidence."[54]

Art knew everything about what he was training her to do. He had the natural talent to make the triple look easy. "You gotta do it just right, or you don't do it. There's only a split second when you get around there, if you ain't there, you're in the net . . . it's a difficult trick."[55] Explaining the trick further, he said, "The triple isn't just a question of overturning the double; the timing wouldn't be right and you'd probably break your neck. It's easy enough to turn three somersaults; the difficulty lies in stopping yourself after the third revolution sufficiently to collect [your] faculties to make the catch."[56] He well knew having the first woman in the modern era to complete the killer trick in his act would increase their paycheck.

The tenaciously determined Antoinette wanted to be known for more than just her beauty and wardrobe. She wanted her skills to be noticed. She diligently worked to complete the trick everyone thought impossible for a woman.[57] She had been doing a triple to the net as her finishing trick for years, but to complete the triple to a catcher was far more difficult. She practiced for hours, day after day, year after year. Virginia Gardiner of the *Chicago Tribune* visited the Farm in Bloomington to watch her practice. During her visit, Antoinette tried nine times to catch the trick and each time, she failed. Gardiner captured the interaction between teacher and student. "Now honey," Art said to Antoinette, "don't break it short that way, particularly with the safety belt on. How'd it feel to you? It was a dandy, a pip. That's enough on that . . . " Art explained to the reporter that she just wasn't there yet. He figured he racked up more than nine hundred attempts before he caught it. He knew she was close to completing it, and after that, it would be only a matter of time before she did so in a performance.[58]

The time for completing the triple occurred during a winter show in Detroit.[59] Tunis "Eddie" Stinson wanted his 1937 edition of the Shrine Circus to be the place where Tony debuted the trick and made her a promise to sweeten the deal. "He told me, 'When you catch the triple, I'll get you the prettiest dress you've ever had,'" Antoinette recalled. "So, on opening night, I remember we had a packed house, people were sitting on the ground even . . . and I didn't know it, because Art didn't want me to be nervous, but Art had told the catcher, 'if everything goes well, don't drop down after the passing trick.' So we did the whole act . . . I looked and the catcher didn't drop down to the net. So Art put the raise up, a bar placed above the pedestal bar to give a flyer the advantage of leaving from a higher point, giving the flyer greater momentum in their swing and a tiny bit more time in the air, and said, 'Let's do it for them.' And we did. We did a real nice one. He [Stinson] went over to the microphone and started telling the people what had just happened. I dropped down to the net and he came over, hugged me, and kissed me—there, in front of God and everyone! Oh, it was a wonderful moment!"[60]

That night, the night when she completed what was proclaimed to be the first triple somersault ever done by a woman, Antoinette was wearing an opalescent outfit that her sister Mickey had made for her. She heard everyone say that she looked like a million bucks, and after she completed the triple, heard the cheers, and got the hugs and kisses, she felt like it. Antoinette's words to her sister about Stinson's gift were gleefully delivered: "He paid off like a slot machine!"[61]

Even though she wanted her accomplishments noted, appearance mattered to Antoinette. Often described as someone who carried herself like a queen, Antoinette's posture was as impeccable as her wardrobe—both in and out of the ring. She possessed a keen eye for detail, adding spangled trim to her short skirts and fluttering capped sleeves so that the spotlight would make her movements sparkle. Newspapers documented the diameters of each bicep, her forearm diameters, and those of her waist, hips, and bust.[62]

Antoinette's hands told the truth of her training. After finding his way to her dressing room decked out with floral arrangements, one reporter watched her trim her calluses that were heavy as corns. "They get like this when we work," she said. "Blisters first. And then they harden. It takes work, you know, climbing ropes, chinning yourself, swinging from a bar. You have to be strong before you can even try this work."[63]

She was exceptionally physically fit and not stupid. She knew her husband was not immune to other women's allure. She confided as much to her sister and confessed what she had done to one of them. Mickey recalled that Antoinette "beat the hell out of a woman in the john with a billy club for fooling around with Art."[64] Antoinette warned the young Concello flyer that if she told anyone how her bruises appeared, she would be beaten again. As it was, the woman wasn't able to work for weeks. Mickey believed the blame for such interactions laid at the feet of a woman because "not very many men could resist a woman." Antoinette perhaps held similar views. Besides, because Art was "her husband, her hero, and her teacher,"[65] the blame for infidelity just couldn't be placed completely at his feet.

The kickoff to the 1938 circus season began back home with a gathering at the Tilden Hall Hotel in Bloomington, coordinated by the establishment's manager, William "Happy" Hunt. The hotel he managed near the downtown YMCA was often used for lodging and as a gathering site for circus people who visited or trained there in the winter. Happy hosted a dinner party well attended by the stars of the circus—its flyers. The Concellos were joined there by their catcher Eddie Ward and the dozen flyers contracted to Art. Also in attendance were single trapeze aerialist Ullaine Malloy, the high-wire-walking Billetti Troupe, and a dozen other flyers.[66]

The Billboard supplied information for performers, owners, and anyone else looking to learn about the world of show business. In early June 1938, it reported little news of the Concellos in The Greatest Show on Earth other than the fact that Antoinette now completed triples in performance.[67] It had, however, lots of reporting about the show's management, its union troubles, and its new executives, John and Henry Ringling North.

When the show premiered at Madison Square Garden on April 8, 1938, there was a new man in charge, thirty-four-year-old John Ringling North. When John Ringling, North's uncle, died in 1936, he named his sister, Ida North, and his nephew, John Ringling North, as executors of his estate. After Ringling died, North borrowed money from various sources—largely from Manufacturer's Trust—and paid off the loan John Ringling had taken when he purchased the American Circus Corporation in 1929. North paid off that debt and others, leveraged stock in the corporation, and put himself into position, by late 1937, to gain the presidency for five years over the Ringling circuses.

North initiated many positive changes for the Ringling Bros. and Barnum & Bailey Circus during its 1938 season. The format of the show had become somewhat stale under the management of Vice President and General Manager Sam Gumpertz. North changed it, imbuing it with new spectacles, new costuming, and new music. For example, the opening spectacle, "Nepal," benefited from a reported investment of $60,000 in costuming.[68] To improve the visibility of aerial acts, especially for daytime performances, North broke with long-standing circus tradition and ordered a dark blue canvas instead of the traditional white.[69]

Frank "Bring 'em Back Alive!" Buck—of jungle, wild animal, and movie fame—was billed as the star of the show. But the real attraction ended up being "Buddy," a fully grown pet gorilla sold to the Norths for $10,000 by his frightened owner. Not wishing to share his own nickname with the beast, Henry "Buddy" Ringling North renamed him Gargantua after a sixteenth-century novel about two giants. The show's press agents went to work supporting in written word what was depicted on thousands of posters: their very own version of the still wildly popular *King Kong*. Inside a steel "jungle conditioned" cage with thick glass to protect the gorilla from human ailments and the patrons from the menacing arms of the ape, "mean, dangerous, and insane" Gargantua prepared to reign as the biggest, most heavily publicized circus attraction since Barnum's famous elephant, Jumbo.[70] With his simian superstar safely secured for the season, Johnny was ready to ascend to the ranks of legendary showmen.

The opening night at Madison Square Garden was a huge success. Glowed *The Billboard*, "A near-capacity house welcomed the Ringlings back to active participation in circus operation, and representatives of the daily press, legitimate stage personalities, Eastern Circus Fans, and a goodly number of the New York public witnessed circus wardrobe and lighting effects that, in the parlance of press agents, is 'magnificent' to say the least."[71] Gargantua, advertised as a million-dollar attraction, circled the hippodrome track, his cage drawn by six horses and escorted by safari hunters in pith helmets, their rifles cocked at menacing angles. The flying act near the end of the program featured the Concellos over the center ring in an east-west configuration, while the Comets and the Randolls were over the outer rings in parallel north-south positions.

Johnny's new job as circus producer was the talk of the town. There was a lingering problem, however, that loomed over the gaiety. For generations, the muscle end of the Ringling show—and all the other circuses—was cheap labor. The men worked long hours for little pay, enduring extreme weather and other rough conditions. The unskilled roustabouts traveled aboard crowded railroad cars with little heat and no air conditioning. The management held back the first week or two of wages for the workingmen. If they stayed the entire season, they got those wages back. If they blew the show before the season ended, the circus kept those funds. This ensured both a healthy bottom line for management and an incentive for the workers' continuing service to the operation. If a circus endured bad weather or other causes of poor business, workers' pay was cut or they were simply not paid. Naturally, labor organizers targeted the largest shows. The Ringling-Barnum workers—well over five hundred who physically unloaded, erected, operated, and dismantled the show at every stand—were ripe for union organizing.

Those who performed for the Ringling-Barnum Circus in the Garden weren't there long before a wage dispute for the workers, not the performers, reared its head. The previous year, the management under Sam Gumpertz signed a five-year union contract with the American Federation of Actors which stated, in part, that workers would get paid sixty dollars a month plus boarding. There was no stipulation, however, for a wage scale when the show was in winter quarters or playing indoors in either New York or Boston. Before the show reached Madison Square Garden, North insisted that he could not meet these terms.[72] Shortly before the season's premiere there, a strike order was issued by Ralph Whitehead, the executive secretary of the American Federation of Actors. A two-day walkout by the workingmen eventually led to a tenuous agreement between the circus and the American Federation of Actors. During those two days, most animal acts were cut and the performers had to do the physical labor. *The Billboard* reported that John and Henry set props and Art rigged his and most of the other aerial acts. The "show must go on" mentality was a tremendous hit with the audience, who kept attendance strong.[73]

A settlement was reached, though Whitehead demanded that those performers who had not yet joined the union must do so. As the show left New York City, tensions continued among the circus employees. Shortly after Ringling Bros. and Barnum & Bailey Circus started touring under canvas, *Variety* reported that receipts had fallen off due to rain and poor business conditions. By the time the circus reached Wheeling, West Virginia, it was reportedly losing $40,000 a week.[74] As the show jumped to Toledo, it was discovered that air hoses had been maliciously severed on some of the circus cars,[75] crippling the braking system. The show limped on through several New York state dates, all while reporting diminished gross receipts.

Then came Scranton. The circus was set up on an industrial lot in the union-friendly Pennsylvania town. Citing mounting business losses, North had earlier announced that show personnel would have to take a 25 percent salary cut—a move Johnny hoped would keep the circus on the road and out of the "barn," as the circus' winter quarters was called. In response, Whitehead again ordered the workingmen to strike. This left the huge circus crippled with no clear-cut way of putting on a show or leaving town. North blamed Whitehead for the impasse and Whitehead blamed North. An emotional plea to save the circus by Mrs. Charles Ringling, widow of one of the founders of the show, earned the respect of the strikers, but it resulted in no resolution to the crisis. North prepared to send the circus back to its winter quarters in Sarasota.

A bad situation grew worse. It started raining. The lot the tents stood on turned into a big bowl of mud. Then the pro-union, pro-labor city shut off water to the lot. No deliveries of ice, feed for the animals, or other provisions were permitted. Picketers stoned Ringling performers.[76] Citing unsanitary conditions at the show grounds as a public health menace, the city's mayor ordered the circus to leave. North balked; all of his workers were on strike—all, that is, except two hundred performers led by Arthur M. Concello, Karl Wallenda, Frank Buck, and other top billers.

The entertainers voted to accept the 25 percent pay cut, but Concello went further. He rented a hotel room in Scranton, drafted a petition stating "undivided loyalty" to John Ringling North's management, and urged the show to go on. Before he could get the petition into Whitehead's hands, an employee ripped it to shreds.[77] Art drafted another petition and, this time, made seven copies of it. Those who signed the petition and Art Concello (who never signed it) agreed to the wage reduction "to be exactly proportionate to the twenty-five percent cut taken by every other member of the organization, if the Circus is to remain on tour."[78] Concello and Frank Buck presented these results to Whitehead. The union refused to recognize the meeting or the vote.[79]

Helen Wallenda, Karl's wife, wrote friends extensively about the situation. English was not her native language, but the essence of her feelings was clear. "So, you see where the blame is, just the Union and that good for nothing Whitehead. He is no good I tell you. . . . You know we—all most [*sic*] of the Performers except a few were willing to take the 25% wage reduction because a good performer wants the show to go on and we all know that Mr. North is a very fine man and he surely would not take such a step when it's not necessary."[80]

After days of seemingly endless wrangling with the union, North directed a skeleton crew of workers to tear down the equipment and load it for the retreat to Sarasota. Still more delays followed after Whitehead demanded special compensation for the teardown crew. A violent confrontation between performers and roustabouts required police intervention.[81] And still, it rained. The precipitation left the canvas heavier than usual. Wet canvas transported for days in the hot weather meant that spontaneous combustion became a concern, too.[82]

Whitehead justified the delays by professing to protect the circus property from further damage. North agreed to pay off the workers—after the circus equipment was safely loaded. According to the *New York Times,* Whitehead's last act was trying to enlist performers to join the union in a suit against the show for breach of contract. "This plea," reported the paper, "was greeted with stony silence."[83] The performers desired to keep the show going.

John North had another plan. His organization's other show, the Al G. Barnes–Sells-Floto Circus, was touring the Dakotas free from labor conflicts. Many top acts and attractions, including Frank Buck, Terrell

Jacobs' wild-animal act, and a lot of the equipment from the closed Ringling show went to the Barnes-Floto outfit, a move that increased the show from a thirty-car operation to a fifty-car one.[84] The Ringling-Barnum big top, cookhouse, light plants, tractors, trucks, horses, some of the sideshow, and Gargantua joined the smaller show. The Concellos, who were on their way to Bloomington when the show went to Sarasota, got word from John to join the revised Ringling show in Redfield, South Dakota, where Art already had the contract for two flying acts.[85] Art jotted instructions on how to get to Redfield on the back of a telegram[86] and when they got there, the Flying Concellos replaced the Covets, managed by Wayne Larey. Larey's troupe was sent to work dates for parks and fairs.[87] On July 11, the expanded circus, billed as "Al G. Barnes–Sells-Floto Circus Presenting Ringling Bros. and Barnum & Bailey Stupendous New Features," premiered on the plains just nineteen days after the Ringling-Barnum Circus closed in Scranton.

Under the new circus title, the Concellos garnered even more newspaper attention. When asked if they talked about anything while flying, Antoinette shared that she and Art exchanged thoughts about the audience, the weather, and their dinner plans when on the pedestal board and in the air.[88] Though she had been turning triples, her taciturn, sandy-haired husband, who often sat smoking a cigar while slouching in a backyard deck chair, got the questions about the trick. He explained to reporters the hardest part about mastering the triple was the timing. The young man who looked like a schoolboy except for his "chest like two barrels" and shoulder muscles so developed he looked hunchbacked tried to put into words what his body seemed to do naturally.[89] "You gotta get that feel of it, the swing, and swing right with it. If you don't, your trick'll go sour."[90] Tantalizingly, the article stated that Art had completed the quadruple somersault with a mechanic on and told readers that Art believed it would never be a regular performance trick. (It wasn't until 1982, when Miguel Vazquez of the Ringling Bros. and Barnum & Bailey Circus did the first quadruple in performance.)

The 1938 season proved disastrous for the circus business. The new Tim McCoy Wild West show, launched with $100,000 of the movie cowboy's own funds, folded suddenly only a few days after opening in Washington, DC, on May 4. The Russell Bros. Circus, a truck show, endured layoffs and a 25 percent cut in salaries. The Cole Bros. Circus ended its season in Bloomington, Illinois, on August 6 because of poor business.[91] Some shows, including North's Barnes-Floto title, would never troupe again.[92]

But North, with Concello's active assistance, strengthened his hand and reputation with the unions and impressed his employees. Art impressed North, too, not only by signing his acts again with the Ringling-Barnum Circus for the next season but also by signing his act and five more with

Shrine circuses for the winter. During the tenting season, Art actively managed eight acts and booked more in winter shows.

The world and the circus would never be the same after 1938. Ahead lay wartime challenges, shifting tastes in popular entertainment, frightening realities of the atomic age—and for the big circus, tragedy in abundance. For now, the great American tradition of the Ringling Bros. and Barnum & Bailey Circus was comforting to the masses and profitable for its owners. In the next few years, the North brothers had problems, but Art had none. Come what may, Art was ready to step out of the spotlight and into the world of bigger money and broader control.

Chapter 3

Counting the House

1939–1942

"Anything that requires skill is dangerous. Life is dangerous, if you do anything at all worthwhile."[1]

—Antoinette Concello

While the Concellos were in Rochester, New York, in 1939, a local paper profiled the dark-brown, curly-haired Antoinette for its readers, which included her mother, stepfather, and half-siblings. The article told of the hazel-eyed flyer's bravery to taunt luck by walking under ladders and wearing yellow—a color, the piece advised its readers, that was bad luck to wear in a circus. Antoinette explained why she chose to do so: "You see, Arthur, my husband, likes yellow tights, and so I always wear them."[2] She said her biggest accomplishment to date was performing the triple somersault, but she looked forward to the coming years when she would hang up her tights to start a family, a reflection that she was very much a woman of her time.

With the 1938 season in the rearview mirror, Ringling Bros. and Barnum & Bailey Circus President John Ringling North focused more intently on cutting costs. He knew a large portion of the public loved watching horses do so much of the necessary work unloading equipment, but he also understood the expense of them, their handlers, and the teamsters. He turned to Concello, his star performer, for advice. Performers rarely took an interest in things outside their own act, and it's remarkable that a show owner would even ask a performer for input on the labor side of the circus. But Concello had always shown a clear interest in the physical end of the show. Concello remembered telling John, "The damn army moves all these heavy ammunition wagons and everything else with Caterpillar tractors. We ought to think about getting some tractors . . ."[3] Concello, whose half brother, Joe, worked in Peoria, the corporate headquarters of the Caterpillar tractor company, made a suggestion to get rid of horses in favor of tractors.[4] The fewer horses used, the fewer teamsters needed to handle them, the fewer union men and railcars needed to transport them all. The Engineer's Report, commissioned by John and Henry the previous year but submitted to them on March 15, 1939, also supported the transition.[5] It made beautiful sense.

The 1939 Madison Square Garden premiere of The Greatest Show on Earth went off smoothly—streamlined to the hilt and the proportionately pruned opening spec, titled "The World Comes to the World's Fair," celebrated New York's hosting the World's Fair; as such, it included the resplendent wardrobe representing the pageantry of the nations. North's approach to the circus was to mechanize and economize the eighty-car show without compromising the quality of the performance. The main riding acts were cut from two to one, other familiar performers did not reappear for the season, and even clown alley was downsized.[6]

Problems still plagued the show. Salaries were slashed from the previous season, and performers resented the American Federation of Actors' collection of dues. The first nine days of the business's income at the Garden was said to be "below par" compared to previous years. By the end of April, *The Billboard* reported that Concello was upset over the possibility of one of his flying acts being cut,[7] but all three troupes remained for the duration of the season.

North pressed ahead with plans to redesign the show's aesthetics. A new oval big top with a blue color pattern had four center poles, not the traditional six. The change resulted in a three-ring format without the two customary stages between them. Audiences seated on the ends could now see more of the action in the center ring. The enhanced lighting effects for night performances and the air-conditioning units that fed cool air through ducts attached to the tent canvas garnered positive reviews, but they added eight mechanical wagons to the fleet.[8] To please horse lovers now that his wagons were pulled by tractors, North devised a "horse fair" tent near the main entrance where patrons could admire the ring stock, or performing horses, that stayed on the show. This smart move earned additional praise in trade papers.[9]

By mid-June 1939, opportunity to assist North arose again. This time, it was the court that created John's need for Art. Sarasota County Judge Forrest Chapman ordered Ida and John Ringling North, both executors of John Ringling's estate, to furnish a bond of $300,000 within one week to guarantee its proper administration.[10] John's attention and assets were tied up in the circus[11] and the "Cavalcade of Centaurs," an hour-long international horse show he produced with assistance from his brother

Henry, Pat Valdo, and Murray Burt at the New York World's Fair.[12] Through legal maneuvering, the bond got reduced to $100,000 and a delayed payment until November 1940. John knew who to tap for money and Art saw the loan as a way to further endear himself to his employer. Management usually went to concessionaires for big infusions of cash, but North knew Concello had the funds.

With the money necessary to satisfy the court's demand secured, and as Europe edged toward war in the autumn of 1939, John's confidence grew. His relationship with unions appeared to be improving. He emerged stronger after Scranton, worked to make friends in the ranks of organized labor, and enjoyed the fruits of the 1939 season with a better labor contract. His show toured over seventeen thousand miles and ended the year with a profit of around $400,000.[13] He dashed over to Europe to sign new acts before the war made travel impossible.

Johnny and Art had drawn closer. Henry Ringling North recalled how he and his brother kept an eye on the Concellos. They saw two exceptionally talented individuals in the ring and a man who had ambition, curiosity, and a "tough talking" practicality outside of it. More than those things, his "brilliant mind and surprising executive ability" intrigued them most.[14]

The aerial stars lived in their own private quarters on the circus train. A third the length of a Pullman coach, it included a kitchenette where Antoinette made breakfast every morning for herself and Arthur—and later, fudge for the other boys in the flying act. A darling in the press, she played down the accidents in aerial work, saying, "They were only little ones and one never thinks about them."[15] Yet those "little ones" often left big impressions on those who saw them. "Livid red lashes of aching fire" crisscrossed "a full quarter of an inch" into the aerial queen's back after hitting the net hard when a trick was missed.[16] Antoinette's response to those who looked horrified after seeing such marks revealed one of her life's tenets: "Anything that requires skill is dangerous. Life is dangerous, if you do anything at all worthwhile."[17]

Throughout the late 1930s and early 1940s, the Concellos tantalized audiences with their daring aerial routines. Starring with the Ringling Bros. and Barnum & Bailey Circus during its eight-month tour, they returned to Bloomington to train aspiring performers whenever they could. Used to constantly moving, they traveled to Cuba for winter dates before returning to the United States for the post-holiday Shrine Circus season in the Northeast and Midwest. Then back they went to Madison Square Garden for the opening of The Greatest Show on Earth.

Antoinette's adolescence in a convent was highlighted repeatedly, as it was likely a facet of the star's story the circus's press agents knew would draw interest and an audience. The novelty of going to a circus and seeing a woman who once studied to become a nun (of all things!) was titillating. If Antoinette grew tired of the attention, she never showed it.

The circus drew attention to Antoinette, not her husband, who seemed rather bored up there on the pedestal board at times. One reporter, Joseph L. Myler, seemed drawn to Concello, not his missus, and filed a story that was reprinted in newspapers across the country. His story opened with "Art Concello slid a callused thumb over the four-carat diamond in his tie pin today and said he guessed he was the 'black sheep' of his family"—a status earned, he said, because he didn't go into the cigar business back in Bloomington." Myler revealed that Art, at the age of twenty-nine, owned three farms, managed eight flying acts, and owned a beer garden in Bloomington. He also detailed Concello's diamonds, saying several were "big enough to go skating on."[18]

Together, Art and Antoinette maintained the circus lifestyle, a rhythm of life unfathomable to their audiences. Visitors to the circus lot may have seen the aerialists in their private dressing tent, being driven around in their chauffeured vehicle,[19] but likely, they never gave thought to where the circus stars had come from, where they went, or what they did after their brief flights through the air. Nor would they have realized how much weather played a part in their craft. When the outdoor temperatures reached into the nineties, the temperature inside the tent could be 110 degrees. The heat and humidity produced by as many as fifteen thousand people caused the temperature thirty feet above the audience's heads to reach astronomical levels. "We were almost suffocated," Arthur said of being high up on the pedestal board in such conditions.[20] At the other weather extreme there was cold and wind. The former hampered movement due to layers of clothing and the latter could ruin the timing of the tricks with sudden wind gusts.

The Concellos were stars of the sawdust circle and, in some ways, seemed like polar opposites. Antoinette moved with a refined elegance and softly spoke in a measured, ladylike manner. By contrast, Art reminded people of a mobster. Comparisons were made to Edward G. Robinson, the Romanian-American actor of Hollywood's Golden Age best known for his tough-guy gangster roles in movies like the one which later became the whispered nickname people used for Art: *Little Caesar*. That film portrayed a tough-talking, fast-moving hoodlum who moved to Chicago and ascended the ranks of organized crime until he reached its upper echelons. At the time reporters from his hometown did nothing to contradict the resemblance while describing Arthur as "a nervous little fellow, about five feet five, with huge biceps and keen eyes . . . continually on the run, pretends to be lazy and indifferent about money . . ."[21] Those keen gray eyes conveyed an intensity some found intimidating, others found alluring, and more than a few thought betrayed his scheming.

Their work brought them to places well-known and to people not-so-well-known—at least, not yet. One such person was Jack Tavlin.

Jack "Abie" Tavlin was born Jacob Tavlinsky in Grodno, Russia (now Belarus), on September 20, 1904. He was the oldest of seven children born to Chazkel (later known as Charles) and Julia Tavlinsky. After Charles immigrated to the United States in the early 1900s, his family followed him to settle in Nebraska, where Charles pursued jobs that included being a salesman, teamster, and truck gardener specializing in horse radishes.

By 1920, Jack had been out of school for four years and had had enough of life on the Great Plains. So on September 1, 1920, when the Ringling Bros. and Barnum & Bailey Circus came to Lincoln for its one-day stand, he left with it. His parents, led by Julia, sued the circus for $10,000, alleging that their son was enticed away. Their attorney argued that his absence led to lost wages the family needed for support. They also sued for the grief and suffering of losing their son to an immoral organization. As testimony, they used letters their eldest had written to one of his brothers, telling him how the life had hardened him morally. In May 1922, the Tavlinskys were awarded $7,500 in district court,[22] a decision that was overturned in the state's Supreme Court by mid-1925.[23]

The dark-complexioned youth of medium height and build hustled to learn as much as he could about tented entertainment. By the time his parents filed the lawsuit against the Big Show, he had secured a position in its cook house tent working for John Staley, who believed the Jewish boy had the first name of Abraham. Reminiscing, Staley shared, "Abie was a young kid full of pep and vinegar. I believe at times he put on a false front of being happy-go-lucky to keep from being homesick."[24] Staley also recalled Abie used his fists and raw strength to win arguments. Gradually, he added words and cunning to his dispute resolution skills.

Earlier in his career, Tavlin managed sideshow acts before turning his attention to other ventures within the entertainment business. By 1938, he had pleaded guilty in Nebraska to gambling,[25] paid the fine, and laid the groundwork to get back on the Big Show in its concessions department in Sarasota. He was doing so by currying favor with George Smith, a man who was short-listed to be its new general manager.

Much happened in the Ringling-Barnum organization in 1938. Early in the year, veteran General Superintendent Carl Hathaway was named general manager—taking the place of Sam Gumpertz. When Hathaway unexpectedly died on January 25, that vital position was left vacant for a short time. Tavlin attended Hathaway's service and was invited to a small gathering at its conclusion. He wrote Smith about it and told him of the politicking done on Smith's behalf with John and Henry Ringling North, the new heads of the organization. Tavlin relayed to Smith that he had all but secured the job for him but advised him to expect a verbal lashing when the offer was extended. "When you get there I suppose they are going to give you a little lecture as I heard them talk about all your bad faults, getting drunk in Sarasota and getting in jail, etc . . . Now, George," Tavlin continued, "I impart this information to you and I don't expect anything for it. However, I do feel if you are able to do me some good that you will gladly do it."[26] Tavlin believed that Smith would not forget to return his favor when the opportunity arose. But for Tavlin, the opportunity and the time had to be right, and this was not the time.

Instead of returning to Big Bertha, as Ringling-Barnum was known, Tavlin turned his attention to other money-making propositions—namely, selling concessions at the New York World's Fair. He made a deal with Billy Rose's Aquacade to sell field glasses, another in George Jessel's Old New York Village to supply concessions in three or four of their stands,[27] and was working yet another agreement with sideshow impresarios Lou Dufour and Joe Rogers. What he needed was money to make all these arrangements click. Specifically, he needed money to buy the "garbage," as concession material was called in the biz, and for that, he turned to Art Concello.

To get the dough, Tavlin sent a telegram to Art in July 1938. He knew what to say to grab Concello's attention. "Dear Art," Tavlin started. "I have a good chance to cut in on a big deal at the World's Fair. I would like to have you as a partner for my share of the deal. Lou Dufour and Joe Rogers will be associated with us. I am willing to put up fifteen thousand, will you go ten thousand. If interested, I'll come up and talk it over . . ."[28] Later, Tavlin asked Art for another $5,100 to buy 150,000 pencils and pennants, rain capes, and opera glasses.[29] Two days after that, Tavlin reached out to Concello again with another telegram which stated, "Don't worry. I am not taking any deals unless we have a chance to make real money . . . I have several good things coming up . . . I hope your [*sic*] sleeping good."[30] The next day on March 23, 1940, Art sent Tavlin $5,000.[31]

As a new decade started, Art was sleeping just fine—when he stopped long enough to do so. The performer turned manager placed his non-Ringling flying personnel with parks, fairs, and other circuses both in the United States and abroad. The handsome income from his flying acts as well as his association with Ringling, Tavlin, and others was deposited in the Corn Belt Bank in Bloomington.

Art and Antoinette stopped consistently catching triples in the air,[32] but on the earth and back in Bloomington, they eyed real estate opportunities to further pad their bank account. On December 31, 1941, Art pulled the trigger to buy a six-unit apartment building for $17,965.25.[33] Pride of ownership compelled them to emblazon the combination of their names, Artonia, into the terrazzo entryway of the building, where it remains today. Since he was gone so frequently, Art tasked his father with managing the property for him.[34]

With the war raging in Europe, the United States instituted the Selective Service Act requiring men between the ages of twenty-one and forty-five to register for the draft on September 16, 1940. The slick-haired and darkly tanned Concello did so when the circus made a stop in Columbus, Georgia, on October 16, 1940. He documented his height and weight—five feet, five inches and 148 pounds and named his father, A. Vasconcellos, as his next of kin. Oddly, he recorded his birth year incorrectly, noting 1912 instead of 1911.

Thousands of men were called up to serve the country in its time of need. Sometimes, Art was able to get short-term deferments for friends and flyers by working with the local board officials in Bloomington. As for Concello, despite his physical prowess and obvious courage high above the circus rings, his decided preference was to stay away from war.

Many of Concello's pals served, both those from his childhood days along with those he made through the circus: people like Tuffy Genders, Tex Copeland, and Laz Rosen. Tuffy, who used to skip school with Art as a child and learned to fly with him in the YMCA, served in the US Navy and scoffed at the men who were reluctant to jump ten feet into the water. James "Tex" Copeland ran away from his home in Texas to join up with the Barnes-Floto circus in 1938 and later decided to train his six-foot-two body to be a catcher. He registered on the same date Concello did, October 16, 1940, and listed as his current address 801 W. Locust Street—the Vasconcellos' home. He served two years in the Army. Laz Rosen, a non-trapeze-flying Bloomington buddy whose Russian-born father worked with Papa Vas was, in July 1942, learning how to fire .30 and .50 caliber machine guns and 37 mm antiaircraft guns, but he was dreaming of the day when he could work in some capacity, any capacity, for Art.[35] Art wrote them all.

As for Concello, he continued flying while creating acts and getting them signed to perform in a variety of venues. Before the war, most of the men he used came from—or at least through—Bloomington. Now, after so many of his boys went to war, he had to train and use people he had no history with, like Dick Anderson, who wrote him out of the blue asking for work.

He penned two contracts with John Ringling North for the 1942 circus season. One agreement stated that Concello was going to supply eleven flyers in three acts plus himself (oddly, Antoinette wasn't specifically named), a high-diving act of six people, and two combination aerial bar acts of three people each. In return, the show would compensate him $1,350 each week. The other contract was for ten women, referred to as "Arthur Concello's Girls," to appear in spectacle, web, elephant ballet, finale, and all production numbers for $320 per week.[36] Altogether, Concello personnel made up nine acts for the 1942 Ringling-Barnum performance, created by the pioneer of industrial design, Norman Bel Geddes, costumed by legendary luminary, Miles White, and staged by John Murray Anderson.

The 1942 season of the Ringling Bros. and Barnum & Bailey Circus was set to open April 9 in Madison Square Garden. When the show's train left Sarasota on the last day of March, George W. Smith was on board, performing his duties as general manager. Hours later, he was out of the job.

Smith started drinking—and couldn't stop—when the show started its annual trek north. John and Henry Ringling North had previously tried to get Smith the help he needed to win his battle against alcohol, sending him to an alcohol treatment center, an enlightened decision for the time and one that spoke to Smith's value to the circus. Henry Ringling North recalled the scene years later in his book. "George was an old friend who knew all the intricate technicalities of moving the circus army. But infirmities gradually overcame him, and he kept getting worse . . . We were on our way from Sarasota to New York with the great, long trains and had just reached the Jersey terminal, where we had to transfer the coaches and equipment to railroad ferries to get across the Hudson. It became evident to me that George was in no condition to handle the complicated operation and get the show up in the Garden." Henry then asked Art if he thought he could take over.[37]

Art remembered the night this way: "Anyway, they had a problem with George and damn it, he's a good man and everything. Some guys could drink a quart a day and you'd never know it. But George would fall down . . . George is dead drunk, falling down, and raising hell, and this, that, and the other. Anyway, we get to New York and John North and Henry called me in and says . . . 'Can you unload the train and get it in the Garden?' I said, 'Shit, that ain't no problem . . . What are you going to pay me?' They said, 'We'll talk.' I said, 'Don't talk about it. Tell me something. I don't want to do this god damned thing unless you're gonna pay me!'"[38]

The hometown newspaper, the *Pantagraph,* ran a story on Concello's new position[39] that stated Art had had a financial interest in the show for more than a year, which might have piqued readers' curiosity. Perhaps an enterprising reporter had learned something about the November 1940 agreement between Ida and John Ringling North, Concello, and Coastal Trading Company that enabled the Norths to assemble the needed money to procure the executor's bond the State of Florida demanded for the settlement of the estate of John Ringling.[40] No original copies of the agreement are known today.

Variety's headline for its review of the circus's debut at Madison Square Garden stated that the production lived up to its "greatest show" billing. It went on to mention specifically the flying acts, which were not as prominent as in past seasons. Busy with his new managerial duties, Art, the review said, cut out his double somersault full twister, while Antoinette skipped her two and one-half somersault.[41] Obviously, his mind was not focused on what he could do in the air; it was more concerned with what to do as general manager.

Concello confessed that he had spent years watching the show load up at night and unload in the morning. "I used to be around here and there, in the front, and all over. I used to be down there and knew all the bosses, and knew where everything went, and everything."[42] He was ready to assume greater responsibility. The North brothers agreed to pay him $7,500 backdated to April 1, which was, Henry wrote him two weeks later, "the day I called you in to assist me in getting the circus in to New York and unloaded for the Garden engagement."[43]

On April 20, he drafted a memo to all department bosses, requiring them to provide him with a list of contents of each wagon on the show. Concello wanted to see all its assets and equipment documented on paper. He made similar lists for all motorized equipment and noted how and where it all fit on the train.[44]

Once the circus started its tented tour, Concello used those lists to make several changes to the loading order to increase efficiency.[45] It was the first summer of America's involvement in World War II, and while there was a shortage of men to help raise the tents, the canvas city was erected as swiftly as possible at every stand.

The 1942 version of The Greatest Show on Earth offered new and newsworthy features. An elephant ballet scored by Igor Stravinsky and choreographed by George Balanchine joined the star acts which filled the program: the Wallendas on the high wire; the Cristiani equestrians; and the Concellos on the flying trapeze—though Art was only on the pedestal board sporadically. The animal superstar, Gargantua, was joined by M'Toto, another gorilla. They wed one another twice daily. The war drove down unemployment and produced audiences that had money in their pockets to spend. The circus—and Concello—wanted some of it.

Multiple-day stands provided an opportunity for circus personnel to settle, to relax, and to retool a bit while also saving travel time and freeing locomotives for wartime duty. Cleveland, a four-day stand, came immediately on the heels of a six-day stay in Pittsburgh. The Ohio lot had a view of the harbor but was too small to accommodate the cookhouse, so that was moved across the street. The first day's business on August 3 was good. The weather was clear and the performances were sharp.[46] An eyewitness to what happened the next day recalled that he had just gone into the cookhouse for lunch around 11:30 a.m. "Before the waiter had time to bring my order, someone rushed in the doorway and shouted that the menagerie was on fire. The word 'fire' is all anyone had to hear to see a wild exodus" out of the cookhouse and toward the flames.[47] The blaze burned fast because the tent had been waterproofed with the traditional mixture of paraffin and white gasoline. The fire melted the wax and then used it as fuel the same way a candle feeds its flame.[48] Through heroics on the part of circus employees, many animals were saved, and through luck in the form of favorable winds, the rest of the tents on the lot were spared. General Manager Concello estimated the animal loss to be about fifty.[49] He wasn't far from the mark.

John Ringling North directed the cleanup crew, called the sail loft in Sarasota for a reserve tent, and told his aides to scour zoos for replacements.[50] The show's vet, J. Y. Henderson, instructed the policeman who accompanied him to relieve the suffering of the animals who wouldn't survive.[51] North confirmed to the press that while the matinee would be canceled, the show would go on as scheduled that evening. More than eleven thousand turned out for the evening performance, three thousand more than showed up for Cleveland's opening night.

Huge chunks of change passed between the show and Concello around this time. For example, four days after the fire, Concello requested a note from John North and got it. In it, he agreed to advance Concello $12,500 charged against his account that would be repaid in the near future.[52] Concello gave this note to the show's treasurer, Fred C. DeWolfe, early in the day on August 10, and he advised DeWolfe that he'd be back later in the evening. He visited DeWolfe around 10:00 p.m. in the ticket wagon and brought North and *New Yorker* cartoonist Peter Arno with him. Concello told DeWolfe to make a check out to Arno for $7,500, saying it was to be applied against the authorized advance. He said that he would get the balance later. Around August 20, Concello told DeWolfe that he wanted a check for $5,000. When Concello received the $5,000 draft payable to him, he signed his initials on the note signifying that he had received the full amount authorized.[53] What was all this about? Why would Arno, the cartoonist who supplied the illustrations in the 1942 Ringling-Barnum program, get a check for $7,500 mid-season and not after supplying the cartoons which appeared in the printed program beginning with their Madison Square Garden opener? Why did his payment come from Concello and not the show? What did Concello do with the $5,000 advance? Answers to these questions, if they are out there, could not be found.

The correspondence files he kept at the Farm demonstrate that Concello took a lot of time to write letters, memorandums, and telegrams to lots of people affiliated with show business. But Art rarely took time to write home and took much less time to visit there. The majority of the surviving letters from Concello's parents come from his mother. She was a chatty correspondent who dished on the flyers who visited town. She gently reminded her son that a year had passed since she had seen him and wrote that she hoped she would see him soon. She sent updates about his apartments managed by her husband and supplied him with all the names of his tenants, suggesting it made good business sense to send them Christmas cards.[54] She also brought him news of his sister, Grace, who lived and worked in Chicago, and his brother, Joe, who worked in Peoria but lived with them at 801 W. Locust. Papa Vas, when he wrote, focused on the income and expenses for the Farm and the Artonia apartments downtown.

His correspondence with Harry Dube who, with Jack Tavlin, topped the Circus Publishing Company that provided the printed program, revealed the character of Concello's on-again, off-again business partner, who traveled with Concello as the show made its way through Iowa that year. The evening performance in Waterloo had just started when Tavlin met up with Edward Mullins, the private detective assigned to the circus by the Burns Detective Agency. The show employed private detectives to keep grift to a minimum. A detective, perhaps Mullins, had shut down a racket that was earlier in the season witnessed by another circus employee, Red Sonnenberg. Sonnenberg recalled, "All the money doesn't come into the Red Wagon on a circus. Witness the case of an electrician [who] was nailed side-walling customers at $1.00 a crack. He had over $400 in singles in his kick at the time they broke up his racket."[55]

Perhaps Mullins wanted to shut down a similar situation in the programs department. If so, he had another thing coming. Concello wrote Dube that Tavlin had one of the greatest thrills of his life the previous evening. Art noted, "He had the pleasure of beating the hell out of Mullins, the head Burns man. He really worked him over. He has been wanting to do this for about two months." Tavlin broke a number of Mullins's ribs and delighted in it. Art continued, "You should have been here when they had the fight, Jack was like a wild man. Knocked him down, kicked him in the face, in the ribs, and gave him a real beating."[56] Clearly, Tavlin hadn't quite relinquished his pugilistic way of settling disputes.

Art's 1942 Corn Belt Bank statements documented every cent that he ran through Bloomington. Four-digit and five-digit figures appeared—a $5,000 check was written on September 23, when a deposit of $20,000 was also made, but no documentation exists explaining these figures.

Meanwhile, wartime conditions continued to challenge daily operations of the circus. A newspaper reported in September that the labor shortage had pressed performers into service with the regular workmen in setting up and tearing down the show.[57] By the end of the season, however, the circus under Concello's management reportedly made a net profit, before taxes, of over $900,000.[58] That the big circus prevailed amid the myriad challenges—including a musician's strike early in the season[59]—was due, no doubt, to good leadership under John and Henry Ringling North, as well as Art Concello, with his shrewd handling of people, his knack for inspiring personal loyalty while increasing efficiencies, and the incredible good luck served him at every turn.

One of the last memorandums Concello penned to the North brothers in 1942 noted how much animal feed was needed, when it was needed, how much it would cost to procure it, and from whom. Near the end of the note, he shared ideas on how to sell decades' worth of old costumes to a costume dealer and suggested that two additional guards should be hired to watch over winter quarters for the first two weeks after the show closed to ensure that show property wouldn't walk out without management's knowledge.[60] Concello let nothing escape his attention, especially if there was money to be made (or lost) or efficiency to be gained.

Concello filed 1942 tax returns for himself, Antoinette, the Artony Partnership, and for Artonia Apartments. Art's earnings from the circus were $13,571.92. The Partnership Return of Income for "'The Artonys,' successors to the Concellos," noted $26,469.84, which was divided equally between Art, Antoinette, Papa Vas, and Grace, giving each partner $6,617.75 in addition to their other incomes.[61] By choosing to disperse Ringling earnings, Art decreased his own taxable income and took really good care of his family. Pay for his flying acts booked elsewhere—for example, the Flying Covets who appeared in Australia for the Wirth Circus—were not itemized on his 1942 tax return, suggesting this income was perhaps not reported to the IRS.

The Ringling-Barnum contract Concello signed in 1943 was identical to the one for 1942 with one notable exception—he was no longer required to appear in his own flying act. In fact, Concello would soon separate from Ringling Bros. and Barnum & Bailey. He was quoted, saying, "so anyway, at the end of 1942, December/January 1st, I'm fired . . . "[62]

Chapter 4

"The World's Greatest and Goddamdest!"

1943–1945

> "Show Business always does spoil a person, I think, but that is what is so fascinating about it."[1]
>
> —Antoinette Concello

In 1942 the Ringling Bros. and Barnum & Bailey Circus, like many circuses, recorded an excellent year financially. Stockholders received a dividend for the second year in a row, and the money owed by the company was paid, leaving it debt-free for the first time in years. The route book published at the season's end informed readers that, with the backing of the country's armed forces and political leaders, John and Henry Ringling North looked forward to running their circus throughout the war,[2] and that perhaps they would do so using a nonprofit model for the United Service Organization.

A different faction of the family disagreed that the circus had enjoyed a good year. Aubrey, widow of Alf T. Ringling's son Richard, and Edith, Charles Ringling's widow, found the "theatricalized" way the show had been run disagreeable.[3] Moreover, they made it known that they wanted a "real Ringling" man to top the company—not a North. A special board meeting of the Ringling Bros. and Barnum & Bailey Circus Co. Inc. was called for January 7, 1943. Before entering the New York offices where the meeting was held, John North confided to Art Concello that he was about to be "ejected from his post."[4] Minutes from that meeting reflect that North made the motion to put the show in winter quarters for the duration of the war because he believed the wartime restrictions would negatively impact circus operations. Board members Aubrey and Edith Ringling wanted the circus to tour. In the end he capitulated to the plan to take the show out for the season and accepted the suggestion to take a leave of absence for the balance of his term.[5] Not unexpectedly, a similar motion was made and passed for Henry. Both men received full pay through the end of the fiscal year, April 1. Their cousin, Robert Ringling, a trained opera singer as well as a senior vice president and director, took over as the executive in charge.[6] He had neither the experience nor temperament for the position.

Discussions at this multiple-day meeting eventually got around to the operational management of the show. Robert Ringling had George W. Smith waiting in the wings and brought him back as general manager. Though out of management, Concello was not out of Ringling-Barnum. He still had the contracts for the Flying Concellos and several other acts, and he was busy at his Sarasota shop directing, training, and flying with new catchers like Dick Anderson.[7] The Concellos's contract did not require Art to appear personally. Perhaps luck or a well-founded suspicion that there would be a family dispute leading to the ouster of John and Henry persuaded both parties to write the agreement that way. Or maybe a contingency plan was in the works.

With the Norths on hiatus from Ringling-Barnum, Aubrey turned her attention to their right-hand man. Specifically, she asked Herb Sicks to confront Concello about show property she felt he had wrongfully kept. Sicks visited Concello at his home on January 19 and asked him if he had the properties, which included a Cadillac, air conditioners, welding machines, and anvils. Cagily, Concello neither confirmed nor denied he had anything owned by the circus. Instead, he reminded him that he was awaiting his bonus and payment for January, February, and March—a sum totaling $4,500—and suggested that it would be cheaper to settle with him than to have the case litigated. As for the automobile, Concello assured him that John North, not the circus, had given it to him. He would give it back only when North himself asked for it. Sicks found Art to be "courteous but firm" in his report marked "Confidential." Before leaving, Sicks asked Art how he got into showbiz. Art shared the story and went on to say that he had made $50,000 the last three or four years. Afterward Concello took Sicks back to town in the disputed Cadillac.[8]

As the time approached for the Ringling Bros. and Barnum & Bailey Circus to leave Sarasota for its annual New York City debut, the Concellos hosted a party at their Cherokee Park house. The guests included a cross section of Ringling insiders and the Concello crew: Performance Director Pat Valdo and his wife, Laura; John Ringling North; Frank McClosky and his wife, Fannie; bandleader Merle Evans and his wife, Margaret; and Jack Tavlin, the circus magazine publisher.[9]

For the first time in memory, *Variety* reported, Madison Square Garden was sold out for the Ringling Bros. and Barnum & Bailey season opener on April 9. Tickets were available exclusively to those who purchased war bonds,[10] but about fourteen thousand extremely patriotic citizens enjoyed the circus staged by John Murray Anderson and outfitted by Frenchman Max Weldy.[11]

The big act near the end of the program, act nineteen of twenty-two, featured trapezists. The Flying Concellos, flanked by the Comets and the Randolls, had the center ring spot again, and Art was there, dressed to perform. But on that opening night, his pedestal board somehow broke before he could perform his top trick, presumably the triple, so he cut it. Antoinette didn't dress for the performance due to torn shoulder muscles. Her place was taken by Ernestine Clarke, the daughter of trapeze legend Ernest Clarke and a great all-around performer in her own right.[12]

While Antoinette soon made it back into her wardrobe, Art rarely donned his costume in the show's first couple of weeks, opting instead to occupy his time elsewhere. "You get tired of going to the office every day, don't you?" he told an old newspaper acquaintance in Bloomington of hanging up his tights. "It's the same way with the trapeze. Some days it's hot and some days you don't feel good. Well, you finally get tired."[13] Antoinette summed up her husband's attitude a little differently. "Art was so bored with flying he hardly ever practiced . . . He hoped he would get bad enough to quit, but he only got better instead of worse. It made him very nervous."[14] By the first of May, he directed his nervous energy away from the pedestal board and invited circus veteran Joe Siegrist to take his place there. Siegrist remained in the act for the rest of the season[15] while Art looked toward the future for other opportunities. The world did not realize he was about to transform from flyer to owner, but *he* did.

Removed from management, Art never planned on making an extended stay in New York. Shortly after being unseated as general manager, he wrote a couple of big checks, one for $1,000 and the other for five times as much. In the left margin of the February 23 smaller check, he wrote, "B.R. [Bank Roll] For New York trip take care of people until paid."[16] He turned over the management of his contracted acts with Ringling-Barnum to his wife in 1943.[17] She cashed that check and used it as directed.

The other check, written against Art's Sarasota Palmer National Bank & Trust account, was made out to Jack Tavlin.[18] Tavlin, fresh from his short stint in the army, produced a show at the Goldblatt's Department Store in Chicago, which perhaps needed a financial boost. Tavlin's knack for ingratiating himself with the right people—making himself useful or essential, bragging his way into their lives, and keeping them informed with the right kind of news they could use in the gossipy world of the circus—drew people like Art to him. Indeed, Art seemed to find it difficult not to partner with the slippery Nebraskan.

Friends and former Concello flyers serving in the United States' military in places like North Africa, Europe, and several undisclosed locations sent letters to their former boss, hungry for mail and news from home. They were scared, uncomfortable, unhappy, and counting their service time down in places termed "the hell hole of the world" or worse.[19] Concello did not disappoint. He informed "his boys," many his age or older, where their fellow show folk—flyers, riggers, property men, and more—were stationed, shared addresses when he could, and dished out opinions, ideas, and news whenever possible.

At the end of April, he wrote Willie Kraus, an acrobat turned trapezist who had spent the last ten years trouping with Concello but was now deployed somewhere in the Near East.[20] Art's letter relayed a real nugget of news: John Ringling North, Norman Bel Geddes, and Jack Tavlin were going to join him in Mexico City, where they planned on opening a permanent circus in a building. They would leave around the tenth of May.[21]

As that letter found its way to Kraus, a letter from J. D. "Jake" Newman came to Concello. A circus man since 1892 and a general agent for Zack Terrell's Cole Bros. Circus during the tenting season, he spent the off-season scouting opportunities for Concello. In March, Newman wrote him with news that a nice little show would soon become available for purchase. When the moment was right to buy, Newman wanted to represent Concello in negotiating the sale.[22]

With this percolating in his brain, Concello continued to tell dozens of people—among them his flyers, seat wagon engineer Bill Curtis, and Peoria construction contractor James F. McElwee—about his plans for Mexico. There was plenty of money, the Mexican peso was "five to one" to the US dollar, and Mexico City "seems to be the only Capital City in the world where nothing is rationed," Concello crowed. He added that North had been in touch with Mexico's president, who had supposedly pledged his full cooperation.[23]

Some of his friends didn't share his enthusiasm for presenting a circus in a foreign country during wartime. Frank McClosky, a man who, up to this point, was most well-known among his peers for having been megasuperstar Lillian Leitzel's rigger in Copenhagen when she fell to her tragic death, warned Art about the venture. Having been with Leitzel on Circo Codona in Mexico earlier, he went on, ". . . It was always tough down there. I remember when we were down there everything that was taken into the country had a high duty on it, even an iron stake."[24]

Most of the letters from Bloomington came from Art's mother, who filled her letters with local news. Circus rigger China Durbin labored alongside Papa Vas at the railroad shops. Elden Day, a former fellow Ward flyer like Art, worked in the Meadows Manufacturing Company with Concello's half brother, Joe. She wrote about Eddie Ward, the Concellos' on-again, off-again catcher, for whom Art had written many letters to the draft board encouraging them to classify him as a "necessary employee" of the circus and, therefore, immune from serving. Having just been rejected by the draft board, Ward came back to town and went to see Roger Getty at Corn Belt Bank about getting $100—debited from Concello's account.[25] Art's mother exposed Ward's actions, ". . . he gets so drunk he don't know what he's doing half the time. Was lighting cigarets [*sic*] with twenty dollar bills out at the Grand Hotel. Guess he is squandering all the money his poor old man left him."[26] She seemed unaware of her son's plans for Mexico.

If Art's mother didn't know about the proposed Mexico City plan, she did know about his big bank balance. Grateful that Art paid the taxes for everyone in his family (except for his half brother, Joe Killian), she communicated her blue-collar perspective with her boy. "I thought I was going to faint," Mattie wrote when she learned how much money was due for taxes. "All of that tax money would buy one nice home. Some people never make that much in their life."[27]

Concello wanted to use some of his stockpiled money to purchase booze—lots of it. He asked Peoria builder James McElwee to find him one thousand cases of whiskey. While McElwee couldn't lay hands on the twelve thousand bottles requested—the government wanted distilleries to transition to the production of industrial alcohol—Concello found most of it elsewhere.[28] It's possible that he wanted to take the hooch to Mexico. Providing liquor on the circus lot kept the workingmen on the show and out of trouble with local authorities and civilians.[29] They wouldn't have to find a bar in foreign territory, and they wouldn't have to find their way back to the circus at night. The same concept proved true with gambling. If a game was controlled by someone with the circus, he could keep the house's share of the profits and also assure the men that the game was square. In circus parlance, the place where liquor and games—craps, dice, and poker, for instance—were located was known as the blue room.[30] It made good business sense to keep the workingmen from straying too far from the show, and blue rooms served to keep them there.[31]

If he didn't intend to take the whiskey with him to Mexico, perhaps he had the booze and gambling rackets on Ringling Bros. and Barnum & Bailey Circus. McClosky partnered with Jerry Collins and Willis Lawson to form Sarasota's Victory Coach Company, which shuttled people between Sarasota and Camp Martin in nearby Myakka City, twenty-five miles away. McClosky wrote Art in April to ask him for black market gas coupons and to share the rumor that Red Larkin was running the game at the hotel where most Ringling-Barnum employees stayed.[32] Concello's response arrived when the Big Show was still playing at Madison Square Garden and most of its personnel were staying at the Belvedere

Hotel. After informing Frank about his impending Mexican circus deal, he addressed both of McClosky's points. "You state . . . Red Larkin was operating a game in the hotel. This is not true. The only poker game is operating at the Belvedere under [train master Ray] Milton."[33] Concello next showed how much he was in tune with the black market created by rationing during the war: "In regard to the gas coupons, the heat is on. Impossible to do anything in New York at the moment. Black market was knocked off about ten days ago."[34]

Art wrote a flurry of letters on April 29. In five of them, he shared news of his upcoming business venture.[35] He informed McElwee that he and his three partners would soon leave the United States for the Mexican capital. The last known letter written on this date was a brief message sent to the Bloomington office of the Selective Service. He obliquely asked for a deferment.

Concello had his physical in New York on May 5. The very next day, despite being in excellent physical condition, he received a classification of 4F, "rejected for military service; physical, mental, or moral reasons." Later, after the war, he was reclassified as 4A, "Registrant who has completed service; or sole surviving son."[36] While he was the only son of Arthur D. Vasconcellos, he was not Mattie's only son.

The US government released a publication titled "List and index of Essential Activities" in December 1942. Divided into two sections, "Manufacturing" and "Non manufacturing," the circus industry was represented in neither category. Yet "Certificates of War Necessity" were issued to circus owners so that their vehicles could convey their equipment from town to town.[37] Circuses, like baseball, remained in the fabric of America during the war.

The North brothers responded to the war in dramatically different ways. John, engaged in settling the estate of John Ringling, looked for opportunities to cultivate the impresario lifestyle his uncle developed. Henry, six years younger than John, enlisted in the Navy Reserve at age thirty-two, shortly after the attack on Pearl Harbor, but deferred his service until after he and his brother stepped away from active circus management. Buddy North recalled, "I wangled my way into the OSS," the Office of Strategic Services.[38] His education—at Yale and in the circus—made him an excellent candidate for the intelligence-gathering secret service, the precursor of the Central Intelligence Agency, that specialized in covert operations.

Though risking his life overseas, Henry always had the circus, its management and well-being, on his mind. In July he wrote a five-page letter to his brother outlining what he'd like to see happen on the circus from a mechanical and operational view. "I believe I have definitely hit upon the scheme to solve our labor and transportation problem,"[39] he wrote before laying out his ideas, which involved increased mechanization by using army-surplus hardware after the war, getting rid of wagons, eliminating coaches from the train, and nixing boxcars for the horses. He advised his brother to get busy on this by scheduling meetings with banks, the government, and the army so that all this could happen as soon as possible after the war ended. "My advice," he counseled, "is for you to ask Concello to make a survey of all existing Army transport and then get Norman Bel Geddes (if he will work himself and not just delegate) or Hans Oberhammer to go to work on the design for conversion and also the design for a new grandstand and big top."[40]

In 1943, Robert Ringling presented a strong, old-fashioned Ringling Bros. and Barnum & Bailey Circus program for flush-with-cash, circus-hungry audiences. The Big Show's theme was wildly patriotic, and the circus, like many others that season, offered free admission to war-bond holders and those in the armed forces. Reviewers offered fawning praise and celebrated the return of the "real" Ringling family to management.[41] But the tour was anything but smooth. Antoinette shared with her husband after he left the show that "things are a bit rough," and Art wrote a friend that "John North and myself were right in our decision not to go out with the show this year."[42]

On the West Coast, the Russell Bros. Circus, owned and operated by Claude and Pauline Webb, was doing tremendous business in Los Angeles under its five thousand-seat tent. Operating since the early 1920s, they had begun "with little more than a pet python, a fat lady, and a diminutive one-eyed elephant."[43] With shrewd management and opportunistic showmanship, they built their production up and proclaimed, by the late 1930s, that they were the "world's largest motorized Circus."[44] They had a number of talented people in upper management positions, yet several times over the course of the decade, advertisements for its sale ran in *The Billboard* magazine.[45] Claude, whose health suffered, wanted out of the business and trusted Pauline to handle the details should its sale become a reality. He clung to one condition: the show should be sold as a whole, not piecemeal. Pauline agreed. The time was right to sell. For her, the handwriting on the wall was the terrible labor shortage caused by the war.[46]

In October 1942, Pauline approached J. D. "Jake" Newman to help find a buyer. Jake wrote a telegram to Pauline on May 10, which asked her for the specific terms for the sale.[47] Her response changed the course of Art Concello's life. At 11:30 a.m., Mrs. Webb sent a telegram to Newman which told him the asking price was fifty thousand cash with 10 percent of that going to him.[48] The next day, May 11, Art wrote John Ringling North a telegram informing him that he would be unable to join their adventure to Mexico City, using words reminiscent of that list produced by the government. "I have 30 days to get in some esseccantial [*sic*] War industry sorry."[49] Art had made the decision to be his own boss and buy a circus.

Jake Newman, on behalf of Concello, and Pauline Webb hammered the deal out over the next ten days in a flurry of telegrams. One sent to Mrs. Webb by Newman on May 22 outlined the specifics for the transfer set to happen at the end of their San Francisco stand on June 28. Concello, always unnamed in the telegrams, wanted to use the title for the remainder of the year and would be out in the first week of June to close the deal with the down payment made via a certified check.[50]

Perhaps Pauline never received that telegram, or possibly she—or Claude—had seller's remorse. After a telegraphically quiet six days, she wired Newman on May 28. "Sorry you delayed so long answering show has been sold [to another party]."[51]

Concello wasted no time hiring attorneys to straighten things out. Leonard Bisco, longtime legal representative for John Ringling North, recommended Concello use Messrs. Loeb & Loeb, Los Angeles–based attorneys for the job. Concello retained them, and Bisco brought them up to date on all the specifics of the case, including copies of all the telegrams placed and received. But trouble loomed.

On June 23, 1943, Concello brought suit against C. W. Webb et al. in the Superior Court of the State of California. He alleged that the Webbs agreed in writing to sell their circus to him on May 14, 1943, but they rescinded the agreement on May 28, and by June 3, would not transfer the title nor deliver the circus to him, even though he had agreed to pay the asking price of $50,000. The suit raised the question of whether or not Pauline could act as the selling agent. Concello's attorneys asked for $100,000 in damages and costs for him.[52]

Like most legal matters Concello was involved in during his career, this matter was settled out of court. By June 26, Art wired Newman to inform him that the deal had been closed. He asked Newman to come out to Stockton, California, to get his commission and meet with him.[53]

The legend circulating around Art's purchase was that Red Larkin (whose real name was Larkin Goldsmith) drove him to the San Francisco stand where Art walked up the short side of the lot, through the back door, out the marquee entrance, and handed a briefcase containing $50,000 cash to Webb to purchase his show.[54] Concello and his canceled checks tell a different story. Red Larkin drove him to the California lot. Once there Webb asked for his $50,000. Instead, Art gave him a check for $35,000.[55] At the end of the season, when it was proven to Art's satisfaction that there were no significant outstanding bills, Webb got the rest of the money.[56]

With a circus purchased, Concello started shopping around for people who might want the privilege of partnering with him or, at the very least, operating the concessions on his show. His first selection was the Miller brothers, Frank and Paul, who ran the Coastal Trading Company, the firm that sold the concessions on the Ringling Bros. and Barnum & Bailey Circus. When they were with that circus in Baltimore, Art wired to ask if they wanted to be his only partner, sweetening the deal by intimating that good money could be made with it.[57] They turned Art down. Concello then found two already working for the Russell Bros. Circus—Lou Berg, who had the lunch wagon and concession stand, and Jack Joyce, who worked as a performer and the ringmaster.

Concello signed an agreement with Berg and Joyce on June 27 wherein Berg and Joyce were to pay $500 each week until the end of the Russell Bros. Circus's touring season. Berg and Joyce believed that this contract, along with a verbal gentleman's agreement to split the season-end's profits on a 10 percent–10 percent–80 percent basis, established them as partners where they were the operating company and Concello was the holding company. In this way, Art limited his liability and protected his assets, a common business model for circuses then and now.

Trouble soon developed between Concello and Berg and Joyce. They claimed they raised a portion of the $50,000 needed to buy the Russell show. Later, after Concello took over, they said that friction developed, Concello barred them from the premises in Denver in early September, and he then refused to account for the show's earnings.[58] The men wanted to not only end their relationship with him but also to sell the circus and share in the proceeds.[59] They believed a lawsuit would accomplish this.

Concello vehemently disputed the men's claims. In his deposition, Concello begrudgingly admitted that he viewed the lease and the gentleman's agreement as meaningless, unless the men could each put up $5,000. He contended that neither Berg nor Joyce ever came up with the cash. Not unexpectedly, there was no final judgment in this case. The suit was settled out of court. Joyce rejoined Concello the next season.

By his own admission, albeit years later, Art did set up a holding company for his Russell Bros. Circus. Concello thought, "Screw this . . . I'm going to have someone else own the equipment and I'm going to run the operating company." He tapped his friend from Bloomington Ed Raycraft, the Bloomington Cadillac dealer, for it. Concello's thoughts continued this way: "If I get sued in Odessa, Texas, Goddamnit, I'm going to have Raycraft come in and say, 'Wait a minute, that's mine. Don't touch that, that's mine.'"[60]

John North missed running his circus; he missed the activity, and he missed the people. Dick Anderson, a performer Concello trained, remembered North always hanging around Concello's shop waiting for him.[61] When the opportunity to operate a circus in Mexico City dried up, John visited with former employees like Frank McClosky and Jack

Tavlin there. Both men and, likely, others reported North's activities to Art regularly. McClosky, who looked after both Art's house and his shop and chauffeured North when he was in Sarasota, wrote that John thought that the time was not right for Art to buy Russell Bros.[62]

News of the Russell Bros. sale to the thirty-two-year-old Concello spread quickly. Congratulations poured in from friends, flyers, and those eager to work for him, do business with him, or just stay on his good side. Art's response to each of them was to humbly suggest that the "nice little show" he purchased had "much room for improvement."[63] A far different tone was used with his hometown banker who oversaw deposits ranging from $5,000 to $20,000.[64] "I told you guys this is a real deal and no one believed me. It is a real winner."[65] He was even more blunt with Frank McClosky. "I think he [North] is very wrong as I have had the show two weeks and it has made nothing but money."[66] While Johnny was sidelined from his family's big circus, Art was running his smaller one up the western coast, earning more prominence, wealth, independence, and status in the world of spangles and sawdust.

Tavlin, keenly aware of where money was at all times, wrote Concello in mid-July: "I suppose you are making so much money that most of your time is taken counting it."[67] Art responded a few days later, after talking with him on the telephone. Art first assured Jack that he wouldn't repeat anything he heard and then asked him to extend encouraging words to John North, who was missing the action. "Give John my regards and tell him I am going to write him soon. I do hope everything is going along nicely for him and tell him to keep his chin up as everything is going to be alright. I know he was upset about the show and time will prove same. I am his best booster."[68]

Tavlin continued currying favor with Concello, tempting him to partner up. He first assured Art that they would make a good team, acknowledged that Art would be boss, and then said he'd invest up to $30,000 to make the partnership work.[69] No evidence suggests Concello took him up on this proposition at that time, but he became a silent partner of Tavlin's by throwing in $4,500 to make his winter holiday show at Goldblatt Bros. Department Store in Chicago work.[70] The theater in the department store seated five hundred and it featured American Indians.[71]

Half the continent away, Walter "Punchy Forbes" Kernan was serving in the army, working with heavy machinery in an engineering regiment that was soon to ship out for North Africa.[72] Art wrote Kernan, relaying rumors he'd heard about his replacement on the Big Show in the summer of 1943. "Understand G. W. [Smith] has started on the bottle again—give them enough rope and they will hang theirselves [*sic*]. Everything will turn out OK for the future. It has started to work out already—just like J. R. N. said."[73] As if sharing this tidbit was a favor, Art asked Walter for one in return. Namely, he wanted intel on the army's air-compressed stake driver. Kernan complied with his friend's request in his next letter.[74]

As for the money Concello spent buying Russell Bros.' Circus, he made his investment back almost immediately.[75] After sending the show up the West Coast, he turned it east to Spokane and points farther east and south. In Idaho, they met stiff competition from Cole Bros. Circus, the show with which Newman was affiliated. A staffer on Cole informed a friend about the situation. "Had opposition with the Concello troupes in Boise, Burley, [and] Twin Falls, Idaho. They showed a day ahead of us in La Grande, two days ahead in Pendleton [both in Oregon], and three days ahead here [in Walla Walla, Washington]. We gave them a good licking, so I think they will stay out of our way from now on."[76]

The season was winding down. Showmen called this final, often-risky leg of a circus's tour the dead man's trail, because the financial gains of the summer could be lost there in the fall. The show had made money. The trick now was to keep it.

Russell Bros.' press agent, Bill Antes, confided to friends that the circus would close early in Denver and then would winter back in Los Angeles. "Mis-management, contention, and disorganization is partly the cause, but then Art's made his wad, so why should he continue?" he wrote.[77] Art's income from ticket sales was great, yet in the deposition given during the Joyce and Berg lawsuit, Art repeatedly stated that he closed the season early because the show was running out of money. He also said that he never deposited profits into his personal bank account,[78] which was simply not true.

But the Russell Bros.' Circus did close four to five weeks early in Denver,[79] publicly citing the polio concerns in Oklahoma and Texas as the reason. Soon after, Concello called Waldo Tupper (his superb general agent) in from the advance and gave his man Elvin Welch (nicknamed "Sheriff") a special task after hearing Tupper's concerns about finding enough truck drivers to take the show's thirty-eight trucks south. He tasked Sheriff with finding fifteen railroad cars and then set the show in Los Angeles. Moving trucks on railroad flats had been done decades earlier, but Art was the first one to do it during World War II. Sheriff leased the flatcars, Concello negotiated with the railroads to transport them, and the show moved back to Southern California to rest for the winter at the old Selig Zoo in Lincoln Heights, northeast of Los Angeles. Concello paid Webb the remaining $15,000 due to him, cut his circus down to be a one ringer, added rodeo elements, and renamed it King's Olympic Circus for a short winter season at the zoo. It offered three ninety-minute shows each day for the admission price of sixty-five cents.[80]

With the year close to ending, Concello's plans for the next circus year grew. Those signed to work for him could not ignore the little man's talent. His press agent wrote friends that Art's show the next year would "make everyone sit up and take notice."[81] Art was going to frame a rock-solid circus, one bigger and better than it had been. He advertised in *The Billboard* and fielded inquiries for employment at all levels. From Bloomington came a letter from flyer Elden Day, who wanted a contract for himself and his wife. He wanted a bit more, though. "I would want something else to do on the side . . . I want to make some of that 'non-taxable' money!"[82] Art always found ways to take care of all of his boys, Day included.

Concello sent letters asking others—many on the Ringling Bros. and Barnum & Bailey Circus—to come work for him. He reached out to medically rejected draftee Frank McClosky, who had given up trying to operate a bus company to watch Concello's Sarasota-based flying practice shop for him. "I can use both you and Fannie here with the show," Art wrote, "Have [a] set-up for you where you can make a buck. Let me know . . ."[83] At Concello's command, McClosky shipped everything from Art's Sarasota shop back to Papa Vas in Bloomington and then headed west with his wife to join the show. Art made him a manager.

Art's brother-in-law, Allen King, was offered a job but was also warned, "liquor and wagon shows don't mix!"[84] Art placed him in charge of reserved seat tickets and put six men under him. Always thinking of business, on Christmas Eve he sent a telegram to Tavlin. "Do you want a position with me next year—concert, sideshow, programs? . . . Advise immediately."[85] Tavlin took the program's top spot.

A lot of Ringling-Barnum people came to work for Concello. One of the biggest stars—if not *the* biggest star—to leave Ringling for Russell was Antoinette.

In the weeks leading up to the 1944 debut of his show, Concello alerted his friend, Tex Copeland, who was serving time in the army that "quite a few of the 'Squeese [*sic*] Mob' are here including Frank and Fannie McClosky, Red Larkin, Bob Reynolds" and nine others. His letter stated that he planned on opening the season March 16 around San Diego.[86] He also wrote his friend Merle Evans, bandleader for the Big Show, and asked him to send any music he wouldn't be using because "this guy's library will probaly [*sic*] be from the 18th century,"[87] referring to the music catalog of Orin A. Goodson, his show's bandleader.[88]

Dude Rhodus, a former Concello flyer, wrote from an army camp in Oklahoma, offering words of encouragement to both Concellos: "I can't see how you'll miss, with Artie behind the wheel and Anti on the pedestal ('head up—break hard & full, Anti') . . ."[89] A congratulatory letter from his first trapeze teacher, C. D. Curtis, received a rapid reply. Delighted to hear from him, Art provided his mentor with an update on what was happening in his life. Then he took the opportunity to share that Tuffy

Genders was waiting to hear back from the army, that Frank McClosky didn't pass his physical, but that Big Joe Remillette, Grace Killian, and Red Larkin were with him in California. He ended by acknowledging he was a poor letter writer but wanted Curtis to keep writing him frequently.[90] He missed his friends. To childhood chum Lewis "Laz" Rosen, Concello wrote, "You mentioned you would like to be here for opening, sure wish you could make it Laz. I wouldn't run you down the road like I used to a few years back. Are you laughing?"[91] Another note received stoked Concello's pride by suggesting his new show would become known as "The World's Greatest and Goddamdest [*sic*]."[92]

Concello's King's Olympic Circus closed before the start of the Southern California rainy season. The time had come to provide the show-going public something different, something bigger, better, and unexpected. The time was right to bring in one of the biggest names of the sawdust ring. And as luck would have it, that star—Clyde Beatty—contacted him first. As Art told Curtis, "Clyde hasn't been out here since 1938 so he should draw."[93]

Proclaimed by many as "one of the greatest wild animal trainers of all time," national celebrity Clyde Beatty reached out to Concello, who had loaned him money back in 1929, when they were both on the Hagenbeck Wallace Circus.[94] It had been years since Beatty—or any big cat act, for that matter—had toured the West Coast, and people there were hungry to see the famous star of films, books, and the circus perform in the steel arena.[95] Through weeks of negotiation mostly managed through a flurry of telegrams and air mail, a deal was made. Though the full nature of the partnership remains a mystery, Concello assured Beatty he would get a percentage of the net profits after the show left winter quarters.

The Clyde Beatty-Russell Bros. Circus went out on forty-two vehicles and eight private living trailers,[96] including "the biggest and fanciest trailer ever built," which housed the performer turned owner and his wife, Antoinette.[97] Every piece of Concello-owned circus equipment was painted ". . . something snazzy. The Red hurts your eyes," Antoinette relayed to her sister-in-law, Grace Killian.[98] The paint wasn't the only new thing. Art outfitted his show with a new 150-foot big top, new uniforms for attendants, and all new wardrobe for performers.[99]

Circus insiders suspected that Concello might have trouble framing his show because rival Arthur Bros. had taken many of the Russell Bros.' staffers.[100] Concello successfully lured many former Ringling-Barnum personnel west to work for him, but even with doing that, the total number of people working for him was reported to be only 124. The labor shortage meant that everyone had to pitch in. A clown recounted that the showgirls set up the chairs in the big top; the candy butchers handled the two middle pieces of the big top's canvas, installed the reserved seats, and assisted in erecting the menagerie tent; and the clowns moved their own trunks and props after putting up their dressing tent. After the finale, the same people worked to tear down what they had helped set up.[101]

Jack Joyce was the equestrian director and Red Larkin, often Art's chauffeur, served as the announcer on the road. Concello surrounded himself with loyal friends he could trust. Joining McClosky in the manager's office was half sister Grace Killian as secretary-treasurer. Ed Raycraft, the Bloomington Cadillac dealer, managed the front door, and Jack Tavlin served as the director of public relations.[102]

Art never forgot his self-imposed financial obligations to his family. With his wife he incorporated the Artony Company in California in early February to operate the show and protect himself.[103] Antoinette choreographed the "Ballet of the Sky," which featured the showgirls performing on the Spanish web. She also occasionally performed with the Flying Concellos, the act that closed the program, but the usual troupe members were Grayci Genders, "Big Joe" Remillette, and Elden Day. But it was Beatty's act that really brought in the crowds. His famous name packed customers into the big top, eager to see the safari-clad star with whip, gun, and chair battle the "natural enemies of the jungle."[104]

Art's circus did tremendous business up the West Coast. The show "had sell-out after sell-out at both afternoon and evening performances," wrote Bill Antes, general press and radio representative.[105] Antes negotiated tie-ins with national radio programs *Truth or Consequences*, *People Are Funny*, and *The Charlie McCarthy Show*, built around the Clyde Beatty-Russell Bros. Circus, which stirred even more ticket sales.[106] The year-end operating statement recorded gross receipts of $917,409.41. Salaries, wages, and commissions, along with the percentages of profits to partners—sideshow operator Pete Cortez and Clyde Beatty—ate up just about half of that amount.[107] But money (and lots of it) was made. It was not unusual to regularly have $15,000–$20,000 on the floorboards in an old tin box before Concello could transfer it to his banks.[108]

The circus got good publicity when Hollywood stars Greer Garson, Bing Crosby, and Wallace Beery—whose own background included circus work—visited the Los Angeles lot[109]; it also earned media praise for benefit shows promoting the purchase of war bonds, politeness to customers, and outfitting the hustling concessions vendors, known as "butchers" in circus vernacular, with signage showing the correct price to be paid for popcorn, cotton candy, and other circus fare. Tucked inside the band of their hats, a cardboard sign read "25¢ Pay No More." With a nod to the extra income always desired by personnel, a reviewer noted that Elden Day, one of the Concellos' star flyers, could be found selling programs to patrons as they entered the big top.[110] Day might have been marking up the price of programs and pocketing the "non-taxable" difference. Concello rewarded loyalty.

He also took care of an early mentor, Chuck Holloway, who had worked at the YMCA with C. D. Curtis when Art was a youngster learning the trapeze. Holloway took pride in guiding young Artie away from wildness and the streets. Sometime after naming his eldest daughter Antoinette after Artie's wife, Holloway left central Illinois for better work in California. His youngest daughter, a teenager at the time, recalled that her family was living in a rented "cracker box of a house" in Naples when Concello came to visit. Art, after giving the house a once-over, reached into his coat and "took out enough cash for a down payment for the three-bedroom house," saying, "For Christ's sake, get yourself a house!"[111]

Los Angeles fire ordinances and painful memories of the Cleveland menagerie blaze two years earlier compelled Concello to be proactive about fireproofing his canvas. When news flashed of the Ringling Bros. and Barnum & Bailey's tragic fire in Hartford on July 6, 1944, Concello doubled down on promoting the precautions he took so as to relieve patron anxiety. A performer with Beatty-Russell recalled the evening of the tragedy in Hartford vividly and said the big top was fireproofed immediately after the last performance of the day.[112]

The Clyde Beatty-Russell Bros. Circus faced stiff opposition from Arthur Bros. Circus but still managed to do tremendous business. Arthur Bros. Circus, a truck show, was owned by Martin Arthur and managed by former Russell Bros. assistant manager Bob O'Hara. Suspecting that Concello was going to run the Clyde Beatty-Russell Bros. Circus up the coast, Arthur Bros. made the tactical decision to play dates ahead of Concello. Antes pointed to the success of the show's wait poster campaign, which counseled the public to wait for the better circus—namely, Beatty-Russell. Space on barns, on the sides of downtown buildings, and in storefronts for colorful poster spreads known as "hits" were jealously guarded and vigorously defended by the bill posters on both shows. Posters for one show were covered in another circus's paper, which led to "billing wars" between competing poster brigades that often ended in physical violence between the rival shows. Art put his faith and trust in his executives to win the marketing war to bring in the business. "I had Red Larkin and all them rough guys around. Hell, I suppose they fought [with Arthur's men] and raised hell . . . I think they did everything to each other, but I backed off . . . I had good bosses . . . they was able to break them up."[113]

Concello's 1944 season was also notable for its audacious geographic jump. After taking the circus up the West Coast and inward to eastern Washington state, Concello told his advance agent, Tupper, to get twenty railroad cars so that the show could jump from Spokane to Nebraska, where he felt there was more money to be made.[114] That's just what they did to play to fresh audiences, people who hadn't seen the Clyde Beatty-Russell Bros. Circus. The show got to Grand Island, Nebraska, six days after closing in Spokane. From Nebraska through Kansas, Missouri, Arkansas, Oklahoma, and Texas they traveled, closing the season in Longview, Texas, on October 30. The circus played 127 cities in twelve states, covered 7,184 miles, and gave 423 performances.[115]

Now thirty-three, Concello termed his 1944 circus season twice as good as his first one as a show owner.[116] Perhaps because he was sick of being in a spotlight or he preferred to stay in the shadows, Concello's name did not appear in the route book produced at the end of the season. But he was the wizard behind the curtain who kept the show playing to paying audiences. He did so by handpicking a trusted team to serve with him.

Art paid off Clyde Beatty at the end of the season with a lump-sum payment of $130,000. "This was more fucking money than Clyde had ever seen in his fucking life," Concello recalled years later.[117] With Beatty paid off and operating his own circus, Concello sought and found another partner—for a forty percent stake—in Jack "Abie" Tavlin for 1945. "Yeah, I sold him a piece of the show and there's your fighting right there. Abie was fighting with them all the time."[118] Art was talking about Tavlin's propensity to fight the competition. That was not Concello's first priority.

Encouraged by a strong season, he wanted to expand. While much of Art's circus laid over at the Louisiana State Fairgrounds for the winter, he and Jack Tavlin purchased fifteen railroad cars from carnival operators Beckman and Gerety.[119] His Russell Bros. now joined Arthur Bros., Cole Bros., and Dailey Bros. as a medium-sized railroad circus. This was a master stroke on Concello's part.

Railroads offered greater flexibility and more efficiency, making quick jumps to areas with larger populations, bypassing small towns or trouble spots and arriving with predawn fanfare in city rail yards. The term railroad show was still magic in customers' minds, denoting size and prominence. For Art, making the leap was easy. He had guided the biggest circus of them all three years before.

Art gave Tavlin free reign to outfit the privilege car where personnel could eat, drink, relax, unwind, and maybe play card games (of which the house always took a cut) or the slot machines.[120] Tavlin named the car the "Trocodero" in honor of the Sunset Strip nightclub where Hollywood stars went to be seen (though he unintentionally misspelled it), and he spent thousands hiring an interior decorator, who equipped the car with stainless steel cooking fixtures, a fancy linoleum floor, special drapes, and flashy color combinations.[121]

Whenever possible, Concello shored up finances before starting a new circus season. After paying off a note early to Ed Raycraft,[122] Concello went back to him in December 1944. This time Raycraft held a $40,000 mortgage on Art's show equipment to protect Concello's assets should another lawsuit crop up.[123]

The management staff changed little between 1944 and 1945. McClosky retained the position of manager, Tupper was the general agent, and Wallace Love, the auditor. C. A. Sonnenberg, head of concessions, handled product and the butchers, while Francis Kitzman had the billposting brigade. Art's biggest hiring coup was luring Ringling's press agent Roland Butler to join Bill Antes in handling the show's publicity. Butler had famously and shamelessly promoted Ringling for decades with bombastic press releases and signature artwork of charging tigers, grinning clowns, and heroic performers—now that legend worked for Art. Orrin Davenport replaced Beatty as director of personnel and added equestrian director and ringmaster to his duties. As such, he signed two of the biggest names among circus performers: the Cristiani family of bareback riders and Con Colleano, "the Wizard of the Tight Wire." Vander Barbette became the director of productions. Henry Kyes replaced Orin Gilson as the bandmaster.

Advertisements in *The Billboard* invited applications from performers, sideshow attractions, concession butchers, drivers, and laborers to apply to work for the show now touted as "greatly enlarged and traveling by rail for the first time in its history."[124] Concello's goal was to give the West Coast public the finest circus ever witnessed. The ad promised a long season with the best accommodations and working conditions. Applicants for drivers, train crew, and other laborers were to write Concello directly at Shreveport. He made all the hiring decisions and then trusted his department heads to manage them.

Because his was a West Coast–based circus like his primary competition, Arthur Bros. Circus, Concello wanted to lock up as much talent and available labor to put them on notice. The "little old trap," as Art later described Arthur Bros., was a fifteen-railcar circus like his, but unlike his, they made money the old-fashioned circus way, by cheating customers.[125] The "grift" was plied by confidence men known in the business as "lucky boys;" their crooked gambling rackets lured gullible towners and usually operated out of the sideshow tent. Shortchanging took place at the ticket windows. Agent Tupper kept Concello posted on the latest news as he made his way through some of the same territory covered by the rival show. "As usual, they left plenty of heat," Tupper had written his boss the previous July from Spokane. "They had four men arrested for gambling and one for carrying a six-shooter."[126] Art expected trouble with the Arthur Bros. Circus again in 1945 but trusted his bosses—and Tavlin in particular—to manage it.

For the first time in their sixteen years together as a married couple, Antoinette was going to have a baby. A friend described Art's wife as the happiest person on earth because she'd wanted a baby for so long.[127] Randall Cope Concello debuted on February 16, 1945. The infant's name honored both Art and Antoinette's families. Art's mother's maiden name was Randoll (sometimes spelled Randal), and Antoinette's grandmother's maiden name was Cope. Ringling bandleader Merle Evans drove Antoinette to Tampa to have the baby, signifying the close bond between the two families.[128] Art commemorated the birth by naming the private railcar he purchased for personal use "The Randy."

It's unclear where Art was while his wife was in labor, but he likely was somewhere west of Tampa. A few days after their son's birth, Art's mother died following a nearly two-month stay in the hospital.[129] Perhaps he was arranging his mother's Catholic High Mass funeral—her good standing in the Church despite having married outside of it was apparently secured—and making arrangements to have her buried in Park Hill Cemetery. Her letters to her youngest son revealed admiration, love, and devotion. Infrequently, she offered advice. More frequently, she asked him to tell her what was going on in his and his wife's lives. Over the last few years, she'd written Art repeatedly on her birthday to tell him that he'd forgotten it once again.

Although emotionally distant, Art held his family financially close. He continued to employ his father to manage his properties in Bloomington. Joe Killian ("Snort," as his half brother was called), frequently arrested and fined for public drunkenness and disorderly conduct, benefited from his younger brother's watchful presence. Believing that hard work might help him stay sober and productive, Art hired him to be in one of the flying acts he named for him: the Snorts. When that didn't work, Art put him to work doing rigging and ironwork for the Spangles Circus in 1943. Unfortunately, Joe washed out of that, too. So Art resorted to moving his brother around the country in a nearly continuous and almost always unsuccessful bid to keep him out of trouble. He employed Grace, the more reliable Killian, as a secretary-treasurer whenever possible.

In the spring of 1945, the war in Europe was winding down as the Allied Forces closed in on Nazi Germany. Americans looked ahead to Japan's defeat and a return to peace. Despite restrictions and rationing of transportation, fuel, and supplies, the years had largely been lucrative for the circus industry. Shows delivered a welcome escape for the weary public. While the overseas war cooled off, the war between West Coast–based circuses was heating up. Concello, who seemed able to foresee and forestall any calamity, could not predict that he was about to take a hit in his most vulnerable spot, his bank account.

Three shows competed for the big Los Angeles-area crowds. Cronin Bros. set up on the well-known Washington and Hill Street lot, forcing Arthur Bros. to find another spot to show, while Concello's circus premiered in the Pan-Pacific Auditorium. When Tavlin and Red Sonnenberg noticed Cronin's posters plastered all over LA and Hollywood, they had a local printer prepare a ribbon "update" that read, "The Location of the Circus has been Changed to the Pan-Pacific Auditorium." [130] With typical bravado, Abie and Red covered Cronin's posters with the strips, which effectively diverted patrons to Concello's location. It worked. Cronin Bros. Circus folded shortly after its season started.

The name of Art's show now reflected the venue where it premiered: The Russell Bros. Pan-Pacific Circus. Art considered a circus could do good business without the hazards—like fire or heavy winds—of a tent. The personnel shortages caused by the war could also be reduced and, therefore, profits increased. The six thousand-seat, art deco–styled arena caused him some initial headaches. For example, before the show opened on March 29 for its eighteen-day appearance, tons of dirt had to be hauled in to cover the floor so the stock could work on it.[131] But his was the first circus to ever play there. No doubt the lessons he learned were stored for later reference.

The third competitor was Arthur Bros. Circus, which boasted the appearance of movie cowboy Ken Maynard. Not to be outdone, Concello brought in fellow former Ringling-Barnum performer "Bring 'em Back Alive!" Frank Buck for the opening stand. Reviewers were awed with Art's show, which had lavish costuming, hosted exquisite acts, and used the auditorium's ice-show lighting to good effect.[132] No one caught on to the fact that the *Russell Bros. Pan-Pacific Circus Magazine and Program*, produced by Tavlin, featured plagiarized articles originally published in the *Ringling Bros. and Barnum & Bailey Circus Magazine* of 1942 until the season was almost over.[133] Concello even hired Peter Arno to create an image for the program's cover.

Earlier in the season, attorneys for the Ringling Bros. and Barnum & Bailey Circus investigated a tip that the Russell Bros. Pan-Pacific Circus was misleading the public into believing Concello's circus was part of the Ringling operation. Advertisements for the West Coast–based circus touted the Ringling-Barnum talent appearing in the smaller outfit as if they were still contracted with The Greatest Show on Earth.[134] Paul Eagles, the advance agent for Arthur Bros., planted the clue.

The Arthur Bros. Circus continued to foment ill will in the communities it played by cheating the public at the ticket booth, concession stands, and in rigged games of chance. Concello's publicity man, Bill Antes, knew something had to be done before all the territory was ruined.[135] Arthur Bros. Circus left such a sour taste in city authorities' mouths that communities were reluctant to welcome another circus. Tavlin was ready to physically persuade Arthur Bros. personnel to get out of Concello's show's territory, at the very least.

Concello didn't want to hear any of it. He told Tavlin and others who may have been involved with fighting the other show, "I'm making a lot of money here, and if they want to fight, the hell with them."[136] It's likely that Tavlin created a poison pen campaign using an alias to help. One "B. Wilson," a self-proclaimed "advocate of the American Way of Life," circulated letters to towns where Arthur Bros. was scheduled to appear. "Wilson" claimed Arthur Bros. Circus operated shell games, three-card Monte, and "many mechanically controlled sure-thing games," not only on its sideshow but also on the midway. Wilson stated that "many cities this season have, after thorough investigation denied them a permit [to appear]." The second page of his letter included copies of newspaper reports about Arthur Bros. with headlines like "Not wanted here."[137]

By August, the Arthur Bros. Circus's character assassination crusade was working. Martin E. Arthur filed a complaint against Concello in Boise, Idaho, asserting that he promoted "false and scandalous" propaganda about the Arthur Bros. show.[138] The judge refused to grant a permanent injunction against Russell Bros. Pan-Pacific Circus, believing the geographic separation of scheduled dates solved the problem.[139] Concello took this as a victory. As for Arthur Bros., it managed to finish the season, but it would be its last.

The Russell Bros. Pan-Pacific Circus traveled over ten thousand miles, showed at 136 locations in eleven states,[140] and fought competition over much of it. But now Concello faced a far greater threat from within his ranks. Late in 1945, Tavlin absconded with over $40,000 of the circus's money—funds intended to cover taxes and other liabilities.

Tavlin did it by taking advantage of his check-signing privilege on the account at the Citizens National Trust & Savings Bank in Los Angeles. That account was established for funds to be available to either Concello or Tavlin if one was off the show when a signature was needed.[141] Tavlin wrote three checks for cash, totaling $40,040 (roughly $580,000 in today's dollars) on October 13. Planning to dissolve his partnership with Art, Tavlin simply stole the money, drained the account, and vanished.[142]

It got worse. As a result of Tavlin's actions, Art's check to the IRS bounced. The agency stepped in to control the circus and seized its assets. Concello's battle with the government dragged on until the late 1940s. It was a hard lesson of misplaced trust for the confident and successful Concello, and it was a lesson he would not forget.

Chapter 5

"Nothin' but Money!"

1946–1948

"Well, I did them in 1947 when I wasn't doing anything . . ."[1]

—Arthur M. Concello

While the Russell Bros. Pan-Pacific Railroad Circus planned to end its 1945 season in El Centro, California, it actually closed its season in El Paso, Texas. General agent Waldo Tupper had slotted the show into the Texas town for October 8–10. On the last day, huge winds, rain, and hail shredded the big top tent. Getting a new top so late in the season was impossible, so Concello decided to winter the majority of the show's equipment and stock right there in the city's livestock exhibition buildings.[2]

The Russell Bros. title never toured again with Art Concello as owner. The show's auditor, Wallace Love, filed paperwork in California to close the circus at the end of January 1946.[3] Wanting to rid himself of any reminder of Tavlin, Art sold the railcar outfitted by him, the Trocodero, to Al Wagner's Cavalcade of Amusements, a carnival. He transported five elephants from the show back to Bloomington, first to his barn and then to the local zoo[4] before he sold them to the Kelly–Miller Circus.[5] The sale led some to think Concello was getting out of the business.

Rumors also swirled of a renewed relationship between Clyde Beatty and Concello. In 1945, Beatty had purchased the Wallace Bros. Circus and toured the truck show under the title Clyde Beatty Circus. Concello, who seemed to know the finances of all the circuses at all times, saw that Beatty "lost his ass" that year,[6] so it came as no surprise to Concello that Beatty sold his show in mid-January 1946.

Beatty and Concello started negotiating terms for affiliation in December, around the time Concello was transporting elephants and Beatty was appearing in Houston's Shrine Circus. According to Art, Clyde had sent him "a big, long wire" imploring Concello to take him on again.[7] By New Year's Eve, plans were finalized. Beatty brought his eight elephants, his eighteen big cats, a Liberty horse act, and a pony drill.[8] Like their 1944 agreement, the big cat trainer got a percentage of the profits after all costs once the show premiered.[9] Concello still believed Beatty was a fabulous draw for audiences and a less-than-stellar businessman.

New cage wagons were needed to get Beatty's felines on the fifteen-car railroad show set to open in El Paso. Concello ordered four eighteen-foot wagons with five compartments in each that were designed to look like trailers, not traditional cage wagons. Wagon makers all over the country turned him down, so he used a shop in Eureka, Illinois, to build them. It would not be the last time he redesigned circus equipment to increase efficiency and a circus's bottom line.[10]

With Art's show—now commonly referred to as the Clyde Beatty Circus but officially called the Clyde Beatty Trained Wild Animal Railroad Circus—wintering in El Paso, he visited his acts booked on Shrine Circuses from Grand Rapids to New Orleans. Antoinette suspended her career in favor of raising Randy. In between familial demands, she corresponded with her show friends around the world. To those in postwar Germany, she sent food packages along with words of encouragement, often sharing how much she missed performing now that she was a stay-at-home mom, like so many others.[11] Back in Bloomington, the Artonia apartment building sold in January.[12] Papa Vas, still grieving the loss of his wife, would no longer have to concern himself with it.

As was the annual norm, people wrote Art looking for work. Concello jotted notes on the letters he received, like "Want this man to day [*sic*]" on Andrew J. "Dummy" Robinson's application letter. A deaf (sometimes noted as a deaf-mute) native of Tuscaloosa, Robinson boxed professionally as "Silent" or "Dummy" Robinson in the middleweight and light-heavyweight division throughout the 1930s before joining the properties department of Ringling-Barnum in the early 1940s.[13] Now Concello had the pugilist with him, as a show of muscle. Art was the intimidator, not the intimidated.

He responded to Charles Clarke with a tentative offer[14] and a firm offer for Charles's nephew Joe Siegrist. The latter joined Elden Day and Jeanne Sleeter as flyers to be caught by Jeanne's father, Red Sleeter, in the Flying Concellos act slated to close the Clyde Beatty Circus performance.

Concello chose Ira M. Watts for the general manager position. Born in Missouri in 1895, Watts cut his circus teeth selling tickets with the James Patterson-Gollmar Bros. Circus. After serving in World War I, he came back to eventually work with and learn from the grifting showman Fred Buchanan. Though Buchanan warned Watts that he wouldn't like working for the squeaky-clean "Sunday School" goliath, Ringling Bros. and Barnum & Bailey Circus, come payday, he sure did. "Mr. John" Ringling liked Watts's work and after purchasing the Sparks Circus in 1929, he set him up as its general manager in 1930.[15] After Sparks, he spent time with other circuses before the flailing economy pushed him out of the Ringling organization. Following a year spent out of show business, he got back under the white tops, but this time for what would be a series of truck shows, including one he co-owned named Parker & Watts Circus,[16] before Concello tapped him for the managerial spot on the Clyde Beatty Circus. Watts summed up his no-nonsense management philosophy this way: "You can't get the money unless you get it [the canvas] up."[17] He was on the same page as Art.

Other management positions were also filled early. Jimmy Albanese had the watchdog role over all aspects of the shows' finances as treasurer. Wallace Love served as the auditor. William Moore fixed beefs as the legal adjuster, Bill Antes directed the publicity department, and Tuffy Genders watched the front door as its superintendent. As paymaster, Grace Killian made sure everyone who worked got paid. Jack Joyce was back with horse acts and as equestrian director.

Written negotiations between Jack Burslem and Concello illustrate the importance Art placed on getting the right man for the job. The correspondence with his managers clearly indicates Concello ran a show with games—poker, dice, and the like—in his pie car.[18] Art wanted the experienced pie-car manager Burslem to oversee the operations there and was willing to increase the percentage of his take to get him; however, Jack, his wife, and her family's act went with Sparks Circus in 1946.

The Clyde Beatty Circus opened on March 22 to capacity houses for both its matinee and two evening performances. From Texas, the show moved through Arizona for six stands before presenting shows in San Diego. It got to Los Angeles for the seventeen-day run on April 11. A truck with an aircraft-type searchlight mounted on its flatbed swept the skies and lured people to the well-known circus lot. The show receipts were $205,000 for thirty-five performances there.[19]

The circus had no meaningful competition as it made its way up the coast through Oregon and Washington. Though slated to continue east from Spokane, Concello changed his mind, similar to the time he scuttled the original Washington route in 1944. He liked to keep his circus's route fluid so that it could play to the largest possible crowds. General agent Waldo Tupper, who had the critical job of determining the show's itinerary, had repeatedly and tirelessly reminded Art that a tented circus had not shown in Canada since Al G. Barnes presented there in 1937.[20] "Canada is all fresh!" Tupper cajoled. He also believed his shirttail connection to the late Sir Charles Tupper, the former Canadian prime minister, would make for easier bookings. When he shared his notes of the incredible receipts the Barnes show enjoyed nine years earlier, the die was cast. The life-changing decision to play Canada was made. Concello relied on Tupper and his team to book it.

Two new partnerships were formed before the Beatty-Russell show went north. Wallace Love topped one of them and was joined by Bill Antes and Harold Genders. The other partnership included Jimmy Albanese, Bill Moore, and Jack Joyce. There must have been a financial advantage for creating these entities—perhaps to spread the wealth and therefore decrease the Canadian taxes owed or to hide income—but no documentation was found explicitly stating why these combinations came into being. No explanation was unearthed as to why Concello's name does not appear in either partnership. Surely he benefited monetarily; it's just not clear how.

The first Canadian stand on Vancouver Island presented more than the usual logistical challenges. Emigration, barge and steamer traffic, and tidal times had to be considered in addition to the customary details like railway and loading schedules. The risk paid off not only on the island but all over Canada as it made its way through British Columbia, Alberta, Saskatchewan, Manitoba, and Ontario. "We did $10,000 a day with a fucking show that cost $2,000," Concello recalled.[21] The show's press agent provided more detail in a letter to friends: "Personally I don't think any show, anywhere, or at any time ever enjoyed such enormous consistent business. The midway is packed from ten in the morning until midnight day in and day out. We gave three performances almost daily . . . and turned hundreds away . . . Have often wondered if we will ever see business like this again in the circus."[22] Circus historians still consider the Beatty show's Canadian tour as one of the greatest financial successes in field show history.[23]

The Clyde Beatty Circus crossed back over to the United States at Niagara Falls on September 27. Stateside, business never reached the phenomenal heights achieved in Canada. The receipts were light but seemed dismal when compared to the income to which they had grown accustomed.[24] The season ended nineteen days later in Brunswick, Georgia.

Beatty was especially disappointed but was more intrigued to hear Concello offer him the show for a cash price at the close of the season. Circus historians relayed the story that Beatty entered the office wagon one day to find Concello sitting behind a table piled with money—both paper and coin. Concello slid the money, said to be in excess of $30,000, across the table with effort, saying something like, "Business has been great, here's your cut." Beatty's reply was to ask if the show was for sale, and if so, how much would it cost to buy it. Concello replied that it would take $100,000. Beatty then asked how much would be needed for the down payment. Concello then reached across the table to sweep all the money back and said, "About $30,000."[25]

That story isn't far from the truth. On October 29, 1946, the Artoney Company, Inc., consisting of Arthur M. Concello and Wallace R. Love, entered into a contract with Clyde Beatty whereby the latter purchased certain circus equipment and assets from the former. The specifics of the deal stipulated that Beatty would pay $35,000 cash as a down payment. Beatty later paid the Artoney Company $55,000 in twenty installments ranging from $1,500 to $7,500, starting April 15, 1947, and ending September 1, 1948. An escrow account was established for this purpose at a bank in Nacogdoches, Texas, where the Clyde Beatty Circus wintered.[26] Beatty's payments were transferred to the United States Treasury Department and applied to the tax due from Russell Bros. the previous year.

In May 1947 Wallace Love, the circus's financial wizard, wrote manager Ira Watts. In that letter—which provides the nearest thing to evidence that the books were cooked—Love wrote, "It is interesting to note the percentage of [net] profit against the receipts. I doubt if any Circus has ever shown a greater Net Profit from a percentage standpoint than we did in 1946. Too, we had plenty of "Extraordinary" expenses."[27] What was not "extraordinary" was that Art seemingly willfully hid profits while pulling all the strings from the shadows. In an all-cash business, many likely did the same. His players made themselves and him a great deal of money but probably didn't report accurate income or inflated their "expenses." Tax problems with Canada went well into 1947, but Concello let his attorney and Love handle them.

Over at Ringling Bros. and Barnum & Bailey Circus, things had gotten messy. At the heart of it all was a family dispute over who should top the entertainment giant. John Ringling North spent nearly every waking moment since walking in January 1943 striving to regain control of the show after the war. Two other men—each from a different branch of the family and each representing one-third of the stock—joined him in jockeying for the top spot. Robert Ringling, son of Edith and Charles Ringling, had held the presidential post from 1943 to 1946. Then James A. Haley was installed as president.[28] Inept decisions and a lack of managerial skills resulted in turbulent years for the Big Show. Many, including Concello, believed it was only a matter of time before North was back in command. A final settlement of John Ringling's estate helped to swing things in John Ringling North's favor, but it was a complicated situation.

The stars aligned for John Ringling North (and therefore Concello) in 1947. The eleven-year battle over John Ringling's estate ended in August when the state of Florida accepted North's offer to purchase all the interests of John Ringling's estate for $1.25 million.[29] The state stipulated, in part, that $500,000 be paid within ninety days.[30] North needed cash—$180,000 of it—to consummate the deal, and he knew Concello never lacked that commodity. In September, Art and Antoinette provided North $80,000, drawn against their Bloomington Corn Belt Bank account. Frank and Paul Miller, concessionaires heading the Coastal Trading Company, provided $60,000; T. D. Buhl, former Yale roommate of John Ringling North, and Harold R. Brophy, a New York attorney who once represented the John Ringling estate, both loaned $20,000. The Concellos' loan was payable in one year at 5 percent interest,[31] though a later due date was eventually negotiated. This cleared the way for North's return to the top spot.

With the $500,000 down payment, North acquired John Ringling's estate assets, which encompassed Sarasota County realty holdings, Oklahoma oil properties, and a one-fourth interest in the Al Ringling movie theater in Baraboo, Wisconsin. Most importantly, it also included three hundred shares of Ringling Bros. and Barnum & Bailey stock.

The Haleys saw the handwriting on the wall and agreed to sell some of their stock to North. North knew if he bought 140 of Haley's shares, he would have 510 shares, or 51 percent, of the Ringling Bros. and Barnum & Bailey company. But to make that purchase, he needed more money. As Henry North recalled, "Eventually, John and our mother put up $100,000. He raised the rest with the help of his favorite flyer, general manager, and true friend, Arthur Concello."[32]

To outward appearances, in 1947 Concello seemed to be everywhere all the time.[33] He continued to place his acts with various Shrine circuses in the winter and for the tented season of April to October, the Flying Concellos act was on the Clyde Beatty Circus. Antoinette was reported to be performing, but friends conveyed the conflicting news that she now hadn't flown in over two years.[34]

The Concellos used Bloomington as their home base over most of the summer,[35] but they traveled frequently. After getting a few lessons from Bloomingtonian Art Carnahan, Art now flew through the air differently—by piloting a new four-seater Bellanca airplane.[36] Never one to follow rules, he did so without a pilot's license until it was issued to him on Halloween.[37] Both alone and with his family, Art visited shows where his troupes were performing to check in on them. Cash flowed weekly to Concello from act managers. One of his groups, which played the West Coast Polack Bros. Circus dates, sent him $8,726.59 over the course of thirty-seven weeks. For comparison's sake, the manager for the five-performer, one-rigger act made $3,340.25 during that time.[38]

Antoinette and Art visited longtime friends on the Cole Bros. Circus lot on two sunny days in Rockford, Illinois, in July. Antoinette and Eileen Voise caught up with each other and swapped sore shoulder stories, perhaps even discussing how best to fix them. They both had shoulder surgeries performed by the same surgeon in the same New York City hospital less than a year later.[39] Meanwhile Art, chewing his omnipresent cigar, squinted while talking with Harold Voise, the man he flew with years before in the Ward barn. Coincidentally, *The Billboard* both reported on the Concellos' visit and touted a new way Voise rigged his acts in its July 26 issue. The rigging had no blocks or falls and included a rachet system that made it possible for one man to guy the entire wire support system out in five minutes.[40] If there was something in the circus business that made the show more efficient, Art sure wanted to know about it.

The circus pages within *The Billboard* well documented Concello's activities. *The Pantagraph*, their hometown newspaper, to a lesser extent, did too. On May 10, the *Pantagraph* reported that Art made a forty-hour quick hop to New York,[41] where he met with attorneys and John Ringling North to strategize how, as John put it, "to get the show back."[42] The trade paper documented several visits Concello made to the Big Show, often with Bloomingtonians Ed Raycraft[43] and Lester Thomas in tow.[44] These trips were hardly just social visits. Arthur had a plan and Thomas was an integral part of it.

Art and Antoinette first worked with Lester Thomas in 1929, but his circus experience extended back further than Concello's. Lester Mitchell Thomas was born in Chicago on January 11, 1903. Les, as he became known, stopped attending school in the sixth grade, and when the family moved to Bloomington, he fell in with the young flyers working out at the YMCA and at Eddie Ward's barn. By 1921, he traveled with the Sells-Floto Circus as Lester Ward.[45] The Dunbar & Schweyer Circus brought the young man to South America in 1928, where it moved by pack mule.[46] Exhausted by that adventure, Les started the 1929 season with Art and Antoinette on the John Robinson Circus, but unlike them, he finished the season there.[47]

More than being a flyer, Thomas became known as a first-class rigger. While he was on the Barnett Bros. Circus, he became associated with Ray Goody, a wire walker who wanted new rigging that wouldn't necessitate drilling holes in fancy floors for indoor dates in places like hotels and resorts. Thomas understood the mechanics of what was needed and completed the new design for a wire-walking frame in January 1939.[48] Goody submitted the drawings and applied for a patent but was not granted one.

Bloomington had been the hot spot for trapeze flyers for decades. Now, in the late 1930s to the mid-1940s, the community was gaining notice as a place where circus equipment, props, and rigging were built. The Hub Welding Company and Kaiser Van Leer Company churned out circus equipment to a star's specifications. Les worked in their modern new machine shop, whose advertisements proclaimed it as being nationally recognized as a fine example of buildings of its type.[49] The deluxe hardware store offered complete service for tradespeople from mechanics to electricians, plumbers, contractors, and farmers. Circus and, specifically, trapeze superfan Harold Ramage (the sales manager) welcomed the business there. Just a few blocks away, Eddie Hebeler, known professionally as the wire walker Eddie Billetti, worked at Hub Welding Company, where he specialized in building equipment for circus performers—from aerialists to elephant trainers and beyond. "It's a funny thing, but no two aerialists will use the same size rope," Hebeler said in 1946, when the local newspaper highlighted the tremendous business he was doing with circus performers.[50] Men like Hebeler and Thomas, because they had backgrounds in circus, had the ability to create the specialized gear people in the industry needed.

Thomas no longer performed professionally by 1944. Trapezists rarely had careers spanning more than a decade, much less two decades. Injuries often forced aerial artists into ground-based jobs. Although Thomas managed a café in Bloomington in the winter of 1945, he still had the itchy feet endemic to so many circus people. He wanted to troupe. Come spring, Concello chose him, the former Ward flyer and trusted Bloomington buddy, to oversee the Russell Bros. Pan-Pacific Circus's pie car.[51]

Thomas heard a lot while selling hamburgers to the working men. Sore backs caused by the hard physical labor of setting up seats under the big top was likely an oft-repeated complaint. Perhaps hearing such protestations compelled him to think and doodle. Eventually, he lit upon an idea for mechanical seat wagons and then, once back in Bloomington, he used his time in the machine shop to build a model of one.

In 1947 he brought his design for seat wagons to Concello. Art liked what he saw and struck a deal with Les. Concello would pay the expenses of hiring a patent attorney who would shepherd the design through the US Patent Office if Thomas would agree to turn plans for them over to him for an undisclosed price. Thomas agreed.

Concello used much of 1947 to entice the Big Show into purchasing the seat wagons. In May he brought the idea to the circus's president, James Haley. The pitch he made was simple. He said, "Gentlemen, this labor situation is getting bad. This will save you a lot of money."[52] He described how the system would use twenty-eight separate steel mobile grandstand wagons that, when erected hydraulically, formed an oval around the big top. The boxlike structures unfolded mechanically. Manual labor was still needed to lock the twenty-two tiers of upholstered blue and red chairs into place, but instead of requiring 250 men over three hours to assemble them, the new seat wagons could be spotted, set up, and ready for an audience in about an hour using far fewer men.[53] Haley turned him down. Concello went back to Bloomington to wait.

Concello used the time wisely. He found the Lewis-Diesel Engine Company in Memphis to manufacture the wagons. "Now Womble," he wrote the company's vice president, "[the seat wagon] must be good and will have to work perfectly with a minimum of labor, so get on the BEAM and get this thing built by the time they close [the season]."[54] Concello sent the initial $2,500 down payment for the first experimental unit with a signed contract for the first vehicle. Womble estimated that each all-steel wagon would weigh around twenty thousand pounds and cost $7,265 with volume discounts for subsequent orders.[55] All Concello had to do was wait to sell North on the concept.

Art brought Les Thomas and the seat wagon model[56] to Ringling-Barnum when it was appearing in Texas and Mississippi.[57] He used the face time he had with North, who was now traveling with the show, to tout their labor-saving (and therefore money-saving) benefits. John seemed intrigued.

Then it happened. In October 1947, North took control of the circus during the Atlanta stand. Attorney Leonard Bisco was there along with a half-dozen other men, including Concello, who had arrived from Bloomington. Haley abruptly left Atlanta in his railcar, leaving behind General Manager George Smith, who found Concello to nervously ask him about his future. "Shit, George, nothing's gonna happen," Art told him. All he was going to do was check the tickets and count the money.[58]

He did a little bit more than that, however. The show was doing turnaway business in Atlanta on Monday, October 27. While standing in front of the marquee, he noticed a circus employee sneaking customers into the show under the side walls in a practice called (not unexpectedly) sidewalling. The hand came up to ask if he wanted to see the show. Concello asked how much it would cost, and the fellow gave him a price fifty cents more than the price of a general admission ticket. While Art was sardonically impressed that the employee tried to price gouge him, two days later the man was unemployed.[59] The message was clear: Concello was in charge.

With the circus season nearing its end, a Ringling-Barnum board meeting was called for November 15 in Sarasota. As agreed upon earlier, North was named president and Robert was given the title of chairman of the board.[60] At the same meeting, and for the second time in his life, Art became the general manager.[61] One of the first things he did was to ask the Ringling-Barnum auditor how much salary George Smith received. Concello asked to get at least $12,000 per year.[62]

With his experience both as a performer and manager, his connections, and his brilliant mind, Concello was entirely ready to once again manage The Greatest Show on Earth. Bill Taggart noted, "When [Concello] was out in the circus as a flyer, he knew everybody," the veteran Ringling trouper recalled.[63] Through his network he became aware of who worked and who didn't as well as who was loyal and who wasn't. He also recognized the right palms to grease. "Art Concello knew how to do it. And he knew how to spread the money around and . . . spreading the money around made the circus move."[64]

Concello installed his most trusted people in key management positions and gave them the autonomy necessary to do their jobs. After the painful lesson learned from his troubles with Jack Tavlin, Art would never again rely on anyone he couldn't vouch for 100 percent. In time, these experienced managers were to become known—notoriously—as the Sneeze Mob. Back in Sarasota, the local paper reported on the now-out-of work activities of the "Anti-Sneeze Mob"—those Robert Ringling loyalists who were no longer department heads.[65]

Art's managers were a who's who of childhood chums, past associations, partnerships, and deals. Among them were Walter Kernan, who kept Art informed of conditions on the Ringling show during his absence, and longtime Bloomington friend and fellow flyer, Harold "Tuffy" Genders, who was assigned to watch the entrance to the big top. Trustworthiness was required from the person who had the front door responsibilities on a circus because ticket takers had more opportunity to steal from the circus than almost all other employees. Another longtime Concello loyalist, C. A. "Red" Sonnenberg, was in charge of selling programs, and Bill Antes headed up the radio coverage.[66] Frank McClosky was Art's assistant. Willis Lawson served as assistant to McClosky. Lloyd Morgan was the lot superintendent. Waldo Tupper became the general agent making the vital decision where the circus would appear and Grace Killian, his secretary. Noyelles Burkhart was hired away from the Cole Bros. Circus to serve as assistant to the legal adjuster, Herb Duval. Venerable Pat Valdo, longtime Ringling veteran, retained his role as director of performance. Together, their duties ran the gamut of the Big Show's daily details. Nothing escaped Art's attention. It was said if you sneezed on the lot, Art would find out about it from his network of informants.

The activities of the blue room, where gambling and booze could be had, kept the working men occupied and more importantly, on the lot. His "persuasive charms with tough itinerants, ne'er-do-wells, and winos" worked the magic that Nena Thomas gruffly teased him about, saying, "You can work a person longer hours for less money and make them like it more than anybody I ever knew."[67]

If Concello heard complaints, he referred them to the appropriate department bosses, who reported everything back to him. At the core of his relationship with others was leverage. "He was smart. He knew everybody's dirty laundry, too, including John Ringling North's," remembered one Ringling veteran.[68] Information translated into money and power for Concello.

Interested in saving the circus money whenever he could, Art tapped McClosky to sell off surplus paraphernalia in 1948—from the menagerie tent to wardrobe, coaches, stock cars, and wagons.[69] Concello watched the small stuff, too, like stationery. An anxious staffer informed him that use of more expensive letterhead was only necessary for a short time because of a delay in the delivery of a less expensive grade.[70]

John Ringling North inked the deal to purchase the seat wagons on the second day of January 1948. The agreement was made between the Ringling Bros. and Barnum & Bailey Combined Shows, Inc. and Arthur Concello, Grace Killian, and Antoinette Concello of the Artony Company. The circus agreed to purchase sixteen wagons for the grandstand chairs around the center ring and twelve for the general admission sections at the ends of the big top. Concello was to receive reimbursement for the $2,500 he paid to have the first unit created. In addition, the circus agreed to pay Artony $20,000 per year for ten years. Concello maintained control by retaining the right to choose three to four foremen and one engineer to supervise the operation of the wagons and had their salaries paid by the circus, too.[71] He installed Les Thomas to oversee the seat department and worked with Womble's men in Memphis to create the wagons in 1948 and 1949.

In his history of the Ringling family, Henry Ringling North lamented the old laborious business of building a wooden grandstand every day and praised Concello's innovation as a part of the effort to modernize the circus.[72] The next spring, 1948, the seat wagons were rolled out to great fanfare. Publicity photos showed the big top superintendent, Leonard Aylesworth, as well as John North, Art, and William H. "Cap" Curtis, inventor of the original seat wagons years before, posing in front of one of the wagons with performers filling the seats and an elephant in the aisle, triumphantly raising its trunk in tribute of the new design—so strong it could withstand the weight of a grown pachyderm. About half of them were used in 1948, with the other half coming the next season.

The promotion of the invention was a secondary matter to Concello. "I don't want publicity. I want money," he said.[73]

The Lewis-Diesel Engine Company wanted money, too. Modifications made to the original design had increased the cost of production the second year, with the result that they just barely broke even on them.[74] The circus still owed money to the manufacturing department of the firm, which Concello promised to forward "at an early date," adding what could be construed as a menacing threat: "I understand your company is fooling around with some type of seat wagons. If this is done by you I want 10% of any sales you make as I have a patent on the seat wagon idea, so keep this in mind."[75] Womble quickly replied and promised Concello he would be brought in on any such transaction should one crop up.[76]

There were issues with the new wagons. Many recognized that the seats were too flat, a fact that made it necessary for people in the upper rows to stand so that they could see the ground acts.[77] Art communicated regularly with Cap Curtis, a designer of seat wagons from an earlier time, but refused to implement the changes Curtis recommended (namely, fixes that would allow the seats to set up on soft lots and raise their elevation so that customers wouldn't have to stand) until the wagons were paid off.[78]

But Concello knew the manufacturing company had to be paid for its work. Years later Concello explained that he got all the money Lewis Diesel needed to build the seat wagons from others. Art identified at least some of the men: Walter Kernan, Bob Reynolds, and Merle Evans came to mind initially, but later he admitted that he likely used some of Ed Raycraft's money, too. Of this he was sure: none of his money was used to build them. "I promoted the money," he said. "I didn't put a God Damned nickel in it myself."[79] It's interesting to note that while Concello paid for the wagons, the circus reimbursed him and gave him $20,000 each year to use them—perhaps as payback for the loan he gave to John North to get majority interest.

North increasingly distanced himself from the day-to-day operations of the circus while Art entrusted many of the daily details to his hand-picked managers. Concello would not ask anyone to do anything he himself would not do. He was still a man who was here, there, and everywhere.[80] Art made no secret of what he believed to be the trick to running a circus well. "A good boss picks himself good assistants. If an assistant complains to me about his boss, I say to him, 'Look fellow, if you can't get along with your boss, you can't get along with me.'"[81]

The three-ring layout of tented circuses had been a treasured tradition for generations and changed little over the decades. For Big Bertha, a sea of "tops" spanning roughly ten acres sprung up on circus day, each housing some department of the show. On the front end, commonly known as the midway, customers purchased Big Show tickets, food concessions, and souvenir novelties. The "banner line" of garish images lined the opposite side of the midway, beckoning people to the human oddities and acts of skill and illusion found in the sideshow tent. After purchasing their tickets and entering the main entrance, or marquee, the patron transitioned into the "free" menagerie, housed under a separate tent adjacent to the big top. This tent became one of Concello's targets.

His plan was to arrange the animal cages, elephants, and lead stock—such as camels and zebras—in the front section of the main tent, just inside the main entrance. Doing this eliminated the need for the menagerie tent. A fifth center pole was eventually added to lengthen the big top to accommodate the additional section of canvas. Roars of the menagerie's denizens mingled with Merle Evans's blaring music during each performance, but the concept worked.

Ever the logistics guru, Concello hit his stride once the Ringling Bros. and Barnum & Bailey Circus opened under canvas in Washington, DC. But trouble reared its head once the show reached Pittsburgh in late May. Though attendance was strong, the circus was set up on an unusually challenging lot with inadequate parking and, worse, a severe thirty-five-foot slope that posed huge rigging challenges inside the big top and resulted in the death of an employee outside of it, when Gargantua's heavy steel cage broke free. Crew member Huston Asher died after trying to singlehandedly steer it away from the crowd. The next day the show's train hit another circus employee.[82] But the show must—and did—go on.

Earlier, in the spring of 1948, *National Geographic* featured a color-packed spread about "The Wonder City that Moves by Night." Authored by the former Ringling-Barnum press representative F. Beverly Kelley, it noted both Concello's strong presence on the show and the changing nature of the circus business. "The warning bell for outdoor shows has sounded," Kelley wrote before hinting that the impact auditoriums had on tented circuses was real.[83]

When the tour took the circus through the lucrative West Coast territory in August and September, the public, if they stopped to think about it, could see Kelley's suggested forecast play out. For the first time, the circus showed inside San Francisco's Cow Palace, where it had tremendous business with gross receipts of $187,000 for its seven shows.[84] Though the Los Angeles date was marked by a gasoline shortage and a polio scare, a fund-raising gala for a local hospital brought out scores of celebrities to help present the show in the six thousand-seat Pan-Pacific Auditorium. Frank Sinatra and Bing Crosby were in clown face while Concello stood by with a trident. Elizabeth Taylor, Lucille Ball, Ronald Reagan, and Betty Grable were all on hand at the event, which was carried live by eight local radio stations.[85] In San Diego Concello was arrested during a performance on a charge of violating state fire regulations by admitting 1,500 patrons, who ended up sitting in the aisles, in front of the grandstand, and in the exit passageways.[86] This was a common practice in circuses known as strawing, as straw would be put down on the ground for the overflow audience to sit on. Although the tent was fireproofed, officials wanted to avoid another Hartford-type disaster. The case was dropped when Concello forfeited bail.[87]

After California, the Ringling-Barnum circus toured Texas, Oklahoma, and the South. It picked up good publicity in Lubbock by agreeing to play the Panhandle-South Plains Fair. The circus's policy was not to play fairs, but the changing nature and increasing vulnerability of the tented-circus business led Concello to take a chance. Though the local press touted the agreeability of the circus and praised its willingness to break tradition, Ringling didn't return to Lubbock again until 1951.

For the Ringling Bros. and Barnum & Bailey Circus, the 1948 season proved to be the best of the postwar years. In a tribute to Art's management acumen, a New England newspaper commented, "This season the show has profited immensely by expert routing, moving on time, and experienced handling of the various departments . . . The 33-day run in New York shattered all records. The week in Boston—cut from two weeks in 1947—was a sellout."[88] The article concluded with a sentence acknowledging Concello's desire to stay out of the limelight by stating if Concello had seen it before it was published, he likely would have nixed it. Nevertheless, the article concluded, "On and off the lot, Concello is in charge and the show goes on in a manner that would bring joy to the five founding [Ringling] brothers."

"How the fuck are you?"[89] Art often greeted his associates each morning. He knew the lot better than he did his own driveway back in Sarasota, and he strode the circus grounds with the unquestioned authority of a crime boss, major politician, or Fortune 500 CEO. The rough-talking, cigar-chomping boss of The Greatest Show on Earth exacted respect and exercised the control of someone who knew exactly what he wanted. He could—and did—operate with impunity. "As general manager, he didn't intend to depend on luck or his charm to get him through the numerous pitfalls faced by a touring circus playing under a giant tent," one historian explained. "He handled everyone . . . with the same self-assured aplomb. He let them know he was the boss and that his word was law."[90]

Showgirl Mary Jane Miller recalled, "He was very crude, very rude most of the time. He'd go around hitting the girls on the fanny all the time. He always did that."[91] Another veteran of that era said that Concello had a reputation for sexually assaulting showgirls. "If they didn't object, it was fine, but if not, they left." He added that Art "was too smart" to try the same behavior with the female star performers.[92]

He regularly used vulgar language and a tough, intimidating style, but he seldom forgot his roots. He now made his Bloomington barn available for rent as a storage facility,[93] and he kept tabs on people who had helped shape him as a youth. One such person was Bill Brown, who once was Art's YMCA camp counselor but now worked in the advertising department of Minneapolis's *Star Tribune*. Concello sent him four tickets to the circus when it displayed there in July, telling him, "You won't have any reason for not coming out to the circus and seeing me!" Brown recalled his earlier relationship with the showman: "I was a councilor (sic) at a YMCA camp. Our boys were from homes where there wasn't money to spend for vacations. One of the kids was a little fellow named Art . . . He was a lot of muscles, not much boy. He had broad shoulders and a passion for the trapeze."[94] That high school dropout had transformed himself into the general manager for The Greatest Show on Earth.

On the best days, money from the thousands of circus goers, like Bill and his family, flowed down the midway like a green tide. They bought popcorn and cotton candy, hot dogs and soda, and cheap flags and trinkets. The "bug man" hawked live anole lizards native to the southeastern United States that changed color from brown to green; these were promoted as "chameleons." From the sideshow stages, the attractions sold souvenir postcards of themselves. The circus giant offered metal copies of his rings that were the diameter of nearly a fifty-cent piece. Likely everyone who sold something to the public kicked back a little something to Art.

"The smartest move I ever made,"[95] said North of getting 51 percent control of The Greatest Show on Earth. He needed money to get the control, and Concello was instrumental in providing it. John North had resumed his presidency of the circus, once again free to play the role of international *bon vivant* and talent scout, late-night socialite, and visionary showman. Concello made sure that the circus city, erected in a different town each day, hummed efficiently. Kickbacks from the people running poker games and other forms of in-house games of chance lined his pockets with the greenbacks he craved. Concello ultimately had "the yes and no," meaning he was the final arbiter on the lot.

Bonded by a mutual operational dependency, the North-Concello relationship was a symbiotic friendship that, if not totally founded on trust, was at least marked by a wary confidence that each would somehow prosper from the business wits of the other. In their own ways, both dreaded boredom. They preferred pursuing the art of persuasion and the science of deal making. While North sought the limelight, proximity to celebrities, and coverage in gossip columns, Art chose to remain in the background, where his influence over the circus was total. His command of logistical details and his ability to size up others translated into resolute authority. His lifelong pursuit of control and money could be further satisfied. From his early days counting the house from atop the high pedestal board, through his profitable ownership of his own show, and now to his return as the manager of America's biggest and greatest circus, Art was approaching the pinnacle of power.

Chapter 6

Hollywood Comes Calling

1949–1953

"We have a way of keeping secrets here on the show that has no equal anywhere else in the world."[1]

—Nena Evans

The postwar decade brought new opportunities to Art Concello. Never one to look back, Art leveraged his increasing business savvy into deals to nurture his bank accounts. Problems like help shortages, increasing railroad rates, union fracases, and lot size and locations, not to mention the exploding popularity of television, vexed the man tasked with managing the tented giant. These challenges were assuaged somewhat by the tantalizing profits the North brothers and Art thought could be made beyond America's shores in the circus-hungry country of Cuba. Outside the circus rings, business opportunities—ranging from real estate to casinos, from dog tracks to carnival rides—piqued the financial curiosity of both Art and John, whose interdependence continued to grow. Art kept a finger on the pulse of everything that impacted the circus's bottom line and developed strategies to diminish any negative consequence these things might have on it, yet he didn't realize that his own proclivities might damage their brotherly bond.

John Ringling North depended on Concello to increase the show's financial standing so that he, as president, could bolster the artistic impact his circus had on American audiences. Hailing Art as "the first real general manager the show has had since the palmy days of the Ringling Bros. Circus in 1907,"[2] North gave him authority to make business decisions on the lot, big and small. Nowhere was this more evident than in the work done to bring the splendor of The Greatest Show on Earth indoors—to movie theaters from coast to coast.

In April 1948, David O. Selznick and John Ringling North unveiled a plan to create a Technicolor circus epic based on the Ringling Bros. and Barnum & Bailey Circus. The proposed total budget for the film was estimated at $6 million, a huge amount, with Selznick as the producer and North as the technical advisor.[3] Though the storyline was advertised by some as complete, the next year, when the show was at Madison Square Garden, Selznick had yet to produce a treatment.[4] Johnny loved the idea of his circus being the centerpiece of a film created by a hugely respected and successful producer, but when Selznick pleaded with Concello for an extension to complete it, Concello said no and North backed him.[5] The option Selznick had purchased from John North for $250,000 lapsed.[6]

With Selznick out, Paramount, MGM, and Twentieth Century Fox competed for the project. Paramount and Cecil B. DeMille won with their proposal in July of 1949, and less than six months later, it was formally approved by the Ringling-Barnum board.[7] The agreement stated, in part, that Paramount would pay the circus $25,000 per year for the next ten years. The circus would also get $75,000 as an advance against the royalties of 10 percent of the film's gross receipts. The royalties kicked in when the film earned back twice its negative costs,[8] which consisted of the cumulative costs of production.[9]

North spent freely to produce a circus that looked nothing short of spectacular on film. This irritated the fiscally conservative Concello. Just when John started visualizing beauty, Art suggested slashing the costume and props budget to a total of $100,000, and not one penny more. He told John this cut would be met with disbelief if not disdain. But, he maintained it was necessary and advised, "Whatever has to be done to work this plan out must be done, regardless of who it effects, including yourself and your relatives, so you better think this over and let me know what your decision is."[10] Johnny pondered Art's request and then provided $200,000 to White.[11] Exasperated, Art told Henry, "I think John is foolish for using people like Miles White, when there are so many [other] designers in the country."[12] Yet Johnny wanted the best, and he believed Miles delivered.

Paramount's top director jumped into preproduction work by joining the show with a small cadre of associates in August 1949 for its trek to Chicago. Constantly moving with camera viewer and notebook close at hand, DeMille fearlessly did whatever it took to capture the essence of the big show, including its language—its slang—and backyard vignettes where performers and large animals interacted regularly and nonchalantly. Henry's August 12 missive to his brother recapped the lengths to which the director went to get details and vantage points. "A few minutes ago, your doughty friend, and incidently [*sic*] this is his 68th birthday, went to the top of the Big Top in a specially rigged boatswain's chair to spot camera angles for the flying acts. He enjoyed the experience tremendously."[13] DeMille's notebook quickly filled with ideas he wanted his writers to transform into a story that could fit any number of scenarios, not just a circus one.

Betty Hutton and Cornel Wilde starred as trapeze artists competing for the coveted center ring spot. Charlton Heston was cast as the circus's general manager, Brad Braden. Jimmy Stewart was a clown, curiously always in makeup, as part of a confusing and superfluous subplot. Dorothy Lamour and Gloria Grahame had supporting roles.

Details were important for the producer-director, who was described as temperamental with production people and courteous with actors. When it came time to portray Concello's part on film, DeMille became obsessed with getting Brad's leather jacket and fedora right—over fifty hats were brought in before the right one was found—just as those props for Indiana Jones were pivotal years later.[14] DeMille's character around circus artists transformed into gracious, kind, and patient, which earned him adoration from performers. Clown Jackie LeClaire recalled, "Well, the circus people fell in love with him. When he spoke, my God, we'd do anything for him!"[15]

It fell on North's capable shoulders to scout Europe for superb talent to perform under the Ringling-Barnum big top. He did so in style, living large in places like Paris and Rome, while Art, described by *Time* magazine as John's "henchman and chief of staff," prowled the circus's winter quarters and later the lots, looking for ways to decrease expenses and increase the show's bottom line.[16] He didn't give a damn how the show looked on the silver screen, and at times, his temper flared. When press agent Roland Butler "blew his top too hard and too directly at Art" during a staff meeting in Madison Square Garden, Artie fired him on the spot, only to rehire him on the same night, opening night.[17] But usually, North's right-hand man maintained his cool, commanding demeanor, knowing that anger wouldn't cut the nut. Deal making could.

Roy Burns was to Cecil B. DeMille what Art Concello was to John North. Burns, as the detail guy, purchasing agent, and unit manager, negotiated and finalized the financial and technical details before filming began. Known as one of the toughest traders in the movie business, for Burns, everything had a price and all prices were negotiable.[18] Like his circus counterpart, he operated in sometimes mysterious and often-shrouded ways to make deals.[19] Burns told Concello not to order anything without his personal approval, even if it was the director who'd asked for it. If approved by Burns, payment (or reimbursement) for the item, whatever it was, would be issued immediately.[20]

Burns met his match in Concello, who believed the contract signed between Ringling-Barnum and Paramount was grossly insufficient. He put buffers between himself and his Hollywood twin. Willis Lawson, Art's confidant, became the conduit through whom Burns had to go to negotiate with him, and even then, Frank McClosky, Art's right-hand man, often provided another layer of separation for the little man with the big cigar.[21] Nevertheless, Concello saw plenty of ways for people to make extra money when the movie crew was with them. For instance, when additional sawdust and lights—"all the God damned lights in the world for the color,"[22] Art said—were requested, boyhood chum Laz Rosen provided them for an added charge.

Art repeatedly refused to be directly involved with the production of the movie, yet he read Burns's daily notes written for DeMille. Doing so, he learned a lot about the creative process, and he never shied away from expressing his opinion or contacting North when he felt it necessary. Two examples illustrate this point.

Early drafts of the film called for someone to do a somersault from a trapeze to the back of an elephant. Concello called Burns in for a frank talk. "What the hell, nobody can do that shit," he barked.[23] After that point, Art became the go-to guy for DeMille, advising what stunts were and were not possible. DeMille paid him an additional $10,000 for his advice. Many of those dollars trickled down through Concello's hands to hardworking, low-paid followers and supporters. When he learned that the movie would feature a massive train wreck scene, he fired a letter off to North writing, "I see in one scene he [DeMille] has about 6 cars piled on top of one another, 27 wagons, lions, tigers, and gorillas running all over the place at the same time . . ."[24] Art implored North to be on site for filming that particular scene to minimize the number of people seriously injured or killed.

Together Art and Antoinette were an entertainment "power couple" before such unions had that name. The correspondence between them shows the deference Art had for his wife's talent. While Ringling's aerial director was back in Rochester, visiting family in upstate New York at the end of the 1950 season, Art wrote from Sarasota to ask if she would consider teaching Betty Hutton how to do one-arm swings and Dorothy Lamour how to perform an iron jaw routine, where the actress would hang by her teeth while moving her limbs to music. He advised her, "I can get you $250/week for this, but you would need to be on the west coast . . ."[25] Antoinette agreed, and a short while later, he informed Burns the price would be $350/week plus all transportation costs, which included a personal car for her. Since her salary came through his hands first, Art likely pocketed the $100 per week difference. After January 22, the price for Antoinette's training went down to $250/week for a period of six weeks.[26]

Hutton described her training as "four months of benevolent torture."[27] Antoinette began by teaching Hutton basic ground-floor acrobatics. From there, she transitioned Hutton to the trampoline and then to the trapeze, while fitted with a mechanic.[28] All this took place in a sound stage that Paramount had converted into a gymnasium, complete with trapeze rigging. For Hutton, every day strange new muscles yelped for mercy at the urging of her soft-voiced instructor, who was always, Hutton said, "poised, smiling [and] full of good cheer."[29] Not used to holding bars, every night she rubbed vinegar and salt into the palms of her hands to toughen them up.

It's likely Hutton learned more from Antoinette than just the technical side of flying. Perhaps she heard the story of the first time Antoinette caught the triple in performance. Eddie Ward Jr., the Concellos' catcher at the time, pulled her up and gave her a congratulatory kiss before tenderly dropping her into the net. Either she learned it and passed it along or, more likely, DeMille did and asked his writers to re-create a similar scene for Betty Hutton in *The Greatest Show on Earth*.[30]

With the stars instructed on the rudiments of flying, a train made its way from Hollywood to Sarasota, carrying three hundred cast members and two writers. The West Coasters joined 1,450 circus employees in the Ringling winter quarters. Filming began in January 1951 and lasted just over eighty days.[31] The total budget for the film—at $4 million—was dramatically less than the proposed Selznick project, but the costs incurred by the circus for the film still stretched the boundaries of what Concello thought was appropriate.

Art didn't care about being in the film, but he was concerned about the safety of all involved, particularly the flyers and their stunt doubles. Art personally oversaw the design and construction of trapeze rigging and made sure everyone was appropriately trained. When a climactic scene called for a trapeze flyer to crash to the ground, Concello rigged the trick himself.[32] "If anybody's gonna get hurt, it'll be me," he growled.[33]

When the day came to test the flying apparatus for the pivotal scene, Concello was there. He took off his jacket, climbed to the pedestal board in his suit pants and oxford shirt and took the fly bar into his hands. He swung a few times and then fell to the hard earth below. In reality, the ground was a net that spanned a pit. DeMille's secretary recalled the scene in her diary this way: "This morning, Art Concello pulled a DeMille by going up and trying the 50-foot trapeze fall first. He landed in the pit—full of water, of course—and was really dunked. Some of the crew standing around, watching, said, 'He won't pay any attention to that—he's a trouper.'"[34] Filthy, he proclaimed the rig was ready for the star, Cornell Wilde, to use it. The general manager behaved like a field-tested general and maybe, just maybe, he missed flying a bit, too. Pat Valdo, a longtime friend and Ringling-Barnum performance director mused, "He says he never gave a damn about flying, but I notice he's always finding excuses to drop into that flying net."[35]

Randy sometimes joined his parents on the set and can be seen sitting on top of a float with clown Lou Jacobs in one of the scenes. Seeming to have inherited a love of heights from them, one day the boy climbed to the top of a tall prop during a break between filming. When Art noticed his son up there, he asked him to jump into his waiting arms. Just as Randy leaped from the prop, Art moved away and watched his son slam into the ground. He went to his crying boy and advised him never to trust anyone.[36] The days when Art had a "big time" with his son and his friends, buying them all Hopalong Cassidy outfits—just a year earlier—were over.[37]

More than a year after DeMille started working on the movie, postproduction work for *The Greatest Show on Earth* wrapped. DeMille invited John and Art to a special viewing of the movie in late November 1951. In a personal letter written to Henry shortly afterwards, Art shared his very brief, very Concello-esque reaction: "It should make some money."[38] The movie was released January 2, officially opened January 10, and was shown nationwide in the summer of 1952. It made $10 million in its first six months, making it one of the top-grossing movies up to that time,[39] and it won the Best Picture Oscar in 1953. *The Billboard* reported in April 1953 that the film had earned $18 million to date and suggested that it may well be the top earner of all time so far.[40]

Art and Antoinette's relationship was complex. Art presented as a tough-talking and often-intimidating guy with an ever-present cigar and hat to give him inches his frame didn't have. When asked who Concello was to the working men with the show, a former one recalled, "He was God!"[41] Everyone knew him by sight, but hearing his name "wasn't an unpleasant experience," said a former work hand who toiled long hours in the menagerie department.[42] But to friends, he was generous—particularly, to those who were good to him when he was young. He gave the Carnahans of Bloomington their first air conditioner, for example.[43]

To the public, Antoinette displayed a more refined persona. Known as the Human Swallow for her seemingly innate ability to fly like one, Antoinette's status as a superstar of the circus was cemented the moment she completed what was broadcast as being the first triple somersault caught by a female trapeze performer in the late 1930s, and her star continued to shine for decades. "You know, she was the girl that flew across Broadway and turned on the switch to light up the world on New Year's Day," her sister said, recalling the event that helped usher in the 1950s.[44] With the mercury hovering around the freezing point, Antoinette flew over the intersection of Broadway and Forty-Sixth Street in New York

City to turn on a huge flashlight, which illuminated that section of Times Square.[45] She refused to let the cold detrimentally affect her performance that night. She had been toughened by trouping in all sorts of conditions, both under the canvas and in the stateroom she shared with her husband and, sometimes, their child.

Woman's Home Companion documented a tranquil, albeit unusual, home life for mother and son. Its August 12, 1950, issue gave readers a view into the Concellos' private railcar with images of Tony making breakfast in their kitchenette, tucking Randy in for a nap, and relaxing with Art in the backyard.[46] By comparison and around the same time, *Greater Show World* posed a question which undoubtedly grabbed the attention of contemporary celebrity watchers: "Is Antoinette discussing her domestic problems with a lawyer?"[47]

Antoinette tried to be an available parent for her son. When Randy wasn't in Sarasota for elementary school, she kept him with them in their private railcar. While touring, Antoinette came back to Sarasota to check in on him whenever possible, and one time she watched him in a marbles tournament. After he missed an easy shot, he cursed profusely. "RANDY!" cried his mother, "What do little boys who swear turn into?" Randy shot back, "Circus men!"[48] He had spent enough time with his father to know that much.

With her husband now back in Ringling-Barnum management, she undoubtedly heard the whispered rumors about him and the other men in charge—rumors which said that money and favors were extended to showgirls who agreed to sexual favors. Others with the circus when Concello was its top manager remember the rumors of "sexcapades" he either hosted or attended. He was known to use a sex toy known as the "honey machine" with women who wanted to "be in good with the boss."[49] Concello and his field lieutenants were known to interrupt business meetings to attend orgies held in roustabouts' quarters.[50] At least once, a botched self-abortion led to a bloody mess that had to be cleaned up.[51]

Through his network of managers, Art controlled nearly every facet of the show, sex and money included. "He was making money with the flying acts and making money with every department. Everybody had to have, like, a kickback to him."[52] This system of kickbacks undoubtedly helped the show run more efficiently. It definitely ensured that all news got back to the big boss on the lot.

The "pay to play" system didn't always work. One plucky showgirl, upon learning that she wasn't getting additional pay for the turns she made in the air when she covered a vacancy in one of the trapeze troupes, went to confront the general manager. "Art, I don't have any money for the flying act," she said. "Ah," he replied, "girls will pay me to do it. I don't have to pay you."[53] When Antoinette found the upset starlet and heard her complaint, she paid her the difference between weekly salaries out of her own pocket.

In the late 1940s, Art made the obvious decision: to contract his flying acts for the Ringling-Barnum Circus again.[54] His troupes hadn't been on the Big One for three years and placing them there laid a solid and renewed income stream when combined with the Shrine circuses, where his acts were also booked. By 1949 Antoinette ached to perform again. So back to the center ring she went with the Flying Concellos. The press department appropriately amped up its coverage of her.

By April 1950, *The Billboard* echoed the arena revolution first speculated about in *National Geographic*.[55] Increasingly, advance agents found it difficult to place circuses in cities. The Big Show could seat nearly ten thousand; a site needed to accommodate the big top, menagerie, sideshow, dressing tents, and so on. It had to be roughly ten acres. Arenas would provide the comfort and convenience the show-going public desired and deserved. Under Art's management the previous year, Ringling-Barnum had played arenas in San Francisco, St. Louis, Oakland, and San Antonio.

With this speculation buzzing through the field-show world, Art wrote a detailed letter to John, stating that three hundred American cities had a population of twenty-five thousand or more. Of these three hundred, he stated that two hundred could not generate income for a circus with a nut (total daily expense) of $20,000 per day or more. Most of the other hundred cities, he argued, would only support a show with that nut every two years, ". . . so if Ringling must keep its present size and cost, I can see nothing in the future that will keep it from going broke."[56] Art well understood that decreasing expenses—he proposed cutting the daily expenses by $5,000 to $15,000 per day—and investing in labor-saving infrastructure that benefitted the show's finances. He had a lot of ideas. He needed time to execute them.

Being a show owner taught him that placing the menagerie in the big top, rather than in its own tent, reduced labor and transportation costs. He was also well aware that North wanted his spectacular and expensive vision brought to reality. Help blending his goals with John's came from the network of contacts he created when he was the anchor flyer, and specifically this time, from Ralph Hunter.

Ralph E. Hunter was raised in Logansport, a town about fifteen miles west of Peru, Indiana, the former winter quarters for the American Circus Corporation. An avid circus fan, his cartoon-drawing skills eventually landed him a job as a commercial artist in Detroit. Now, Hunter and his wife, Thelma, regularly wintered in Florida, not far from Sarasota.

Hunter's name popped up in a letter from Henry to his brother on a hot summer day in August 1949. Buddy referred to Hunter as "Arthur's industrial engineer friend" and informed Johnny that Hunter planned to reduce the production number designs for things like floats and spectacles to sketches that could be reviewed by all parties, who then could approve them or send them back for revisions. Buddy, like Art, believed this would cut costs by facilitating discussions about the expensive, spectacular musical routines before they were created in full size.[57] Broadway designer Miles White was slow to create his sketches, so using Hunter was more efficient and provided White more time to finish his designs for the circus.

More savings came when Art transitioned to lighter quarter poles and ring curbs. Using aluminum reduced their weight and required fewer men to transport them. All the poles needed to keep the canvas up—except for the center poles—were aluminum[58] and were manufactured by the Aluminum Company of America,[59] headed by Arthur Vining Davis, who would later play a role in John North's life (and therefore Art's) in the 1960s.

On the other side of the equation were ticket sales. Concello also always kept an eye on them. Recognizing that the show-going public demanded more comfort, he urged John to spend money updating the primitive restrooms, saying, "You can no longer just have a bucket."[60] Brash language got results. Two "well-equipped and neat" thirty-five-foot show-owned wagons housing restroom facilities were placed just inside the entrance in time for the show's Washington stand in 1952.[61]

A couple months later, Concello reminded John that the American war in Korea would likely cause another shortage of labor. John rebuffed Art's concern, stating, "I thought with your new arenas . . ."[62] but Art knew transitioning to arenas would not be quick or easy. In the phone call between the Norths and Art about this, tensions escalated between Art and John, while Henry tried to calm the waters between the two. John's focus remained on making sure the show looked good—through its costumes, props, and by means of its cast's daredevil acts. Clearly frustrated, Art again advised him that circuses and carnivals weren't doing great business,[63] and that spending $12,000, for instance, on harnesses for a few horses was foolish, particularly when harnesses could be purchased for a fraction of the cost—and be just as good, if not better—elsewhere.[64] Their verbal tug-of-war ended when Art said, "Don't spend any more money or you won't have a circus. You can't have your cake and eat it, too." John fired back, "If you don't have a circus, you won't have any cake."[65]

Art responded by bullishly guaranteeing additional funding would not come from him, should it be needed. "You have not asked me, but just so there will be no misunderstanding later, I will not be able to put up any money myself and I will not be in a position to raise any money from my friends, so please plan accordingly."[66] He had every reason to be concerned about cash flow for the Ringling Bros. and Barnum & Bailey

Circus. After years of legal wrangling, a settlement was reached with people impacted by the dreadful circus fire in Hartford, Connecticut. George Woods, a New York financier, member of the Ringling-Barnum board, and friend of the North brothers, wrote Art on August 1, acknowledging the close bond between them while bluntly stating, "Far be it from me to intervene in a friendly family argument between you and John . . . but in view of the fact that we are going to have a tight squeeze, I would hope that you would continue the good job you have been doing in the elimination of unnecessary expenses. I would be pretty ruthless about it."[67]

By mid-October 1950, Art's obsession with cutting expenses led him to write a letter to John, who was staying at Paris' Ritz. In it, he detailed how he saw the next few months proceeding. While Concello, McClosky, and Lloyd Morgan would stay in Sarasota to "kick different things around and get the show chopped down in size," John and Henry would oversee the show's second engagement in Cuba. Henry and Art had closed a deal the previous year for the Ringling-Barnum Circus to display there that winter for four weeks.[68] If their return visit went like their initial foray, the circus-hungry crowds would demand three shows daily on the weekends and two each day during the week.[69] Knowing that day-to-day management was not John's strongest suit, Art advised him to be at Havana's Sports Palace an hour before the first show started and told him to stay in the building until the last one ended "because if you don't, you will find out at the end of the engagement you won't have any money."[70]

It's possible that John didn't respond to Art's letter or if he did, he did so in a way that didn't address Art's financial concerns. Whichever the case, the tone of Art's letters to John now verged on anxious. On November 18, 1950, Art drafted a memo of the points he wanted to make with the elder North. He wanted to know answers to questions ranging from when to open winter quarters in Sarasota and how much admission to charge there, to how many acts to book for Cuba (in about one month's time) and for the 1951 edition of the circus. The final paragraph of this memo shows the depth of Art's frustration with a boss who spent six months of the year in Europe and was often unresponsive. He advised that when John left Art in charge, he'd have to live with the decisions Art made "because I see no other way to operate a business. If you know a way, then I would be happy to hear your system. If you are not satisfied with the way the circus is operated, I would suggest you get somebody else that can satisfy you."[71]

John's continued silence prompted Art to send yet another missive to him in Cuba. "This show is only a good piece of property if you can move it, get it up and down, and show twice daily and I do believe this [Korean] war preparation is going to make that impossible, unless you cut it down . . . so sometime when you are sitting up in your room alone, turn these things over in your mind."[72] Though he was concerned, the letter nevertheless closed with his standard brotherly salutation of "Love, Artie." Along with anxiety about the show, the $115,000 of promissory notes John Ringling North had with Art and the Miller brothers had to be renegotiated again.[73]

Those promissory notes could not be repaid, because North often tied his money up in tantalizing new business opportunities he thought self-evident. Together, John and Art investigated purchasing land in Sarasota, putting $2,000 earnest money down on ten bayside lots.[74] John also asked Art to review the option to build a fifty-room hotel on Long Boat Key.[75] Though ultimately nothing came of these projects, North funneled funds through Concello to Rudy Bundy, who leased the Lido Beach Casino for four years for an average of $32,150 each year.[76] Concello provided the performing talent, usually showgirls booked to dance there.

On his own, Art purchased land and constructed a house trailer park near the Sarasota winter quarters, and he told his employer that the money coming in would be slow but steady after the project was completed in January 1951.[77] Concello wanted North to agree to the use of the Ringling Bros. and Barnum & Bailey name for this property. In this instance, Art took John's silence as a lack of consent and instead named his property Circus City Trailer Park. The compound was rimmed by apartments made from old circus railroad sleeping cars that had been placed on foundations, plumbed, and permanently roofed. Several were split into two units consisting of kitchen and bedroom and bath units separated by a mutual fiberboard bedroom wall.[78]

There was also the matter of the North brothers' interest in Rockland Oil Company in Ardmore, Oklahoma. John Ringling purchased the property late in 1912. After a few years, oil was extracted. Eventually, interest in the asset trickled down to the Norths. While accompanying circus bandleader Merle Evans's dead wife's body back to Sarasota from New York where the circus was premiering at Madison Square Garden, Art offered the Norths some managerial advice about it. "You need someone there 52 weeks/year. Without that, you'll never know what's really going on there," he wrote.[79] Perhaps they listened. The oil profits made it possible for John to start repaying the Miller brothers and Art in late June 1951.[80] Art worked hard to find solutions wherever problems surfaced, and the oil fields proved no exception. When seven-inch pipe was needed for the oil drilling operation, he started with his friends at Sarasota's Circus Supply and Hardware, a business created to help sell old Ringling-Barnum equipment and run for years by his boyhood friend, Laz Rosen, and staffed by Eddie Billetti. He also tried, unsuccessfully, to get it from the Bloomington hardware store and machine shop, Kaiser Van Leer Co.[81]

In addition to his obligations to the circus, Lido Casino, trailer park, and oil, Art was also involved with two other business ventures in the early 1950s: a carnival ride called the Rotor and a dog racing track in Cuba. Circus program publisher Harry S. Dube, Concello, and John North brought the ride over to the United States from Germany. Invented by Ernst Walter Hoffmeister, patented in Sweden, and manufactured by Carl Friese in Germany, the Rotor was a ride designed to use centrifugal force to hold twenty people along its cylindrical walls while the floor beneath them dropped. Scaffolding around the ride supported roughly seven hundred spectators, who watched and waited their turn. *The Billboard* reported that the North-Dube-Concello triumvirate held the US manufacturing rights to the ride,[82] but because of legal disputes overseas between Friese and Hoffmeister, their only Rotor (installed in 1951) was at Palisades Park in New Jersey. Though each man invested $5,000 to bring it there, they never recouped their initial expenses on this venture and got out of the carnival ride business by 1958.[83] Concello lost $8,000 on the deal.[84]

Concello, Frank McClosky, and Walter Kernan conspired to manage a dog racing track in Cuba. Writing North in July 1950 from Danville, Illinois, Concello set the bait to lure him into the partnership. First, he told Ringling-Barnum's president that he was definitely moving forward with being in the dog track business. Then, he told John that he had to be in a position to put up money to be included in the deal. Finally, he wrote, "I am letting you know now so that later on you won't be crying that you were not given an opportunity to go along with this thing . . . This track we are going into did six million dollars last year gross."[85]

By October, North was involved, but the plan had changed. They were not going to take over an established track, they were going to build one. To do so, they would use Jerry Collins, who was in the midst of building a dog-track empire in the United States, and William L. Huntley Sr., who promoted the deal with Collins. They formed a Cuban corporation named Havana Greyhound Kennel Club, S. A. Art and associates—North, Dube, McClosky, and Kernan—would have 50 percent of the common stock issued after each put up $20,000. The other 50 percent went to Collins, who kicked in $100,000. Huntley also put up $100,000, and $300,000 worth of preferred stock was to be sold, making it a half-million-dollar deal. The location of the track was across from the Yacht Club in the Marianao borough of Havana, and construction was to begin immediately. They hoped that the track would be open by January 15, 1951, and would run for ninety days before weather turned unfavorable for racing.[86] They never met that deadline.

Things did not go as planned for Art or the North brothers in late 1950. In early December the dog racing track floundered in Cuban red tape as Ida Ringling North, John and Henry's mother, lay hospitalized in Sarasota.[87] Both her sons were with her December 3, but John was with the circus in Havana when it opened on December 8. Ida died on December 21, with her eldest son in Cuba and her youngest in Europe, still recuperating from World War II. Art remained in Sarasota, trying to cut the nut down for the show's next season. Doing the job of general manager and not particularly enjoying himself while doing so, John (near the end of the show's Cuban run) penned a letter to Art in which he shared his exasperation that the circus, his circus, wasn't better received by locals. He felt abandoned by those whose jobs were designed to promote and make the public believe they were seeing The Greatest Show on Earth. Worse, he felt Concello intentionally set him up to fail. He wrote, "I love you Arthur & I think you love me and if for some reason or other which seems inexplicable to us, we have come to the end of the road let us not spend any part of the [*sic*] these precious years left to you and me trying to out f—— one another."[88]

The scrawling nature of John's writing, along with his word choices and editorial scribblings, suggests John may have had too much to drink before taking up his pen. But it's clear John thought highly of Art, perhaps even considering him like a brother as others did. The fact that this letter, one of a very few lengthy ones written entirely in North's hand, remains in the Ringling archive in Baraboo suggests that Concello received it, though no response to John was found.

Art's first managerial act of 1951 was to arrange for John's annual checkup at the Mayo Clinic.[89] After that, he extended the Havana date by one week, even though business was off from the previous year,[90] and he paid his respects to the person he called "the best general agent the Big Show ever had," Waldo Tupper.[91] The sage advance man had proposed an auspicious plan in which a local fraternal group—the Shriners, for example—would buy out the performance or take a percentage for handling some of the details for the circus. Tupper died of a heart attack on a train back to Los Angeles before both of these plans were fully vetted.

With Tupper gone, Concello concentrated on producing, for John's approval, various routes for the show to play and determined when the show would next visit Cuba.[92] John wanted to pack more into the performance there, while Art reminded him which acts literally couldn't fit into Havana's Sports Palace, and with input from Valdo, he advised John which acts ran too long, making a three-hour show impossible. Concello held his ground on routes but gave ground with the latter, writing, "Last year I argued with you in Havana about the length of the show, but this year I will not say a word."[93]

Throughout this time, Art looked after his friends. Bones Brown, yet another flyer from Art's youth, wrote a note that shows the lengths Concello went to repay loyalty. "I appreciate the fact that you kept me around and paid me whether I worked or not . . . however, I am not at all personally happy working under those conditions."[94] Art responded by informing Bones he would have a job for him if he wanted one.

Herb Duval and Fred Bradna also benefitted from their friendships with Concello. Herb "Judge" Duval was a one-time general manager for the Kit Carson Wild West Show in 1913 but, later, became a legal adjuster with American Circus Corporation shows. Duval joined the adjuster ranks with the Ringling Bros. and Barnum & Bailey Circus after the strike in 1938. An old-timer who undoubtedly saw more of the underbelly of circuses than most, he came to be not only respected but cared for by Art. When Concello learned the Judge, as he was called, was unwell but yearned to be with the show, Art wrote and offered his frank advice: "If you don't feel A-1, you are a damned fool to come around this hustle and bustle of a show . . . No one would be sorrier to see you come around the show and wear yourself out and get sick, so take some advice from a fool, Judge, and take it easy as you have been doing."[95] Judge followed the advice.

Ringling-Barnum Equestrian Director Fred Bradna served circuses from 1902 to 1945, when a near blowdown in Dallas sent a tent pole careening so close to him that he fell and fractured his pelvis, which ended his career. Now a tottering Sarasota retiree, Art asked the man who had directed him when he was a young flyer (and hundreds of others who performed with him) to blow the whistle one more time during the season's final performance in Sarasota. Nena Thomas, Ringling-Barnum's secretary to the Norths, reported to Henry, "He looked wonderful and [his wife] Ella was with him, all dressed up. Freddie had his white pants, top hat, black coat, gold headed cane and all . . . he was thrilled to be there."[96]

Soon thereafter, the circus headed back to Cuba with John and the rest of the show, including Press Representative Bill Fields. The nights John spent in Cuba in 1951 were wild. In a December 26, 1951, letter to Buddy North, Fields reported that John ended up staying awake for a few days straight—gambling, partying with the Hemingways, and visiting various nightclub hotspots—suggesting an incredible endurance for a man now nearly fifty years old. Once more, Concello stayed in Florida, focusing on cutting down the circus's expenses.

The Concellos celebrated Christmas that year by giving Randy his very own house, placed in their backyard and built to fit their child's dimensions. The house was a miniature of their own, reflecting a very modern Dutch style. The paneled interior was furnished with maple tables and chairs, electricity, and a telephone. The local newspaper captured Randy's initial response. After bringing his family's doormat to his own tiny porch he stated, "Little boys are awful messy and all they do is track, track, track."[97]

Art was regularly called upon to help the North brothers with various personal relationships. With John, he provided comfort and support to a former girlfriend, Gloria Norris, who wrote frequently, often beseeching her former paramour for financial help. These letters were often forwarded to Art for response (and payment) and over time, her letters show the depth of her gratitude.[98]

Hollywood and literary royalty—Ernest Hemingway, John Steinbeck, and Bob Hope, for example—also heard from Concello when the North brothers couldn't be reached. Concello responded to the men, keeping them apprised of their whereabouts while also keeping the Norths informed about who was trying to get a hold of them.[99]

Year ends are typically a time to reflect on the past and plan for the future. Art did that in 1951. He wrote a long letter to John and included a numbered list of the improvements he brought to the show since his return in 1948:

1. Seat wagons
2. New big top with no obstructed views and air conditioned
3. New animal arena weighing 250, not 3500 pounds
4. Distribution ticket wagon
5. Metal (aluminum) ring curbs
6. Show moves on 70 cars, 38 cars less than the 1947 show
7. More efficient one-day stands
8. Advance ticket setup where tickets can be purchased 6 days in advance of any show
9. Big Show and Menagerie in one tent
10. Central Purchasing Center for Cookhouse
11. All bull elephant tubs nest, a tremendous space savings
12. Steel discs over outside tires so they cannot be cut by railroad gunnel walls
13. New folding gates for main entrance
14. Created 750 more $6.00 seats into Madison Square Garden—if any show is sold out, that's an additional $9000 per sold-out show
15. Cut stealing down to a minimum; "Your uncle John once said, 'you can't get it all' and I am beginning to believe him"
16. Made good deals with Paramount
17. Aluminum quarter poles and
18. Something to be shared when we can meet privately[100]

The dog racing track finally opened in early February of 1952, around the same time that Art and Antoinette went to the Mayo Clinic—Art for a routine physical and Antoinette to have her back examined. Returning to winter quarters, Art had everyone jumping at his commands.[101] As for Antoinette, she stayed at Mayo after having "quite a little job done on her back. Something about a disk, which was fractured, and so they removed this and perhaps a little bone grafting was done."[102] Antoinette would return to work, but the days of Art being involved with the Cuban dog track were numbered. In fact, the track seemed to have disappeared years before Cuban dictator Fulgencio Batista was removed from power in 1959, because no more information on it could be found.

Antoinette loved performing, but now, after flying for most of two decades, her body was giving out. The decline started months after she completed Hutton's training, when she reinjured her bad shoulder. Having successfully completed a trick during her flying routine early in the 1951 season in Washington, DC, she felt her shoulder give "as if a suction cup had been pulled off a wall" when she went to lock wrists with her catcher.[103] Her catcher recalled believing that somehow, she had made one of her arms grow eight inches. Once again she had separated her shoulder,[104] and once again she pursued treatment to repair it at the Mayo Clinic.[105]

She went back to southern Minnesota for more treatment the following February, around the time of her son's seventh birthday. His big birthday party was held at Nina Cristiani's house, where he had been staying while Antoinette was being examined.[106] He got a bow and arrow and nearly destroyed her house playing with it.[107] To keep the energetic boy busy and out of trouble as much as possible, the Concellos enrolled him in riding school.[108] Perhaps in an effort to strengthen the connection between them, Art tried learning equestrian skills along with him. "You should see me riding a horse," he wrote Henry North in a self-deprecating way. "Wonders will never cease."[109] Antoinette's back likely wouldn't tolerate such activities, but with a constitution as tough or tougher than any of her male counterparts, she was back to her aerial director duties in April 1952.[110]

Throughout the early 1950s, Art was the Ringling show's lead negotiator, be it with Paramount Pictures or unions. There were many involved with circuses: the American Guild of Variety Artists (AGVA) represented performers, and then there were the Costume Designers Guild, Teamsters, Scenic Artists' Union, and more. In the early years, North sometimes had Art with him for negotiations, but as the years progressed, he increasingly trusted Art to act alone. He realized Art seemed particularly skilled at coming to equitable agreements with them.

Strikes often had a jolting effect on the traveling entertainment industry. The 1952 United Steelworkers of America's strike against US Steel had a major impact on circus ticket sales throughout the Midwest. The strike lasted fifty-three days and ended July 24, but its effects were felt for months as evidenced in the letters Concello wrote to the Norths. On August 1, Art noted that business in Dayton, Ohio, was very poor, with only 2,500 people in the stands for the matinee.[111] As days turned to weeks, the financial scene looked so bad that Concello delayed paying the Federal Amusement Tax due in June. This led the federal government to serve Ringling's Sarasota office with papers informing the circus that a lien was going to be placed against the properties in five days if payment was not made immediately. After consulting with Wallace Love, Noyelles Burkhart, and Frank McClosky, Concello paid the tax bill because he believed the bad press received for not doing so would have had dire consequences for the upcoming multiday Chicago stand.[112]

Though irritated with his boss at times, Concello retained his exceptional focus on increasing the show's, and therefore his, bottom line. Never one to let poor ticket sales prevent him from thinking about how to increase revenue, Art pursued the idea of expanding the show's tour into a new market: South America. Perhaps this was Art's big idea, number eighteen on his 1951 list. With a steel strike raging in the rust belt and national ticket sales flagging even on sponsored dates, Concello tapped Harry S. Dube to examine the costs of bringing the show to Caracas, Venezuela. When Dube reported that transportation costs would set the show back $40,000 each way, Art thanked him for his work and then advised John that taking the show to South America would be too expensive—at least for now.[113]

By the end of 1952, Concello had slashed the operating budget for the circus. He had brought the costume bill down to $100,000, cut the costs of the floats in half by having them built in Sarasota at Circus Supply & Hardware, a subsidiary of Ringling Bros. and Barnum & Bailey, now under Eddie Billetti's supervision,[114] and he reduced the spectacle bill to $45,000 by closing a deal to bring former Ringling-Barnum costumer Max Weldy back. To hire Weldy, who was based in France, Art had daily negotiations with the costumers' union until a deal was brokered, which stated that all act wardrobe would be produced and fitted in New York City by either Eve or Brooks Costume Company. Finally, if Weldy was promised a shop in New York or any costume design or production work, the deal was voided.[115]

In 1953, a rumor surfaced among informed members of the circus community that the Ringling-Barnum Circus would be split into two units. Ringling would play one area of the country, while Barnum would play another area.[116] Perhaps the genesis of this rumor came from the investigation done to bring a show to South America, but as is the case with rumors, that cannot be substantiated.

What wasn't rumor was the fact that the movie, *The Greatest Show on Earth,* continued making lots of money at the box office. Art reported to John that Paramount "still owes us about $200,000 by the end of 1952."[117] Circuses had been using marketing tie-ins for a century or more, and at this time, at least one advertising campaign—that of clothier Alfred of New York—piggybacked on the popularity of the movie. Art and John were both featured in print advertisements for that company's shirts in 1953.[118] These sport shirts were billed as "the Cadillac among sportshirts," and by using two Ringling-Barnum executives, the company was obviously reminding people of the movie.

The North brothers' need of Art grew through 1953. For Henry, still recovering from his war experiences, Art provided guidance and support through his divorce proceedings that, under Henry's oversight alone, faltered repeatedly. Once he was a bachelor again, Art shared some of his aggravation, "I am supposed to be working trying to run the circus, but it seems like I wind up with all your brother John's and your problems." But his closing remark was a brotherly one: "Now that you are divorced, for Christ's sake, don't get married next week. Remember the trouble you had the last time you were married."[119]

Though no longer a principal flyer himself, Art remained an advisor for up-and-comers in the art—at least those he deemed worthy of his assistance. Such was the case with Betty Hutton and Del Graham. Betty Hutton, the star of the circus movie, had her mind set on taking a trapeze act to London. Yet while practicing it in New York City, something went wrong every time she got up on the bar. Infuriated, she fired all her riggers. By coincidence, Art was in Ringling-Barnum's New York offices at that time. Concello visited her, supervised the re-rigging of her apparatus and sent over his Bloomington rigger turned catcher, China Durbin, who smoothed out the trappings so that she had no further worries. When Hutton was asked who this man was, she responded, "I don't know any other name than China. They all have such wonderful names, China, Tuffy, and Arky. What wonderful people."[120] Similarly, when Del Graham wrote Concello to ask if he could have the old rigging and net that was laying outside either in Bloomington or Sarasota, Art replied immediately that it was fine for him to take them.[121]

He also helped defray negative press for the circus whenever possible. One incident occurred with show publicist Roland Butler. A circus aficionado flashed his Circus Fans Association of America card to Butler, expecting to be admitted to the backyard early in the 1953 season. The fan felt rudely rejected and wrote a letter of complaint to Art. Art sent the letter to Butler and, typical to Concello, advised him to "send this guy some kind of bull shit letter that you were sick or something" to smooth the waters.[122]

Tenderness and business savvy was on display in a rare surviving letter from Art to Antoinette dated September 3, 1953. It's not known exactly where Antoinette was, but it's possible, given her stepfather's illness that led to his death on September 24, that she was in Bloomington caring for him or settling the estate of her mother, who'd died there on May 2. Wherever she was, Art sent her a detail-rich letter starting with an update about their son Randy, who joined him on his return to Sarasota. Upon waking up again in Florida, "Randy had to get his tent, bicycle, and machine gun when we arrived in Sarasota to take out to Circus City so he seems to be having a good time."[123]

He shared that while he was in Chicago, he had checked in with his half-brother, Joe Snort, and found him to be living a sober life at the YMCA. When he learned Art was in town, he "hightailed it over to Palmer House and didn't leave my side."[124] Art brought him along to Sarasota, set him up at his Circus City trailer park, and asked one of the men working for him to get Snort food whenever he needed it. After providing him a list of chores to do, he warned Joe that if he got drunk, "he'd be run out of town."[125] Art wanted to help his brother stay sober and now thought that threatening him would do the trick.

He informed Antoinette that he would soon go back to New York City to settle the Scenic Artists union dispute and then would rejoin the show. Lastly, Art relayed that he had checked on her house and found everything—except patches of her lawn, which he planned to have re-seeded—in good order. His choice of pronouns suggests they weren't living together at the time. He wrapped his letter up with "hope everything is going along fine. Love, Art and Randy."[126]

While that letter was chock-full of detail for his wife and partner, Antoinette, it understandably lacked details concerning the other woman in Art's life at the time, Margaret Smith. It's unknown exactly when Art met Miss Smith, but it's possible he did so when she was with the Mills Bros. Circus in 1952. Born and raised near Coventry in war-torn England, Smith was enrolled in dance school at a young age.[127] From there, she found her way to circus impresario William Peter Boulton "Digger" Pugh. Pugh's reputation preceded him as someone who could get young girls out of England and into America. Once in America, the determined Brits, as part of Pugh's Wallabies act and unbeknownst to him, worked all of their assets to become showgirls on the 1953 version of The Greatest Show on Earth as part of the Abbott Girls, an acrobatic troupe.

Initially, Margaret was put off by Art. But eventually, their relationship blossomed into a full-fledged affair. The world might never have known the depth of their relationship had a bullet not found its way into her abdomen.

The story of how that bullet got there was deliberately obscured.

The October 10, 1953, *El Paso Herald-Post* broke the story that Margaret Smith, twenty-two, was shot in the thigh at three thirty that morning in the Santa Fe Railroad freight yard. Smith told police that she stepped into the vestibule of the car where she lived and was knocked down by the bullet. No witnesses came forward, and Smith didn't see who shot her.[128]

Subsequent reports added more detail. Two days later, a news story revealed that the bullet entered the back of her right hip, ranged upward through her pelvis, and lodged near her kidney. In this article Concello said he was walking with Maggie to get a drink in Juarez, Mexico, but thought better of it and turned back to get a drink in car 369, instead. This story stated that they had spent about fifteen minutes in the bar car and she was walking back to her sleeper when she was shot. Presumably with the bullet lodged in her and with blood streaming down her leg, she "ran down the tracks and told Concello." He called W. H. Reynolds, chief of circus police, who took her to the hospital. The newspaper story reported that "Miss Smith has given four versions of what happened."[129]

The next-day's report of the incident twisted it a bit more. This time, Concello admitted that he was handling a gun that went off accidentally around 3:30 a.m., and as a consequence, the bullet lodged in Miss Smith's body. It was reported that Concello joined the circus police in taking her to the hospital. Charges were dropped, the story reported, because it was an accident and Smith wanted to forget all about it.[130]

Over two hundred miles away, the *Albuquerque Journal* reported that the pretty young aerialist was accidentally shot in her railcar living quarters. She was lying on her back, the article stated, while Concello was examining a gun. His earlier comments, the ones that said he was not present when Miss Smith was shot, were explained away by him saying he didn't want bad publicity for the show.[131]

Perhaps a tenacious El Paso newspaper reporter demanded even more explanation because the *Herald-Post* supplied more details in its last story on October 14 about the shooting. It boiled down to this: Art said he returned from Juarez with Antoinette to their private car around 11:00 or 11:30 p.m. After reading for a few minutes, he decided to go for a walk. He ran into Margaret Smith and asked her to go for drinks. They went towards town but decided to come back to car 369, the bar car on the show. When she laid down, Art started playing with the .25 caliber gun and accidentally shot her. After the shot was fired, the two of them agreed to make up a story to protect the show. Miss Smith refused to prosecute, the story related, because she understood it was an accident.

Just a few weeks later in Sarasota after the season ended, Antoinette was back driving her pea-green, hardtop Cadillac convertible through town. Son Randy was enrolled in a private school to "prevent his academic life [from] being disrupted by too much circus razzle-dazzle."[132] Though she enjoyed speaking to the press and she had a "gift for pantomime and a lively repertoire of slang, circus jargon, and her own verbal inventions,"[133] she never once mentioned the incident publicly. Privately, she insisted she never shot the gal but wanted to.[134]

Since no charges were filed, the official investigation was dropped. Many stories still circulate about what retired circus performers and its historians simply call the shooting. The consensus among them is that Antoinette pulled the trigger, but consensus does not necessarily translate to truth. Years later, Herb Duval, the show's lawyer, told a circus historian that the toughest situation he ever had to fix was "when Antoinette Concello shot Maggie Smith in the ass," though he never divulged what exactly he needed to fix.[135]

With his personal life in turmoil, Concello made a play to have more control in his professional life by demanding that John decrease the size of The Greatest Show on Earth. The show travelled on seventy railcars, and Art wanted to get it down to sixty. Due to the increased unrest in Cuba, he also wanted to forgo the annual engagement there. John disagreed, thereby forcing the hand of the man so like a brother. Art responded by writing a note on December 2, 1953, which read, "My dear J. R. N.:—I resign as of today. Thank you for many favors. As always, Artie."[136]

Chapter 7

Out from Under the Canvas

1954–1960

"All right, Clyde, I'll tell you what I'll do. I'll take a chattel mortgage on the show, everything you've got, and I'll put a guy over there to collect my money every day . . ."[1]

—Art Concello

Stories swirled around Concello's departure from The Greatest Show on Earth at the end of 1953. Some people, like Bloomingtonian Clyde Noble, who had been one of Art's mentors years before, told friends that Art was simply fed up with trying to keep the show going.[2]

Concello did not leave the show to seclude himself from show business. By 1954, he was calling a railroad car parked on a Seaboard Airline spur in Sarasota his headquarters,[3] where the sagacious, ever-moving man was far from resting. He crisscrossed the country, visiting his flying acts booked on various Shrine shows as well as Ringling-Barnum. With Randy, he even visited the Royal American Shows, a carnival, as it was gearing up to head out for the season.[4] He was hunting additional money-making opportunities. He found one while quietly meeting with former partner Clyde Beatty.[5]

The cash-strapped Beatty initiated the negotiations early in 1955. Concello took a chattel mortgage on the animal trainer's show, which gave Beatty $100,000 operating capital for it.[6] As usual, Art wasted no time figuring out what to do. He redesigned the grandstand seats and the bandstand.[7] His new seat wagons were nine feet shorter than those he provided to Ringling-Barnum in the late 1940s and were side-folding like Cap Curtis's design years before, not end-folding.[8] Nevertheless, the labor saved by using them significantly improved the bottom line.

The trade press and circus fans expected fierce competition between Ringling-Barnum and the Clyde Beatty Circus in the coming season, but the real competition wasn't between circuses; it was between Concello and Beatty. Beatty was ruled more by showmanship and heart than efficiency and financial restraint. Eventually, a deal was hammered out between them: Beatty had 51 percent control, but Concello held the financial reins—at least until he was paid back.[9]

To ensure he would get his money, Art put Tuffy Genders at the front door of the show. Along with Tuffy, Roland Butler, Wallace Love, and half-sister Grace Killian went out west to help run it. The first year, $40,000 plus interest found its way to Concello. But the next spring, Beatty's circus wasn't making any money. Some other deal would have to be made.

While Concello and Beatty sparred for control of the Clyde Beatty Circus, North was busy eyeing new talent for his executive team. He elevated Frank McClosky, a seasoned circus executive, to Concello's position in 1954. He continued the rackets brought back to the Ringling show when Art had returned in 1948. The kickback system ensured money lined the pockets of McClosky and his department heads—money that North believed should have gone to the circus.

North hired Michael Burke as the permanent replacement for McClosky in 1955. Burke was an elegant gentleman who served in the Office of Strategic Services (the precursor to the Central Intelligence Agency) with Henry Ringling North during World War II. His postwar professional pedigree consisted of being a movie writer and then an advisor to the US high commissioner in Germany, making his circus experience as nonexistent as his time in high-level management. Nevertheless, John tapped him to be the executive director and personal representative for him.[10] Like Concello, Burke was not only given charge of the circus but also to look after the Norths' oil and real estate interests.

Burke saw himself as "second only to North" and understood that it was his task to clean up the show, to create a "new circus" by eliminating the Sneeze Mob and its Chief Sneeze.[11] Burke defined these terms in his autobiography, *Outrageous Good Fortune*. "The Sneeze was Circus argot for the men who controlled the rackets on the show: dice, whiskey, beer," and the Chief Sneeze was the circus's general manager and longtime Concello crony, Frank McClosky, who stayed on with the organization.[12] Even the press of the time noted that nearly everyone with the circus had a racket.[13] A former performer provided an example of it: "In the car I was in, there were 40 men. The porter got $5 from each man—plus what he made from selling us sandwiches, beer and whiskey. If we didn't pay, we didn't get the better berths. Our beds weren't made up. Little things happened to us. You can call it extortion if you choose to, but the fact remains it has always been that way."[14]

Burke learned a lot about these schemes, which pervaded most departments. "Working men could borrow five dollars, but only got four and had to pay back five," recalled a timekeeper assistant.[15] Beer "was sold to the captive people on the Circus train at a five hundred percent profit," and the dice games and whiskey sales were run by the ushers and ticket takers.[16] Those dice games caught the attention of Vincent Alo, also known as Jimmy Blue Eyes of the Miami Syndicate, who deemed them significant enough to attach one of his men to the circus to watch over it all. When Burke realized the circus was housing and feeding the attaché, he threw him off the show.[17] Time and time again, Burke tried to rid the circus of these long-standing scams, never realizing that while burdensome, those rackets were necessary to move the giant show. Favors in the form of cash kept everyone working to move the circus day after day.

Frustrated by his inability to create a new business model for the old Ringling-Barnum Circus, in early August North gave the directive to Burke to fire the Chief Sneeze, McClosky, and the managers under him, Walter Kernan and Willis Lawson.[18] Curiously, the resignation letters in the corporate archive reflect that the key Concello guys—McClosky, Kernan, Lawson, Bob Reynolds, and eighteen others—resigned from the show in late July,[19] tendering resignations almost verbatim with Concello's in 1953.[20]

Regardless of when those managers' letters were submitted, they walked off the show in St. Paul on August 4. When the prop men failed to show up to remove the animal arenas after the first act of the night's performance, the show was cancelled. Burke told the audience that ticket money would be refunded. Noyelles Burkhart, Ringling's legal adjuster and the former manager of the Cole Bros. Circus, rallied the workingmen to get the show's properties back on the train so that they could appear the next day in Minneapolis. The circus made it there, but because things had been packed up by inexperienced hands, the matinee was delayed.[21]

With the Sneeze managers gone, Burke perhaps thought his management troubles were over, but that was an illusion. A new specter arose in the form of the Teamsters Union, who sent union organizer Harry Karsh to their stand in Denver.[22] Burke believed that the Sneeze found their way to Jimmy Hoffa as revenge for being fired from the show. When confronted by Karsh, Burke laughed, saying, "a Teamster contract with the circus? . . . We don't want to be organized by the Teamsters."[23] Karsh stormed off, promising that wasn't the end of things, but the circus ran its entire season with no significant management or union troubles.

While Burke rode the rails with the circus, Art was trying to outmaneuver him in New York City. Ringling-Barnum's contract with Madison

Square Garden was due to expire. Knowing this, Art began to negotiate with Garden executives about putting The Clyde Beatty Circus there instead.[24] He couldn't get a deal.

North realized there was union and management trouble brewing around his circus, and whenever trouble reared its ugly head, his first impulse was to find Concello. Sure enough, a meeting between the men occurred late in October 1955. Speculation erupted that this was the beginning of Art coming back into the Ringling-Barnum fold,[25] but the timing wasn't right.

Ringling-Barnum's Madison Square Garden stand throughout May 1956 was picketed by both the performers' union, the American Guild of Variety Artists (AGVA), and the Teamsters for unfair labor practices. The circus's executive secretary broke the news to Henry Ringling North (then serving his country again, but this time as part of the Central Intelligence Agency in Rome) that the unions would unite to have their own circus running in opposition to the Big Show in Boston.[26] She also reported that Burke seemed more interested in outfitting the new, expandable office wagon than addressing this challenge. Every time she saw the plans, she said, the wagon was more plush and elaborate—"a far cry from the old-time circus."

The Union Circus opened in Boston the day before Ringling-Barnum was set to perform there. While only a few hundred attended the AGVA premiere, the show's presence and the sour publicity it brought hurt Ringing-Barnum's receipts.[27] Indeed, union harassment—picketing, litigation, and violence—dogged the circus almost nonstop throughout its 1956 tour. Broken-down stake pullers and misfiring generators caused late starts or missed shows.[28] Personnel suffered too. Observed a longtime observer of circus activity, "The pickets have been beating up the working crew and have been causing railroad delays. [Lloyd] Morgan is on as manager but has no authority, only with the working crew. The train crew is inexperienced as well as the lot boys, and the show goes up and down very slow."[29]

Union activity against circuses was rife coast to coast. At the same time the circus was appearing in Boston, AGVA members struck the Clyde Beatty Circus in Burbank, California, for $15,000 in back wages.[30] The strike, along with a blaze of bad grosses,[31] forced Beatty's circus to close just a few weeks after it opened. The day after the Clyde Beatty Circus folded, Concello—tipped off by Tuffy—showed up on the lot, sparking unfounded rumors that he would take over the show. He had the first mortgage on Beatty's National Circus Corporation, when it filed for bankruptcy a few days later on May 18, 1956.[32] Clyde and Jane Beatty also owned the Monarch Circus Equipment Company, which owed Concello money—$25,000 to be exact—and that note was being called for by June

18. One way to satisfy creditors was to sell equipment and turn over the proceeds, but there was no sale. Instead, they reached an undisclosed agreement at Beatty's winter quarters in Deming, New Mexico.[33] Documentation shows Beatty agreed to assign all his future contracts through 1960 to Concello so that he would get money from Beatty's act whenever he appeared.[34] When McClosky and Kernan joined forces with Jerry Collins and Randolph Calhoun to purchase Beatty's circus, the lien held by Art Concello was dissolved. Concello had lost control of the Beatty show to two of his former underbosses.

By 1956, John Ringling North was sowing seeds of discord through his haughty nature. Merle Evans, Ringling's bandmaster since 1919, had little respect for North's ability to lead the circus.[35] Others shared Evans's opinion. An old trouper judged North this way: "I know a candy butcher who used to loan Johnny a dollar or so every week when North was a checker at the candy stands. Now he walks right by this boy with his head in the air and doesn't even speak to him."[36] Old-timers drew comparisons between North and his late uncle, John Ringling, saying, "Old John was a despot and many circus veterans today believe that Johnny North has carefully patterned himself after his uncle."[37] North's vanity wasn't lessened when he was repeatedly approached by bestselling biographer Alden Hatch to write his life story.[38] Johnny seemed oblivious to both the negative feelings about him and the overtures to capture his life in a book penned by Hatch. His circus had made good money, even though it was now hog-tied by union troubles and poor management.

The weather certainly didn't help. The main tent blew down in Geneva, New York, making it impossible for the circus to show under canvas during its next few stands, but no one could have predicted that less than two weeks later at Pittsburgh's Heidelberg Raceway, the Ringling Bros. and Barnum & Bailey Circus would fold its mammoth big top for the last time. A railroad car breakdown delayed Pittsburgh's initial matinee performance four hours. AGVA and Teamsters picketed outside its big top. AGVA demanded circus management pay weekly per capita into a "welfare" fund, something rightly seen by Burke and North as nothing more than a shakedown. The end came on July 16, and North made it official with a written statement released to the press, which read, "The tented circus as it now exists is in my opinion a thing of the past."[39] North, to his credit, was with the show, although he never left his railcar. Michael Bailey Burke (he used an invented middle name meant to convey credibility as a circus man) was 370 miles away in New York City.[40]

At least figuratively, Burke remained at the helm, dictating memos such as the one to the managers under him, which said there would be "an absolute prohibition of gambling, beer, whiskey and other rackets which were part of the old Circus. Immediate dismissal for anyone engaging in these activities."[41] The season had been a losing one for the morale of nearly everyone with it.[42] Edicts like this were like a captain giving orders from the safety of a lifeboat after his ship had sunk.

After the tent billowed down for the last time, North granted an interview with *Variety*. In it, he explained the situation this way: "The moment labor and other factors started to make us 'the latest show on Earth' was when I thought it wise to return to winterquarters" and retool for a "hardtop auditorium tour."[43]

Then he scouted for Concello. Artie and Tuffy Genders were messing around with trapeze rigging in the training barn in Bloomington when the news of the circus's closing came over the radio. "Let's blow this joint," said Concello. "You and me has got no right foolin' around with fly-bars and catch traps now anymore."[44]

Days after the circus closed, *The Orlando Sentinel* reported that North and Concello met for many late-night discussions.[45] "I want you with me, Artie," said John. "It's a challenge. It will be fun. Let's do it."[46] In exchange, Concello agreed to suspend payments on the ten-year seat wagon contract with North until April 1957.[47]

Art knew he had the upper hand when he cut this deal with John. "I told him my terms was simple. There could only be one boss of operations—me."[48] He also demanded 10 percent of everything North owned: the oil wells, the circus, and the property.[49] The deal was sealed with Concello's non-shake hand-clasp, said to be "as enduring a contract as one engraved in gold."[50]

On October 17, 1956, the Associated Press reported that Art Concello was back in an executive management position for North's Ringling Bros. and Barnum & Bailey Circus.[51] Burke had to go, Concello told North. "No two ways—it's him or me . . . If you're serious about wantin' me you're gonna have to tell Mr. Michael Burke it's all over but the shoutin' and redlight him."[52]

North's circus was $1.6 million in debt. Concello informed North $350,000 was needed to get the circus rolling. When North got it from his Oklahoma oil, he let Burke go.

Now with the title, Executive Director, Concello announced that the circus had to reduce its number of employees across the board—from performers to auditors, from roughnecks to train porters. This cut was necessary because he was going to move the circus on trucks, not the train. With the tent gone—and its annual $100,000 price tag[53]—Concello looked for and found more ways to cut costs. Using locomotives and railcars was expensive. The cost of moving by rail had increased annually and exorbitantly after the war. In 1942, the Ringling-Barnum railroad bill was $115,000. By 1956, the bill was over $600,000.[54] Moving the show by truck lessened the circus's bills, though railroad passes and Pullman tickets were still handed out to first-class talent (elephants and horses included, though they moved on system stock cars) and animal hostlers at the end of every stand—to get them to the new one. Trucks moved the rest of the equipment and people. Sleepers were designed to be thirty-two-foot to thirty-five-foot van-type semitrailers.[55]

Concello exuded confidence bordering on the grotesque with his omnipresent cigar, not always lit but always chomped, and spat on floors—carpeted or not.[56] His team included regulars like Pat Valdo, who retained his position as personnel director, Rudy Bundy who headed public relations, and Leon Pickett as the general agent. Nothing was sacred to Art, including the route and the length of stands. Concello revamped those, too. Ringling-Barnum would now play a thirty-week circuit consisting of three distinct tours in one year. To help him execute the itinerary, Concello used his longtime buddy Tuffy Genders to help scout locations, both indoors and out.

Arthur's idea was this: The show would play the eastern United States in the spring for ten weeks, the West in the fall for three months, and the Midwest in the winter for two months.[57] Among his directives to his staff, he stated that all equipment sold, scrapped, or traded in must be approved by either Genders or himself.[58] As always, Concello had trusted and loyal men around him.

With a leaner organization, a different mode of transportation, and a route based on arena and ballpark availability, Concello told North the time was right to negotiate with unions. Concello seemed wise to the ways of St. Louis's Harold Gibbons, vice president of the Teamsters, who had made a large payment to Harry Karsh, "who later emerged as head of a movement, blessed by Gibbons and Hoffa, that brought unionization of circuses and carnivals by methods described as shakedowns."[59] "There is no yardstick to tell you," Concello told North, "what it'll cost you to be fightin' the unions all the time. I'm gonna make a deal with them."[60] He knew if he couldn't beat them, he had to join them—or at least make the best deal possible with them. And deal he did.

In January Concello met with AGVA representative Jackie Bright and the union's attorney in Bright's New York City office to work out an agreement with both AGVA and the Teamsters, even though there was no representation present for the latter organization. His successful talks led to more calls to the table with other unions like the Billposters Union and the American Federation of Musicians, Local 47, who were staging to picket the circus's use of nonunion musicians while they were playing their ten-day stand at the Hollywood Bowl.[61] By the end of 1958, the show was nearly 100 percent unionized.[62]

All the while, Art (or Little Caesar, as he was coming to be known) walked purposefully around, looking for ways to improve efficiency, decrease costs, and increase profits. Everything was a solvable problem. He reopened the sail loft and asked tentmakers to create a giant backdrop four hundred-feet long and eighteen-feet high for outdoor dates.[63] Aware that animal cages needed to navigate narrow corridors, tight corners, and steep ramps, he designed new barred ones that held one animal and had doors on each end that fit together to form a chute leading animals into and out of the performance arena.[64] An Associated Press article described Concello's mannerisms in a way similar to some of the big cats contained in those carts: ". . . He prowls around winter quarters, asking questions, watching, and hatching ideas . . . [he is] the main spring, the vital force" of the circus. He never mentioned the past, the article stated, but "let it be known that as long as Concello is around, circus is not dead."[65] Art thrived on driving change.

The 1957 season opened as it had for decades in Madison Square Garden. From there, the show embarked upon a ballpark tour, where it played at sites for longer than the usual one or two days. Having longer stands while reducing the number of production numbers cut the daily expenses by two-thirds.[66] Concello recalled playing fairgrounds and just about "any God damned thing that first year."[67] He shuttered the menagerie and sideshow after its display in Boston's Garden, which further decreased expenses.

Booking more indoor dates made sound financial sense. Concello had been experimenting with that idea since his time as owner of the Russell Bros. Pan-Pacific Circus in 1945. Towards this end, he scheduled a meeting with John Hickey of the Arena Manager's Association to find out how many usable arenas were available and where they were. He affirmed his belief in arenas to *The New York Times* by explaining that the circus had been in five businesses: Railroad, restaurant, construction, hotel, and entertainment. He wanted to get that number closer to one. Hundreds of thousands of dollars would be saved in moving, feeding, and housing the tented behemoth.[68] Concello further clarified things to popular anti-union columnist Westbrook Pegler, "We had to put up a theater of 10,000 seats and knock it down almost every day when we were under canvas. But there are 102 buildings in the country where we can fit in and play a week," he said. He also shared his thoughts on the number and costs of workingmen: "We had to carry from 900 to a thousand roughnecks and feed them and sleep and haul them and pay them fifty or seventy-five dollars a month. Now we will deal with stagehands."[69]

He stationed Harry Dube in New York to act as an agent for the show and gave him the title of national director. Specifically, his job was to identify local sponsors or promoters who could make the arrangements with arenas. Sponsorship deals were structured so that the circus would get the first $20,000 profit. Any profit above that amount would be split

80 percent–20 percent, with the show retaining the larger percentage. The sponsor was responsible for procuring the licenses and permits, police and fire protection, and water. They were also to provide both the ticket booth and the place where it would be situated. The cash settlement would occur at 9:15 p.m. on the day of the show and would take place in the Red Ticket Wagon. The Shriners were the first choice for sponsors, followed by the police or firemen's pension or retirement organizations.[70] The goal was to get the daily nut down to around $7,000.[71] If a deal was made with a specific venue without a sponsor, venue management was expected to supply manpower like ushers, ticket sellers, and musicians. While The Greatest Show on Earth continued to play ballparks, stadiums, and arenas in 1958, they usually did so without sponsors.[72]

Part of Art's indispensability was, of course, his shrewd money-making ways that were the foundation of his management style. "I never take on anybody that doesn't guarantee to do exactly what I say without any back talk."[73] Backchat wasn't welcomed, but reminders or suggestions were. Dube recommended that Ringling-Barnum use local promoters or organizations with successful histories of booking shows in arenas—like H. Werner Buck's Show Management and Irvin and Israel Feld's Super Shows, Inc. Details like advance expenses and building rentals fell on the promoters' shoulders. Naturally, some angled for higher percentages of the net income when expenses surpassed daily income. Dube's memo to Concello detailed a strategy used by H. Werner Buck, the promoter who booked 1957's West Coast dates. "Buck played you and me against each other last year, hoping for a better deal. Feld claims he lost $54,000 [last year], while Buck claimed he lost $15,000. Feld took this like a man while Buck cried for a refund."[74] Art's response was to award Feld with a better deal for the 1958 season—fifty / fifty.[75]

The circus's last stand for 1957, an international one, extended into the first week of 1958. For the first time, Ringling-Barnum played Mexico City for nearly thirty days. They were day-and-dating (a circus term for playing the same city at the same time) with Atayde Hnos. Circus for at least part of the time. While Atayde played under canvas, Ringling-Barnum played in the Auditorio Nacional, a venue which sat 17,500. Its first night's performance benefitted the Red Cross and was standing room only. The other nights qualified as full houses and (to coin a Concello phrase) "they were making nothing but money;" in this case, pesos—over 350,000 of them on their biggest night.[76]

Arenas posed structural challenges for the circus—from floor to ceiling—because the rigging for any number of acts, particularly aerial ones, needed to be secured to both. Additionally, some venues—like Philadelphia's Convention Hall—had hardwood floors, which would be ruined when the circus poured tons of dirt over it. After thinking it through, Concello tapped US Rubber to create the solution he had in mind: twenty-by-six-foot sheets of quarter-inch tire rubber laminated to canvas, "tough enough for horses to run on it."[77] When a sample of it arrived at quarters, Art "did a series of round-off flip-flap backs across it" even before performing horses and elephants tested it.[78] When elephant dung was scrubbed into it and it sprayed clean, Concello ordered "fourteen tons of it, $15,000 worth, enough to cover 16,436 square feet."[79]

As for ceilings, new rigging had to be designed to connect to anchor points. Pointing up, Art explained, "You gotta have six points for them crow feet to work," so that the aerial riggings could be placed over each ring.[80] Concello tasked his "best damn mechanic, engineer and builder of circus gear in America,"[81] general superintendent, Eddie Billetti, with creating the rigging for both arenas and ballparks. After about ninety-five drawings of plans, one was chosen, which meant men could hang a show in four to five hours.[82]

As more and more hardtops, as North called arenas, popped up around the country, more and more arena architects and managers contacted Concello for guidance on where to place latch points for rigging in the floors and ceilings.[83] Arenas from Green Bay to Knoxville, from Seattle[84] to Madison Square Garden,[85] and beyond benefitted from Concello's and his staff's work.[86] When Los Angeles architect Kent Attridge reached out for advice on how to make the arena he was designing circus friendly, Concello responded immediately. He hyped the work done in California specifically: "I have . . . furnished the Cow Palace their floor plan when they decided to put in their new concrete floor."[87]

Concello raved about arenas to Ed Raycraft, his old Bloomington friend and exclusive Cadillac dealer to circus executives, saying it would take about a year to catch on. The benefits of arenas were many, extending from controlled heating and cooling, improved seats, and a location with a permanent address and nearby parking. About the latter, Art said, "People don't have to look for the lot out in Minnie's pea-patch or some goddamn cornfield they never heard of, and get stuck down some jerk country road. This way is a lot easier, especially on women with a flock of kids."[88]

The circus ended its third portion of its 1958 season in Miami before returning to Sarasota. The Miami date was poorly attended by both the public and upper management. *The Billboard* reported that neither the North brothers nor Concello were with the show since its return to Florida in early February.[89] Insiders wrote friends about this situation, saying, "Reports from a few [are] that North and Concello stayed out of Florida in order to dodge that trial that was postponed about four times. . . ."[90] The fact that the trade publication didn't pick up on the fact that Art had been back to Florida earlier is an indication of how good he was at staying away from the spotlight—and process servers.

Concello's legal troubles ramped up in 1956. While he was back in Sarasota, jackpotting —circus slang for swapping stories, sometimes even true ones—outside the Hotel Sarasota with friends that February,[91] his half-sister and wife met with attorneys to file a suit against him on behalf of the Artony Corporation, the business that built the seat wagons for Ringling-Barnum. The suit alleged that Art did not keep proper accounts of the corporation and that he "ha[d] appropriated large sums of money for his individual use" and refused to share the accounting with them, his partners. Most damning, the suit stated that Art would "do all within his means to hide and secrete the books of the partnership and substitute other inaccurate records in their place."[92] In September the suit was dismissed with prejudice, meaning it was dismissed permanently; it could never be brought back to court.

While that suit was settled out of court, chaos reigned in Concello's family life. Years of marital disharmony and infidelity led Antoinette to file for divorce on the grounds of cruelty on February 22, the day after Antoinette and Grace filed their mismanagement suit against him. During the divorce proceedings, Antoinette showed by competent evidence that Art was guilty of not only extreme cruelty but also "guilty of habitual indulgence in a violent and ungovernable temper" towards her.[93] As part of the September 1956 divorce agreement, Antoinette received several pieces of property in Sarasota, the trapeze "farm" in Bloomington, and full custody of their eleven-year-old son Randy.[94]

Art's response to his divorce is unknown. Comforting words came to him from his former sister-in-law, longtime friend, and fellow circus performer, Mickey King, who anonymously sent him a poem, which read,

> You're never poor, my noble friend,
> when love is by your side.
> Because if you can claim true love,
> untold wealth is your pride.
> You may be poorer than mere words can tell,
> and you haven't got a cent.
> But the more love you give, the more love grows.
> Its gold is never spent.
> So be alert, and never hurt the loved ones you adore,
> because the richest man in all this land, without a love, is poor.[95]

She thought if her words got through to him, he might go back to Antoinette.

Concello stayed busy with work. Newspapers and trade publications show that he was, as usual, on the move, visiting smaller circuses throughout the country. He may have also personally looked over his assets, which now included 10 percent interest of two oil wells in Ardmore, Oklahoma.[96]

Previous circus-related lawsuits brought against him to date were trivial compared to what was coming. In February 1957, Mrs. Hester Ringling Sanford, daughter of Charles and Edith Ringling and cousin to John Ringling North, started raising questions about the accounting practices of The Greatest Show on Earth. Her son Stuart Lancaster was named a vice president at the June 12 board meeting, when Concello took a spot on the board. John North was chairman at the time, and brother Henry served as a vice president—one of four vice presidents.[97] Seven months later, Sanford's questions morphed into a $20 million lawsuit filed by Stuart Lancaster and her on behalf of the Ringling Bros. and Barnum & Bailey Corporation. By then, this faction was called the 49ers because they owned 49 percent of Ringling-Barnum. North controlled the other 51 percent. The suit accused John Ringling North of mismanagement, misconduct, diversion of funds, malfeasance, misfeasance, and nonfeasance, which they claimed cost the corporation $20 million over the course of the previous ten years. Henry Ringling North and Arthur M. Concello were named as participating and sanctioning John North's actions. Because the three were allegedly in cahoots, the suit asked that all three be removed as officers of the corporation and an accounting be made. It also stated that the circus allowed loans to personnel at a staggering 10 percent per week rate.[98] Concello made no official comment but shared his view of this lawsuit with Henry: "I must say that your cousins Hester and Stuart are doing everything they can to make this thing not run."[99]

This legal action hit during the 1957 season, when Art was with the show. Old friend Merle Evans wrote him on September 20, advising him to stay away from town lest he be served with papers.[100] Art responded, saying that while he had been in town, he couldn't stop in to visit because ". . . your house is to [*sic*] close to the Sheriff's office to be comfortable." In the same letter, he later divulged, "I understand Stuart Lancaster called on Antoinette to find out if I was in town."[101] Though divorced, Art and Antoinette were still close.

Concello couldn't stay out of the reach of the law forever, though. When representatives of the court learned that he would be back in Sarasota for a meeting on February 22, 1958, law officers met and served him papers on the $20 million lawsuit.[102]

Early in 1958 Nick Schiavone, the circus's comptroller, divulged two things to *The Sarasota Herald-Tribune*: that the circus had recently decided to sell surplus animals and properties, and that it was considering moving their winter camp to a new location.[103] Simultaneously, Stuart Lancaster requested he be informed in advance of any sale of show-owned properties, animals, or equipment.[104] A day later on February 26, *The Herald-Tribune* reported that North was willing to sell his shares of Ringling stock. Lancaster and Jerry Collins, owners of the Clyde Beatty Circus, were identified as potential buyers.[105]

Concello met with Lancaster and Collins, but he refused to be photographed with them.[106] "We have received no offer from no one," he said about the rumors of a sale.[107] He vociferously reiterated that the circus was not for sale, that John North was not selling his stock, and that the winter quarters in Sarasota would not close permanently. Further, he told reporters that all statements about the show would come from him and no one else.[108]

Within two weeks of this hushed-up meeting, the Sarasota court approved the circus's proposal to sell surplus materials and animals. Afterwards Concello reminded the press that the circus itself wasn't for sale, just some of its surplus properties, materials, and animals.

March 1958 found Concello in all sorts of meetings. He met with the Teamsters in Sarasota,[109] prepared to close up the Ringling-Barnum training quarters there for the season, and he formally asked the court to have his name dismissed from that hefty $20 million lawsuit.[110] Strong support for Concello voiced by an unnamed insider ran on the newswires: "It's strange to hear stockholders calling for Concello's resignation. You'd think they would have learned that if the circus is indispensable, then Art is indispensable to the circus."[111]

The first hint that Art acknowledged mortality came when he met with his attorney to write his will in March 1958.[112] Now at nearly fifty years old, he thought about settling affairs after his death. For a man who ascended the entertainment-career ladder like few others, he perhaps felt like his family life was falling through the net. He was paying for his ex-wife's new home; keeping his on-again, off-again girlfriend, Maggie Smith, employed as choreographer and aerial director in The Greatest Show on Earth; moving a troubled teenaged son to different schools to find one he might be interested in attending; and trying to take care of his half-brother, who constantly struggled with sobriety.

Yet Concello made really good money. In 1958 his salary was $30,000, doubled from the $15,000 he was paid in 1952.[113] He accepted payment of that entire amount on May 1, 1958, and instructed the show's accountant, Fred McKenna, to deposit it in "two or three banks."[114]

He used some of that money to care for his half-siblings. Brother Joe was ushered out of Sarasota, sent first to Houston via a first-class ticket,[115] perhaps, to keep an eye on Stuart Lancaster, who was there to raise money to continue the hefty lawsuit.[116] Art wrote a letter to Grace accompanied by a check to reimburse her for the expense of Joe's airline ticket.[117] He later assured her ". . . don't worry about [Snort's] cost for living, doctor bills and so forth—I will pay them."[118]

Concello distanced himself from his son, Randy. He wrote "My dear Anto"—his nickname for his former wife, which he kept using for the rest of her life—in a letter at the end of May. In it, he apologized for missing their son's eighth-grade graduation ceremony from Farragut Academy and explained that business was his first priority. Then he shared the takes from New York (big), Boston (good), and Providence (off) before ending his letter with "do take care of yourself and tell Randy I will see him soon if he is in Florida. Love, Artie."[119]

While his son prepared to graduate, Concello dealt with problems big and small. He sent a quick memo to North, informing him that Harold Ronk, the show's announcer, had just left the show with no person to fill that vital role. They didn't know it at the time, but Ronk had gone to Indianapolis to star in a live-theater production.[120] Performers Don Forbes, George Michel, and Trevor Bale pinch-hit as announcers and ringmasters.[121]

There's no indication that North ever responded to Concello's Ronk-related dispatch. The next letter Concello wrote to North, now in Paris, took a decidedly stronger stance and one that, for the first time, showed Art's artistic opinions. Art went into great detail (for him) describing the acts he believed North should sign. For example, of the Yong brothers and their acrobatics, Art wrote, "I think these two guys are out of this world and you won't find anything half as good." His tone then shifted from deferential on all artistic matters to informational before ending his missive with the sterile salutation "sincerely," instead of his usual "love."[122] Concello was now the "one boss" he wanted to be.

Arthur's communication skills were good with entities outside the circus, but they left something to be desired within it. Late in 1958, he fired Dube from his job as general agent and installed Paul Eagles in his place. He did so seemingly without first telling Dube. When news of Eagles's impending arrival into New York hit *The Billboard*, Dube's response was to say that he knew Eagles was coming, but he "did not know what his title or capacity was to be."[123]

Now, in 1959, he used his skills to create deals for the circus with television people and major manufacturers. Early in February, he inked a deal with the ABC network to bring a one-hour *Highlights of the Circus* television special to the airwaves on behalf of the Ringling Bros. and Barnum & Bailey Circus. Ford Motor Company's Edsel Division sponsored the production after the circus agreed to use Ford's 1959 Edsel Ranger in its televised clown stunt.

Concello later worked with CBS television to produce *Ringling's Christmas Party*, which aired on December 10, 1959. It netted the circus a profit of $135,000.[124] Television was hot and Concello liked being where the action was. The success with CBS encouraged more television executives to approach him with even more potential deals. His tone in his communications with North reflected his mixed feelings about them. "I have been offered $150,000 net for a one-hour circus TV show . . . it's hard to refuse this kind of money . . ." This particular offer wasn't for a one-time television special, but rather a one-hour television series for thirty-nine shows. Concello wasn't in favor of it—at least, not yet. He also had talks with David Selznick's attorney regarding a closed-circuit theater program that could be produced once each year. While Concello didn't believe Ringling-Barnum was ready for that type of deal either, he was intrigued enough by it to inform John that he would continue to negotiate with Selznick through his people.[125]

With Art entrenched in the Big Show executive management, Antoinette moved into a new home in Sarasota. She received what she considered a great honor: being inducted into the Minnesota State Fair's Showbiz Hall of Fame. Antoinette, who retired from flying in 1953, graciously granted interviews about this distinction, reiterating how she got her start in the spangled world of sawdust and admitting that at that time, "I don't suppose I had ever seen a circus."[126] Of her various injuries, it was reported her bicep was broken first in her right arm and then she developed a loose left shoulder socket, not from falls but from the frenetic pace of her act. Of course, falls happened too. "Sometimes it was the fault of the rigging, sometimes the wind threw us off our timing." She didn't see falling as a negative experience, saying, "I think it was good for us to fall once in a while, it kept us more alert."[127]

Antoinette's son and father were East Coasters in 1959. Randy attended high school at the Lawrence Academy in Groton, Massachusetts. Her father, Toussaint, lived in Burlington, Vermont. The *Sarasota News* ran a story on Toussaint on November 15, when he was there visiting his daughter. He claimed he had been a rum runner during Prohibition, worked in silk and cotton mills, and was a lumberjack, an army cook, and a cook for the railroad. The scars on his head were from an ax injury received at the hands of his brother who lost his grip while chopping wood.[128] Little was reported about Antoinette, except that she lived right next door to her former residence.

Arthur Concello assisted John with non-circus-related matters like negotiating the sale of most of the land obtained from his uncle, John Ringling, after his death in 1936. Arthur Vining Davis's ARVIDA corporation purchased the land in May 1959 for the sum of $13.5 million. Included in the two thousand-acre deal were several parcels on the mainland of Sarasota, a major portion of Longboat Key, all of Bird Key, Cool Key (with the exception of the Sarasota Yacht Club), Otter Key, and a "substantial portion" of Lido Key.[129] It's a sure bet that Concello got his 10 percent.

Five months later ARVIDA bought Ringling-Barnum's 157-acre winter quarters and gave the circus six months after closing to vacate the premises.[130] Ringling-Barnum had closed the compound to outside visitors in 1958—at a time when about two hundred thousand people visited it annually—and used it primarily for storage. When John Ringling bought the land in 1927, he told friends he paid twenty-nine cents per acre for it.[131] Now, that land brought the Circus $340,000 in the sale of it.[132]

Cecil R. Montgomery was the overseer of winter quarters and, early in 1959, spent most of his time there drinking. Concello gave him his pink slip by instructing John Seawell, a longtime staffer, to ask him to leave. Concello told Seawell that William W. Perry would be handling the sale of property equipment from winter quarters, with prices set by Jimmy Ringling or Concello himself.[133] "He is an old crook but a good man for the money he gets," Concello said of Perry.[134] Art instructed him not to let anything out without first getting his written approval.[135]

Bill Perry was forty-five years old, the son a prominent attorney in Sarasota, and had spent years working in newspapers before becoming the first full-time publicity director for the Sarasota Chamber of Commerce.[136] Hired to be Concello's right-hand man and administrative assistant at winter quarters, his personal interactions with him may have been few, but they were memorable. He wrote Henry North about them, saying, "It has been my good fortune to have worked with some brilliant minds and some notable 'greats'; but the opportunity of seeing AMC 'click' is literally another world and—even at my age—I learn something new every day!"[137]

Art didn't forget about Henry's need for financial guidance and assistance while working with his increasingly egocentric brother, John. This included extending Buddy a much-needed personal loan. After ARVIDA's purchase, Art told the younger North that he would use the profit he received from the real estate deal to pay off Henry's debts. Art's letter also revealed that he understood the waters needed to be smoothed between the brothers. "If there is anything I can do to help out with this situation, Henry, please call on me and I will be happy to sit down and do what I can with your brother."[138] Henry fully appreciated Art's assistance—financial and familial. Henry responded, "Indeed, I appreciate your interest in my affairs but then you have been helping me lo these many years."[139]

The memos Concello wrote in his fifties to circus personnel beneath him show a decidedly harsher tone. In March he demanded that Tuffy provide him with statistics relating to buildings in Birmingham, Washington, DC, and Baltimore.[140] The next day, he ordered Rudy Bundy, the show's treasurer, to pay the Hotel Belvedere in New York City, disclosing, "I've been staying there on and off all winter, but have never paid them."[141] The next month an even more strident note went to Bundy regarding the show's recent annual statements: "Let's get this together now because I am sitting around with my finger in my ass trying to find out how much [business] we did in each of these towns and at the same time trying to decide what towns to book."[142]

Concello took time to bring Henry North up to date on circus matters. He informed him that Maggie Smith, Chet Toliver, and Bob Dover framed the new show because "the price was right."[143] The critics liked everything except the music, Art told him. He engaged in good meetings with Alden Hatch, who was working with Henry to write the Ringling family history. He ended his commentary with, "Enough said about that old whore called the Circus"—a sentence reminiscent of the opening for *Circus Kings*, the book published by Henry North and Hatch in 1960.[144]

Arthur went to Europe in August in preparation for bringing The Greatest Show on Earth there in the early 1960s.[145] In 1956, Umberto Bedini, European talent agent and personal friend of John North, suggested the American impresario bring his circus to Paris. At the time, North relayed this information to Burke, who said he would follow up with a friend of his who had been recently appointed to the State Department's International Cultural Program.[146] Burke left, but apparently, the idea never strayed far from mind, and now John pushed the button to activate the plan. He started by insisting that Concello look things over, meet with people, and make plans over there.

When it came time for Ringling-Barnum to dismantle its winter quarters and leave Sarasota, the newspaper reported Concello's reaction: "Sitting in a comfortable chair outside his private car, Concello watched the destruction of the winter quarters without the slightest trace of sadness. 'Let's face it,' Concello said, 'I don't think Sarasota wants us anymore. We have several attractive offers from other places and when I get ready I'll make my mind up. We don't need much space, just a place to rehearse for a couple of months and a place for our costume department.'"[147]

Ringling Bros. and Barnum & Bailey moved to Venice, Florida, late in 1959. The circus leased about ten acres for $1,000 an acre with an option to add on an additional eighty. The site at Venice was near its airport, a fact which necessitated the Federal Aviation Association's approval, which they got.[148] Max Weldy's costume shop was the first building built.[149]

When the circus arrived "home" on November 29, 1960, they did so in Venice. A parade proceeded to its new winter quarters, where Concello received a hero's welcome with all available employees and a crowd of five thousand.[150] When completed, its new fifty-five-thousand-square-foot arena,[151] designed by Concello and Lloyd Morgan, was the largest building in Sarasota County.[152]

The show came home on a railroad track. After three years of using trucks, Concello realized that they were not as cost-effective as rail. Cars and trucks broke down, and when those vehicles belonged to performers, sometimes performances were detrimentally impacted.[153] The press heralded "Generalissimo" Concello as the man responsible for transforming the "huge, temperamental empire into a well-organized and efficient entertainment production,"[154] which moved on fifteen eighty-five-foot-long railroad cars, four of which were tunneled out and made into open shells.[155] These were designed to fit snugly together as one unit 340 feet long with "but a light space between each car." [156] Inside the tunnel cars were the wagons—now aluminum, low slung, and equipped with airplane tires—that shuttled wardrobe, props and equipment to the venue after being hooked together and pulled in and out by one rubber-shod tractor. The cars were originally hospital coaches and the price paid, according to the newspaper, was $1.25 million. Eight cars were used for staterooms and personnel, with three cars for animals.[157]

As Concello looked over the financials for buying the railcars, the hefty $20 million mismanagement suit was dropped at the request of the plaintiffs, the Charles Ringling family. The judge dismissed the case in June without prejudice, meaning it could be presented in court once errors were addressed,[158] but it was never brought forward again.

Laz Rosen, a friend from Concello's Bloomington days, worked for Harry Dube in Ringling-Barnum's New York City office at 10 Rockefeller Plaza. He informed Concello about a proposal to bring the Russian Circus to the United States in 1960. Frank Moore, who booked rodeos into large venues like Madison Square Garden, had visited Rosen and told him that Russian-born impresario Sol Hurok was working to bring the State Circus of Russia to America. Rosen posited that if this happened, bookings in arenas would get tight.[159] Five days later he again wrote Concello advising that the State Department had cleared the way for the Russian Circus to appear in the United States. Rosen saw this as "a political football as well as competition for the coming season,"[160] but Art saw it as an opportunity. He tucked the idea away for further thought.

For now, however, *Variety* reported that Ringling-Barnum would make the leap to Europe in the near future.[161] By the end of 1960, Concello had made three trips to Europe, scouting locations for Ringling's Barnum & Bailey Circus—a name change dictated by the legal advisors and those who recognized "Barnum & Bailey" was far better known in Europe. While Concello toured Europe, he sent Lew Rosen to Russia.[162] Arthur likely sent the first-generation American, Russian-speaking friend to the old country to scout, listen, and learn on his behalf. There seemed little the Little Giant of the Circus Biz couldn't do. Wrote one of his friends, "When asked why a thing can't be done, Art always answers, 'Why not? In my circus dictionary I have never been able to find the word "can't."'[163]

Back in the States in 1960, the circus was thriving financially.[164] Nearly all the Ringling-Barnum performances were held indoors and handled by promoters like Irvin Feld's Super Shows, Inc. (SSI). He started with the circus by promoting just a few dates, but by 1960, Ringling's agreement stated that Feld's organization was to promote Winston-Salem, Chicago, San Francisco, Oakland, Los Angeles, Dallas, Louisville, and Detroit. Parties had a fifty-fifty split on concessions and a fifty-five to forty-five (circus to SSI) split after advertising costs were deducted from gross receipts. In addition, Super Shows was to have the option of first refusal with the same terms and conditions for the same dates in 1961 and 1962 after all dates were played in 1960.[165]

Concello bullishly believed in the relationships forged with promoters. *Amusement Business* shared his thoughts on the matter: "Feld's Super Shows in Washington [DC], Harry Lashinsky of Charleston, West Virginia, Martell Brett of Birmingham and the Arena Managers Association—that's all we need. They handle all but one or two dates for us. We don't fool with guarantees, either, so every deal is a partnership. If they win, we win, or vice versa. But the promoter has every incentive to work like the devil . . ."[166] Eventually, he had a preference for working with Feld over other promoters because while "Feld spends too much money on his dates . . . he will take all the lemon promotions along with the good ones."[167] Feld made it clear that he wanted all the cities, but Concello would never cede such control. "Oh shit, you ain't never gonna get me in a position where you get them all," Concello told an interviewer.[168]

In 1960, *Circus Kings, a Ringling Family History* by Henry Ringling North hit bookstores to favorable reviews and solid sales. Memories of the tremendous money made by DeMille's *The Greatest Show on Earth* film undoubtedly spurred interest from moviemakers to turn this book into a film. While Henry and John were in Europe, Art inserted himself into the negotiations to do just that. Henry's European agent, John C. Mather, brought Concello's interference to his client's attention. "I know you have great faith in Concello, and I know he is a very fine businessman. My only misgiving," Mather informed Henry, "is that I can see he is working entirely for brother John . . ."[169]

The book went on to enjoy several printings and a paperback edition in 1964, but the movie was never made. After reading it, preeminent circus historian Dick Conover wrote North and identified a number of historical errors in it. Interestingly, North apologized for the errors and admitted that he hadn't yet read the finished work. He stated that he couldn't bring himself to do so, because he didn't want to wallow in the family's discord, union troubles, and more.[170]

Transcripts of daily phone calls detail the numerous times Concello tried to rein in John's expansive ego and proclivity to sign more and more acts, but they also highlight the free-flowing ideas bandied about between the men. Such was the case late in 1960, when Art broached the idea of a school where circus performers could be trained and then booked with the Ringling Bros. and Barnum & Bailey Circus, likening it to a baseball farm team scenario that developed talent for the big leagues. Concello suggested it could be called the "John Ringling North Circus Academy." North initially balked because he wanted to see Concello's name on it, too. They verbally sparred, but ultimately, John deferred to Art's wishes.[171]

Concello refined his ideas over the course of the next couple of weeks after speaking with and listening to a cadre of Ringling executives, including the general manager, Genders; treasurer, Bundy; board member Jimmy Ringling; administrative assistant Bill Perry; and secretary, Norma Wright. South American circus impresario Carlos Vasquez was brought into the conversation when the idea arose that the academy talent could be hosted by a second unit of Ringling to tour South America. They debated the idea of a second unit managed by Ringling executives and sprinkled with its performing talent, who would help train newbies that would tour Brazil and Argentina with the Cristiani Bros. Circus under the banner Ringling Bros. and Barnum & Bailey International, Ltd. Though nothing crystallized, Concello was thinking about how the circus could grow its own talent and expand its reach. The Ringling Bros. and Barnum & Bailey Circus looked to expand again—this time, internationally.

Art at sixteen and a member of The Flying Wards with Hagenbeck-Wallace Circus, 1927. Note how he signed his name. *Illinois State University's Special Collections, Milner Library.*

Antoinette Comeau poses for a snapshot in the backyard of Sells Floto Circus, 1928. *Courtesy of Fred D. Pfening III.*

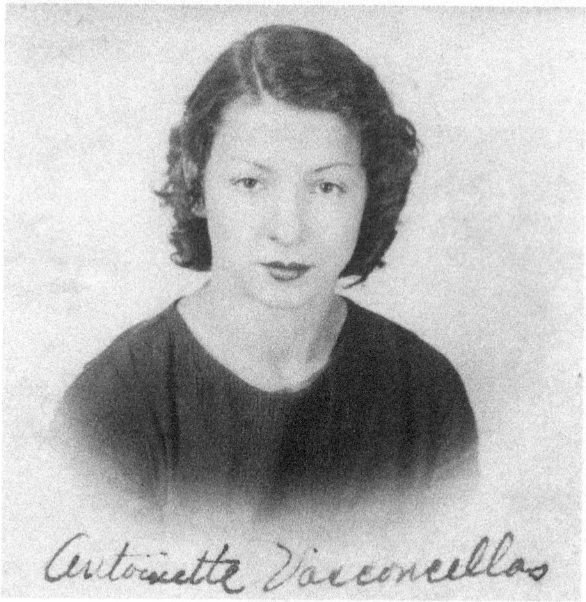

Arthur and Antoinette Vasconcellos' 1931 passport pictures. They rarely used his legal surname. *Illinois State University's Special Collections, Milner Library.*

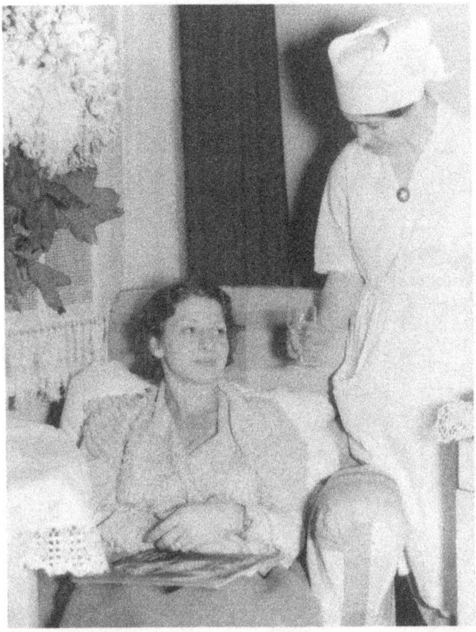

Antoinette in the hospital after she injured her shoulder in Berlin, 1932. *Illinois State University's Special Collections, Milner Library.*

Alfredo Codona, the world's best flyer, known for his triple somersault, incredible grace, and showmanship, faces off with the up-and-coming Art Concello. Jack Johnson, former heavyweight champion, gamely poses between them in this 1932 photo taken in the Scala, Berlin. *Illinois State University's Special Collections, Milner Library.*

A 1936 lineup of friends who perfected trapeze skills in Bloomington, Illinois: Everett White, Wayne Larey, Harold "Tuffy" Genders, Art and Antoinette Concello, and Gracie Genders. *Illinois State University's Special Collections, Milner Library.*

The specially built training space in Bloomington, Illinois, where so many youngsters learned the art of flying trapeze. Art purchased the Ward barn property in 1935 and often referred to it as "The Farm." *Illinois State University's Special Collections, Milner Library.*

Mickey King, Lew "Laz" Rosen, and Antoinette in the backyard of the Ringling Bros. and Barnum & Bailey Circus. Newark, New Jersey, 1937. *Illinois State University's Special Collections, Milner Library.*

Art snaps a picture of Antoinette shortly after taking a fall into the net, which left its "waffle weave" pattern on his back. *Illinois State University's Special Collections, Milner Library.*

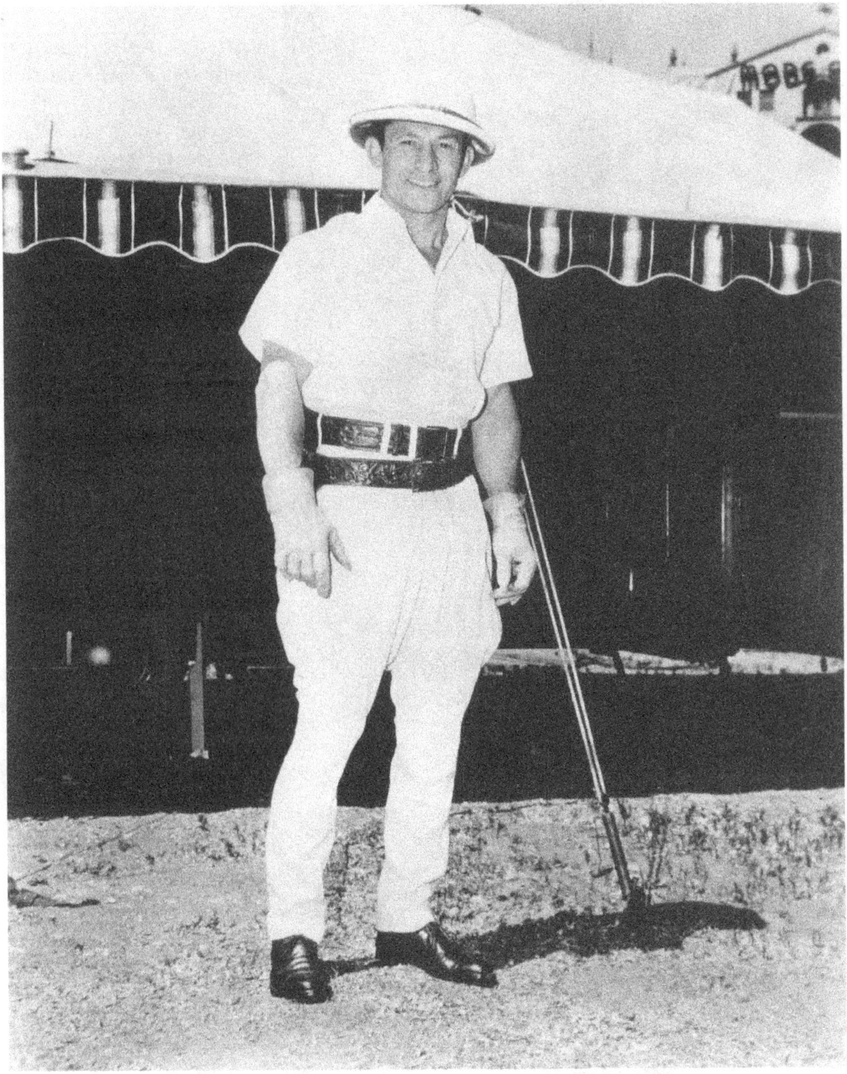

Clyde Beatty, the fabulous big cat showman and Art's on-again, off-again business partner. ***Illinois State University's Special Collections, Milner Library.***

Art and Antoinette perform the crowd-pleasing passing leap to their catcher Eddie A. Ward for The Greatest Show on Earth's opener in Madison Square Garden, 1940. *Illinois State University's Special Collections, Milner Library.*

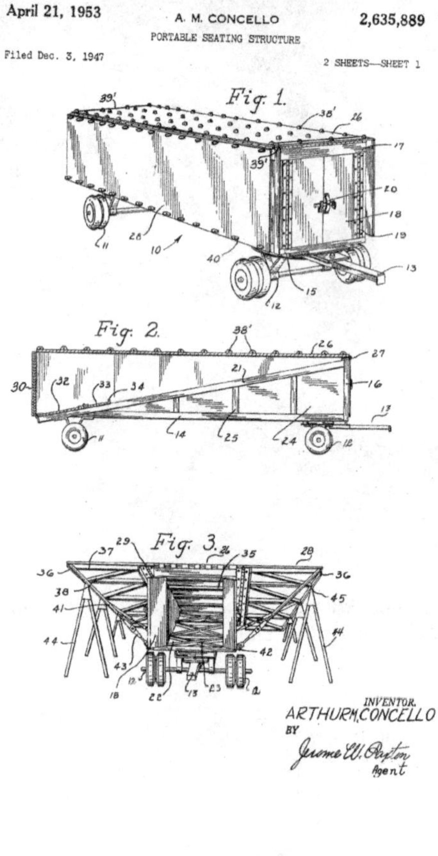

Three drawings from Concello's patent application for his seat wagons, filed December 3, 1947. *United States Patent & Trademark Office.*

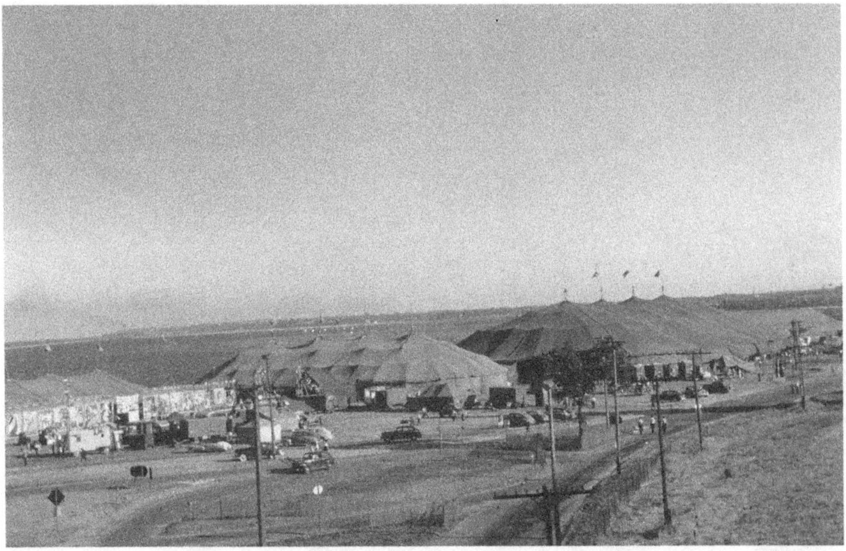

Ringling Bros. and Barnum & Bailey Circus lot, Milwaukee, July 24, 1948. The big top on the right could seat up to ten thousand customers. *Illinois State University's Special Collections, Milner Library.*

Brothers Henry and John Ringling North. Between them, a framed photo of the five Ringling brothers, who brought their first circus out from Baraboo, Wisconsin. *Illinois State University's Special Collections, Milner Library.*

Randy Concello stands between his grandparents, Papa Vas and his second wife Ollie Mae Vasconcellos, in front of their Bloomington home in 1960. *Illinois State University's Special Collections, Milner Library.*

Frank McClosky, former rigger, Concello confidant, and on-again, off-again business partner. *Illinois State University's Special Collections, Milner Library.*

In 1963, Desilu Productions brought their color program *The Greatest Show on Earth* to television. Jack Palance's character was based on Concello. *Illinois State University's Special Collections, Milner Library.*

"The *only* Mrs. Art Concello" backstage in 1969 with Rudy Bundy, vice president and executive director of the Red Unit, Ringling Bros. and Barnum & Bailey Circus. Though nearly sixty years old, Antoinette carried tights and a leotard, so she could fill in on the pedestal board if necessary. *Illinois State University's Special Collections, Milner Library.*

Art, with his omnipresent cigar and his longtime girlfriend, Maggie Smith. They wed shortly after Antoinette passed away in 1984. *Illinois State University's Special Collections, Milner Library.*

Chapter 8

The Ugly American

1961–1964

> "I don't want to do the God damned European show. I don't know anything about Europe and I don't want to do it!"[1]
>
> —Art Concello, to John Ringling North

The 1960s were a tremendously active time in Concello's life. As the executive director of the Ringling Bros. and Barnum & Bailey Circus, he worked with the show's attorneys to sue a rival circus, explored and developed ways to bring the circus into several new international markets, refined the promotional strategy for bookings into buildings, and settled the circus into its new winter quarters in Venice. He brought the American Circus to Soviet Russia and Ringling's Barnum & Bailey to Europe. And then, he was fired. Not one to let something like employment termination stand in his way, he developed the Continental Circus for the New York World's Fair and brought the Moscow Circus to America. How did he keep every player and every deal straight? He kept a diary.

Art's 1961 date book provides insight into something he generally didn't acknowledge having: feelings. Nowhere were his emotions closer to the surface than when he wrote about Randy. Inheriting stubbornness from both his parents made their son an even more difficult child to raise.

In 1961 Randy, at sixteen, was newly licensed to drive the pink station wagon given to him by his dad. Arthur penned a typical entry during his time at home in Sarasota just three days after his son's birthday: "Sunday, February 18, [1961] Sara-Venice. Up at 11:00 to Venice, no one was working. I gave them hell. Talked to lite [*sic*] man—figured out furnace. Drove back [at] 6:00 to my RR car. Cleaned up. Will stop by Randy place. He had a party—boy stayed all night out on Beach. This is no good. Leads to drinking and Trouble. I stayed till 6:00AM so his Mama could get some sleep."[2]

By this time, both Art and Anto had spent years trying to give their son a childhood that they never experienced themselves. They lavished gifts on the boy, and in return, their son lived the life of a hellion. Because of his parents' indulgences, he had experienced many things other children only dreamt of, like having his own house—albeit one in his parents' backyard—with little to no responsibility for it. There he could be on his own (sort of) with his own rules while his parents were away with the circus.

Randy took his father's path where schooling was concerned, choosing truancy whenever possible. His parents enrolled him in Sarasota schools up till junior high, when they transferred him to Farragut Academy in St. Petersburg, a residential military school that served grades K–12. Cadet Concello was lauded for his cornet playing abilities—which, school publications noted, he had learned years earlier from Merle Evans.[3] After graduating, he was moved to Lawrence Academy outside of Boston for his freshman and part of his sophomore years of high school. There he excelled as a halfback on its junior varsity football team.[4] Anto felt she should be close by while he lived on the East Coast, perhaps to try to keep him out of trouble, so she moved into a Beacon Street apartment paid for by Art.[5] By early February 1961, both were back in Florida. Art wrote an ominous entry that may explain why Randy left the Academy: "Anto said she had a call from girl's mother in Boston. Girl in trouble."[6]

"Fixers" were a fixture on circuses. Often attorneys, these men had the job to solve all sorts of problems. Both Concellos had experience watching how fixers, also called legal adjusters, worked (El Paso, Texas, was the ultimate fix). They knew the power of greenbacks in tight situations. Art wrote about resolving his son's situation: "Randy got fixed to go back to school. That is good. Don't know how long it will last."[7]

Randy's good behavior rarely lasted long. His father documented his disappointment in his day planner. "Randy was to meet me at home [but] he did not wait as I asked him to in note. Disappointed me. He has no consideration for anyone but himself," Art observed less than a month later.[8] Frustrated, Art tried several tactics to rein in his son's behavior. First, he cut off Randy's allowance. When that didn't work, he assigned his son a curfew—10:30 on school nights and 1 a.m. on weekends. He also demanded that his son produce a doctor's note should he not feel well enough to attend school. If this rule wasn't followed, that pink station wagon would be taken away. When Randy disobeyed, and he did so frequently, Art spent the late nights and early mornings with Antoinette, listening to the "tales of what Randy does."[9]

Just two months after Randy started at Sarasota High, his parents decided the boy would be better served by a European boarding school, where he could learn several foreign languages while being assimilated into a more culturally diverse landscape. After a notable rejection, they placed him at Monte Rosa near Montreux, Switzerland. It took some persuading for him to attend, but he eventually caved. Once established at the school, he wrote his mother asking for money. Art read that letter and wrote of it in his diary: "She is a fool if she sends him any. But no doubt she is a fool."[10]

With her son out partying, Antoinette joined her friends from her Bloomington days, Willie Kraus and Earl Shipley, to volunteer at Sarasota's Sailor Circus, an amateur high school circus.[11] After her second year helping the high school, it wasn't a story about her that ran in the local press. Instead, a story about her father, Toussaint, appeared in the *Sarasota News*. Now nearly 102 years old, he reiterated his work history from published reports years earlier, and he added that he had survived being struck by lightning and was partially blinded when gunpowder had exploded in his eyes.[12] The press didn't acknowledge that his daughters, photographed with him for the story, were equally tough.

Randy wasn't the only source of disappointment for Arthur. His half-brother Joe was, too. On December 23, 1961, the day before Art and Snort were due to appear at a dinner with Randy and many of Antoinette's family, Concello found him in a drunken stupor. He ". . . left (and) told him to try to straighten up so he could appear tomorrow, but he did nothing but drink."[13] The next day, when he went to pick his brother up from his newly renovated railroad car that he had spent the year turning into a home, Joe was in no shape to go anywhere. By December 28, he was in jail. When local authorities called Art to bail him out, "I said keep him." He was released New Year's Eve.

Lawsuits were nothing new to the circus or the men who ran it. The 1960s started with Ringling Bros. and Barnum & Bailey Circus taking legal action. Their attorneys filed a $250,000 suit in the New York Supreme Court against Clyde Beatty-Cole Bros. Circus and its management, comprised of Walter Kernan, Frank McClosky, Jerry Collins, and Randolph Calhoun,[14] the same men who were former partners with Concello and North in the Cuban dog-track-racing venture in the 1950s. The action revolved around Beatty-Cole Circus's use of a globe depicting the earth with the superimposed words "Greatest Circus on Earth" in its marketing materials. Ringling-Barnum had been using a similar globe with "Greatest Show on Earth" over it for decades. The suit charged unlawful appropriation of the pithy and memorable phrase and stated that Beatty-Cole's continued use of it would cause irreparable damage to Ringling by leading the public to believe that the two circuses were one and the same.[15] Following two years of legal maneuvering, Ringling-Barnum got an injunction that stopped the other circus from using the slogan and globe. After winning the case, Ringling-Barnum trademarked "Greatest Show on Earth" and the globe image.[16]

While the logo and slogan issue was being litigated, arenas continued to tantalize Concello. "They were all laughing at me when I laid it out for them," Concello now said of the time when he first suggested how to play in them. "Think of it. Anywhere we want to go, we make it at 70 mph. No trouble. Most cases our rigging goes up in hours. And, the lower nut—it's a godsend."[17] To newspaperman and circus writer Gene Plowden, he said, "We've licked a lot of problems and we've come back stronger than ever. There are 150 buildings like this [a convention hall] in the United States and Canada where we can move in and put on the show. We got rid of ticket sellers, ushers, concessionaires, sawdust and mud. All we have to do is move in, put on the show, and move out."[18]

In 1961 the Arena Managers Association published a directory chock full of statistics about current buildings and new arenas that were popping up all over the country. Each venue's capacity, rental and insurance costs, concessions potential, and more were detailed. Concello read it cover to cover, looking for new or better places to route the show.[19] Of the show's artistry, Concello commented, "Is the show any good this year—how should I know? All I know is numbers; we're making money, that's what I care about."[20]

The money he made included payments from his network of friends and underbosses. Eddie Billetti, for one, acknowledged he needed to "take care of you for the 10% I promised you,"[21] though he never provided more details in print. Concello's notes in his daily planner are equally vague. On April 12, 1961, he wrote, "Made a deal with Adv't man to kick back $7500."[22] With no further reference to this, nor a route book to determine who was on the Advance team at the time, it is impossible to know more. But let there be no doubt, Concello expected and received kickbacks.

Arthur M. Concello, as he signed his name these days, had a macro view of the entertainment business landscape. He watched national ticket sales but also considered new, international markets to increase profits. After toying with Manila and Tokyo,[23] the decision was made to go to South America with the help of Carlos Vasquez, the Latin American impresario and local promoter who brought the Moscow Circus to South America in 1960.[24] Now Vasquez wanted to bring America's Ringling Bros. and Barnum & Bailey Circus there.

That started when Ringling-Barnum agreed to loan the Cristiani Bros. Circus equipment and costumes. In exchange, the Cristianis agreed to take their show to South America under the title of Ringling Bros. and

Barnum & Bailey International. Their 1961 route went from Rio de Janeiro to São Paulo, Brazil, and then to Buenos Aires, Argentina, with each stop lasting about one month. Paul Eagles was general manager; Lloyd Morgan was superintendent; Raymond Escorsia was bandmaster; and Justino Loyal was equestrian director. Merle Evans, Bob Dover, Dick Barstow, and Margaret Smith traveled with the show to Rio to work out the kinks.[25]

Only after this second unit of Ringling-Barnum left the country did Concello learn that a levy was placed on "The American Circus Co., Inc." doing business as the Cristiani Bros. Circus.[26] Concello tried to clarify the relationship between Ringling-Barnum and Cristiani Bros., telling a firm that was researching the smaller circus's tax debts that there had been no merger between the two shows. Instead, he stated, Ringling-Barnum was simply operating a circus in South America which employed a number of Cristianis. When asked for their whereabouts, Concello said he had no idea where the Cristianis were at the moment.[27] It's probably true that Concello didn't know *exactly* where the Cristianis were, but he likely did know that their show, its loaned equipment, and personnel were due back in the United States by May 28, just nine days after he responded to the firm.

By mid-June, it was time to reconcile the South American books. In his 1961 datebook, Art noted that he had many people over to his railroad car to help him do that. He sometimes wrote reminders to himself and provided specific details to jog his memory later. Such was the case with Paul Eagles: "Paul Eagles had words with Helen [Steinwachs] and Grace about everything. He ask[ed] 'em, 'why don't you let me go on home to Calif.'"[28] He continued writing notes to himself about his plans, "I will as soon as I get this S.A. Business straight. I have got to let Paul go. No work for him to do."[29]

Concello worked hard and demanded the same from those around him. Sometimes he rewarded all with an alcohol-infused celebration after the work was done. On June 29, a group of seven wrapped up their work on the accounting books. "S.A. All set," he wrote; then the liquor started flowing.[30] The party didn't stop until after 4:30 a.m. Art got back to work the following day, though he started it later than usual: "Warm day—I was up at noon down to talk to Belmonte & Lucio Christiani [*sic*] re S.A. deal there is no more $ for them. Said I would go over figures in 30 to 60 days when auditor has the bill . . ."[31] This also was the day he dealt with Eagles. "Sent Paul off to Calif. He is done. I spoke to him on phone."[32]

Concello sought a more favorable South American agreement for 1962. In May, a memorandum of understanding was negotiated and signed by Concello and James C. Ringling on behalf of Ringling-Barnum and Carlos Vasquez,[33] in which Vasquez agreed to create a touring circus with costumes and some props rented from Ringling Bros. and Barnum & Bailey.

This time Vasquez was forbidden from using the Ringling name. In return, the circus received 10 percent of the net profits each month.

Media coverage helped to drive ticket sales. In the States, Concello recognized it made good business sense to get the circus out in front of all media to stir interest and sell tickets. He continued throughout the early 1960s to have conversations and negotiations with various television executives about the Ringling-Barnum Circus specials that aired regularly. He knew circuses long relied on its press agents to get word about them into the hands (and better, the hearts and minds) of the show-going public.

Bill Fields served as a press agent for The Greatest Show on Earth starting in the early 1950s. This tall, lean Texan with a soft drawl was not the typical press agent. He was not flamboyant or prone to superlatives and promises. His press releases had to be backed by facts, and the fact was that he loved circuses and the people connected with them.[34] One of the last projects he worked on was getting a piece about the circus printed in *Newsweek*. The article focused on the new iteration of the show, how it differed from the circuses of the past but was still exciting, still thrilling, and still fascinating for children of all ages. It touted the popularity of the circus, stating that in Greensboro, North Carolina, then with a population of 75,000, it played to 118,000 people in three days, and in Haddonfield, New Jersey, population 11,000 in 1960, it played to 54,000 in two.[35] Concello, for the first and only time, wrote the magazine and congratulated them on "one of the most enjoyable circus pieces I have ever read."[36] He likely did so because Fields was fighting a battle with cancer that he would soon lose.

Coincidentally, Mae Lyons's praise for the *Newsweek* article appeared directly above Concello's in its May 9 issue. She filled Bill Fields's shoes as Ringling's press agent after his death. Mae was a seasoned publicist who first met Fields during the war and married him shortly after it. It was a "circus first" to hire a female for the position that controlled a tremendous advertising budget, kept publicity communications channels open with media (television, radio, newspapers, magazines, and books), and created press releases exciting enough to get stories about the circus into them. In one of her first media blitzes, she conveyed that in 1962, the circus "grossed more than in any year in their history."[37] As far as the "circus first" part, media were given this: "No official word is forthcoming on this, but manager Art Concello, himself a colorful character in his own right, is said to have crowed, 'I told you it was a good idea to hire a woman!'"[38]

Ringling Bros. and Barnum & Bailey received even more television coverage in early 1963. Desilu Productions, owned by Desi Arnaz and Lucille Ball, announced that it would air a new series on ABC, starring Jack Palance and titled *The Greatest Show on Earth*.[39] The show, which Desilu had in the works for over two years,[40] was scheduled to run in the 9:00 p.m. slot on Tuesdays and was the only hour-long color production on the network at the time.[41]

Palance played the circus taskmaster Johnny Slate, a Concello-based role, and Stuart Erwin played Otto King, the circus owner. Coproduced by Ringling Brothers TV, Inc.,[42] the series had guest stars each week with scenes shot both in Venice and along the show's route.[43] Concello, Pat Valdo, and Bob Dover worked with the production team, and throngs of spectators—about ten thousand it was estimated[44]—watched the filming in Venice. Like when the eponymous movie was shot, Concello was close at hand when it came time for the flying-trapeze scenes. *The Sarasota News* reported, "Concello scampered up the rope to the pedestal to give actors a first-hand lesson about flying" and did so in street clothes.[45] Though he was there to assist actress Ruth Roman when she became entangled in the edge of the net, he could not save the show, as it was panned by critics and only ran for one season.[46]

The press agent position was now known as the international press representative. Its office was in New York's Madison Square Garden, but for a month every year, Lyons visited Venice.[47] The corporation's campus sprouted five new buildings built by G & G Metals, headed by Gene Vercheski.[48] The New Venice Arena—designed to be a miniature Madison Square Garden[49] and ballyhooed by its designer, Concello, as a "miracle of construction" and "a model for the future of building such structures"[50]—took an incredible amount of effort to create. When the arena was in its conceptual state, Art had written Tuffy Genders, now the circus's general manager, asking for the exact measurements of a contemporary flying rig so that one could be permanently installed[51]—reminiscent of the setup they both used as boys learning how to fly decades earlier in Bloomington's YMCA. It's also possible that he consulted with C. D. Curtis, the former youth director there, when his former mentor visited him in August 1961.[52]

Vercheski, a transplant from River Rouge, Michigan, and a self-described "very, very private" person, repeatedly worked with Concello.[53] Art's mechanical and practical mind kept churning away on ways to increase efficiency, and Vercheski brought Little Caesar's plans to life. Describing his process, Vercheski said, "It's a one day at a time deal, you draw plans in the dirt by the side of the car" and then create it.[54] When Art heard people say things couldn't be done, his immediate response was "Fuck 'em."[55] He collaborated with a man who had a much less combative stance. Vercheski believed: "Everything I do is fun. If it's not fun, I don't do it. I live seven days a week, I haven't worked in thirty years."[56] Because of his masterful and dedicated workmanship and his relationship with Concello, Vercheski created the tunnel cars, baggage wagons, and props for the Ringling Bros. and Barnum & Bailey Circus and, eventually, the Moscow State Circus.

It wasn't just circuses that benefitted from Vercheski's fun. In 1962, Concello convinced Morris Chalfen of Holiday on Ice to use part of Ringling-Barnum's winter quarters as the site of its transportation facility and set Bill Perry up to act as a technical advisor to the popular ice show.[57] Tunnel cars intrigued Chalfen, who had booked ice shows into buildings since the 1930s,[58] and he eventually used them to transport props, too.[59] Vercheski produced Chalfen's wagons, modified his Jeeps, and created a unique telescoping stage, designed by Concello, which could be erected in two hours. What once took six Holiday on Ice men eight hours to assemble now took a fraction of that time.[60] Over time, G & G Metals, with input from Concello, made not only Holiday's tunnel cars (based on Ringling-Barnum's) but also the Ice Capades' the next year.[61] It's unknown if payment went to the show or Concello directly, although an informed opinion is that Concello put some of the ice show money in his pocket.

When the circus played New York's Madison Square Garden in 1961, John Ringling North rewarded Art for his exceptional service with a surprise party, where he presented his executive director with an oil portrait and a silver goblet which read, "To a great showman, Arthur M. Concello, from Ringling Cast, 1961."[62] On this date, April 17, Art wrote in his diary, "Worked all day at office. Party at Hotel. They gave me a Photo of myself and a Cup from Ringling cast."[63] After he jotted notes like this in his date book, he read the dailies. Whenever he was in New York City, tabloid publications like the *Daily Mirror* and the *Daily News* were part of his bedtime routine.[64]

North knew Concello was a busy, busy man in 1961. When he'd asked Art to come back to run the show inside buildings five years earlier, he had agreed that he would be a hands-off boss and he tried to abide by that—for the most part, he gave Concello free rein to run the circus. Concello, for example, represented the circus in the five lawsuits brought against the show that year.[65] To do so, Arthur needed to look and feel his best. Concerned about his weight—his goal was to get the scale down to 145 pounds—he consumed a pink, sludgy diet drink called Metrocal and visited his New York City tailor, who could minimize the look of the twenty or so pounds he always tried to lose. He also made sure to get his annual three-day checkup with Charlie Mayo at his clinic in Rochester, Minnesota.[66]

Concello believed in a strong chain of command and knew if the managers weren't healthy, expenses could escalate. Therefore, he sent staffers like Margaret Smith, Willis Lawson, Eldon Day, Tuffy Genders, Merle Evans, Rudy Bundy, Eddie Ward, and Bob Dover to the Mayo Clinic for regular physicals. He received written reports about each of them, read them, and filed them for future reference.[67]

He also pushed for speed, preferring a quick-moving show over one that dragged.[68] Even more, he cared about how rapidly it could set up in and move out of arenas. Though he read the reviews of the Madison Square Garden premiere, he cared less for artistry and showmanship[69] than efficiency. He was all about how quickly he could get his portion of the circus's profit.

Perhaps juggling four circuses had something to do with this attitude. In addition to touring The Greatest Show on Earth, North charged his executive director to bring an American circus to the Soviet Union as well as Ringling-Barnum's show to Europe. North also had aspirations to have a circus in the 1964 New York World's Fair. As for Europe, Arthur had very little interest in taking the circus to John's international playground. North kept hammering the point. He wanted his circus in Europe, and by God, he wanted Concello to run it. "For three or four years, I kept stalling and stalling," Concello recalled about ten years later.[70] He intended to wait John out.

With so much to do, Arthur spent more than twenty-four weeks of 1961 traveling. He crisscrossed the country, visiting cities from coast to coast: New York to Seattle and many communities in between. Internationally, he journeyed to Geneva, Zurich, and Frankfort.[71] He documented in his day planner how long it took his train, plane, or automobile to get from point A to point B. While he was once accustomed to traveling on the show's train, those later days he sacrificed sleep because he "wasn't used to it anymore."[72] He had an energy about him, a presence or aura that pervaded every space he occupied. The Ringling administrative secretary wrote that regardless of where Art happened to be, "one senses a difference in everyone."[73]

On the road he collided with family and friends—and perceived foes—of years' past. In Bloomington, he took his father and stepmother, Papa Vas and Ollie Mae, to dinner, and he listened to a World Series game with them before dropping them off back home. There he also made time to visit Ed Raycraft and former fellow flyer Leo Hendryx. He ate at the Grand Hotel, a restaurant that specialized in mouthwatering fried chicken and which sat in the house in the foreground of the trapeze-training barn Antoinette received as part of their divorce. The restaurant got its name from the circus tradition of raising a flag emblazoned with the word Hotel every time a meal was ready to be eaten.

He also ran into supposed adversaries such as Michael Burke and Jack Tavlin. He saw Michael Burke in the Zurich airport. All he wrote in his diary of that meeting was, "Saw Burke. He looks good."[74] Concello and Tavlin, who had stolen lots of Art's cash decades earlier, ran into each other in New York City on June 6 and set up an additional meeting for the next day. By this time, Tavlin was president of Exhibits, Inc., an advertising company, president of the Race Track Advertising Association, and president of Coliseum Seat Renting Service, an organization that supplied seating.[75] Together, Concello and Tavlin attended Roosevelt Raceway and toured Tavlin's business. Afterwards Art noted, "He has signs," meaning he had a billboard business.[76] Though he had a long memory, Concello didn't have time for resentment or grudges, and though he was informed by the past, he never looked back. "It's just business" was part of his creed.[77] Memory informed Art to never go into business with Tavlin again. Their visits now were merely social.

Concello used his date book to keep details straight. A typical entry for 1961 reads: "N.Y.C. I worked around office. Got a suitcase and small zip bag, brought straw hat, went to tailor's. Meet H.S.D. at tailor's, so I made dinner date. I worked with Rudy Bundy. He got checks and changed money. I went to hotel. Vasques called, I meet with him 5:15PM for 1 hr. Ate with Dube at Billy Gwons. Left there to Hotel and pack & had nap. Left hotel at 12:00 midnite [*sic*] for airport. Left airport via Swiss Air at 1:45. Flying time to Geneva 6 hr 30 mi."[78]

That flight was the second time in 1961 that Concello went to Switzerland to meet with his boss, and, coincidentally or not, it overlapped by four days with his son and ex-wife's visit there. When he met with North, he made a last-ditch effort to dissuade him from touring his three-ring circus through Europe. Concello felt he didn't know enough about the place to make the endeavor a success. "God damn it, I don't want to do it," he said.[79] But North persisted. Once told that he had no choice, Art started laying plans. Preoccupied with trying to get a show put together in a place about which he knew little (and couldn't care less about), he did very little sightseeing. He recorded some thoughts of his visit to Paris. Obviously, he hadn't taken much time to be a tourist the first time he was there as a flyer performing in Cirque Medrano and d'Hiver. Now almost thirty years later and with a more mature perspective, he wrote, "Went to Eiffel Tower in afternoon it is okay."[80] The next week he bought himself a Rolex in Zurich,[81] but he made no other comment about the city or its sights. He reviewed meals far more frequently; particularly, the heinously expensive steaks he enjoyed in Baden-Baden, Germany.[82]

When Arthur worked on circus-related matters, he did so with precision and focus, not stopping until the task was completed to his satisfaction. Now juggling multiple circuses, he relied on his keen attention to detail. One evening in December 1961, Concello decided he would route the 1962–1965 editions of the US-based Greatest Show on Earth. He noted in his day planner that he performed the task with less than five-hours' sleep in twenty-four hours' time.[83]

A decade later in the interview with circus historian Tom Parkinson, Art maintained he was always against the idea of a European circus, but documents show he eventually supported it. Concello penned a letter to John on April 19, 1962, in which he outlined his thoughts on what it would take to successfully operate the circus there. First, he suggested that a European show company be formed in Switzerland with the stock to be held as follows: one-third to John Ringling North, one-third to Dan Gordon Judge, and one-third to himself. Then he identified twenty-two buildings where the show would fit and remarked that there was a great deal of money to be made in West Germany, France, Northern Italy, and the Low Countries. "I propose we do this European company on the following basis: All monies to be furnished by a company owned jointly by JRN and Dan Gordon Judge." Concello told North that he would supply the sweat equity, the "know-how," to organize, build, and see that the show operated successfully. As if Concello thought his boss might have forgotten, he reminded North that he, North, was behind this plan 100 percent, as was Judge.[84]

Concello asked Morris Chalfen for help identifying venues that could seat between five thousand and fifteen thousand people[85] in places like Hamburg, Copenhagen, London, Paris, Amsterdam, Frankfurt, and Geneva. Concello then suggested to North that the circus tour for ten months before returning to its European corporate headquarters in Lille, France, to regroup and retool for about six weeks before heading out for the next year's European tour.[86] At John's behest, Art was muscling The Greatest Show on Earth into Europe, and in 1963 he informed the press that they expected to continue to tour the continent for the foreseeable future.[87]

A lot of work had to be done. With a tour covering so many different countries where various languages were spoken, a combination bookkeeper and interpreter was identified as a top need. They found one in Katherina Marti. Kathy Sabino, as she is now known, worked the reception desk at Hotel Ascot in Zurich. She recalled how she was chosen: "They [Art Concello and Lloyd Morgan] were talking at the reception desk and saying that they needed someone who spoke a number of languages and they needed someone who could come and work for them. I overheard them and I asked them [about a job], because I had a green card, and I needed one."[88] She remembered meeting both of the Concellos. "The only thing I distinctly remember is that his wife told me to be very careful because he liked women and I assured her that I would keep [away]."[89] Though they had been divorced for five years, Antoinette still introduced herself as Mrs. Arthur Concello, a fact which perhaps confused young Marti.

Before Europe, the circus first had to go where no US circus had gone before: the Soviet Union. It wasn't Concello who negotiated a circus trade between the world's foremost superpowers. It was Chalfen. He had that long history of taking his ice show to markets around the world, and in 1959 this included the Soviet Union. Concello and, presumably, North trusted Chalfen to work with the US State Department's Cultural Exchange Program to bring an American circus to the Soviet Union and a Russian circus to America in 1963. Part of the cultural exchange guidelines stipulated that the name of the show be changed to the American Circus. Additionally, performers were to be employees of Chalfen's Holiday on Ice, not Ringling Bros. and Barnum & Bailey Circus. Their plan, as it developed, was to have Ringling's performers first present the American Circus in Russia and then extend their overseas tour into Europe under the Ringling's Barnum & Bailey Circus title.

Forty-six performers and four staff members, Concello included, left Chicago on a chartered KLM flight on June 30, 1963,[90] with lots of instructions about what they could and couldn't do in Russia. Clown Jackie LeClaire's first impression of Moscow revolved around the ubiquitous soldiers he saw: "It looked like they were dressed from the Wizard of Oz," with their long coats nearly touching their ankles. At night, streets were dark because the lights, while installed, were not lit—it was assumed the communist government couldn't afford to do so. About the performance, LeClaire thought, "Art couldn't care less. Some of the acts we had were atrocious . . ."[91] Chalfen openly expressed that they would lose money in the Soviet Union—as much as $200,000.[92] The show opened in the Moscow Circus Arena on July 4 with no ringmaster and ran about three hours. This forced Concello to cut the running time of acts to meet the desired two-hour performance window.[93]

The American Circus worked one show every weekday (except for Tuesdays, which were dark), two shows on Saturdays, and three on Sundays. The tour moved by rail and lasted about eleven weeks, going from Moscow to Leningrad and then on to Kiev.[94] Though official Soviet reaction was stoically favorable,[95] Muscovites clamored to get into the two thousand-seat arena, where tickets had to be obtained on the black market.[96] After Kiev, many performers made the leap to the European show as planned, including loyalist and former Concello flyer turned Australian act manager Wayne Larey, who served as the personnel manager in both places and Chalfen's right-hand man in Russia.

Lloyd Morgan led the Ringling operations team in Europe, and Bill Bailey served as secretary-treasurer. "He really was the person that determined what was happening," Marti recalled of Morgan.[97] More than $1 million was committed to bringing North's circus to Europe. Chalfen routed the European show and asked his Holiday on Ice employees to provide their expertise to make Ringling's Barnum & Bailey successful there.[98] From Lille, where the circus premiered from September 18 to 25, it moved to Paris from September 27 through November 11. After Paris, it was scheduled to appear in Frankfort, Hamburg, Copenhagen, Kiev, Brussels, Rotterdam, Dortmund, Stuttgart, Zurich, West Berlin, Cologne, Essen, Milan, Geneva, and London.[99]

Trouble began while trying to get performers into Europe after their Soviet Union dates concluded. Marti remembered, "We spent a lot of time trying to get the Lippezanner horses back from Eastern Europe. We had circus animals that needed to get veterinary care. It was a very stressful time for people."[100]

The circus's opening in Lille was not a huge success in the eyes of the public or the critics, who were used to elegant one-ring circuses. Troubles that were expected to be worked out by the time the show premiered in Paris weren't. Curiously, Concello instructed Merle Evans and his wife to tour Europe for two weeks after rehearsals and before the show debuted.[101] Why do this when the steadying hand of Merle could help smooth the musical waters for the debut? The internal view of the European show matched LeClaire's opinion of the Russian counterpart. In Paris, the brothers North were in attendance, and both were utterly unimpressed by it; in fact, the elder North was infuriated.

In early October 1963, Ringling-Barnum treasurer, Rudy Bundy, and his wife, Katie, boarded a boat bound for France. Bundy enjoyed being the treasurer of The Greatest Show on Earth during a year when it grossed well over $5 million in the United States, and he was looking forward to a two-week European respite.[102] About halfway across the Atlantic, Bundy received a phone call from North, who told him to cancel his plans. He would be put to work trying to right a show Concello left in shambles. When the Bundys got to Paris, Katie went to the Continental Hotel while her husband went directly to the Palais Des Sports, a venue that sat four thousand spectators. Bundy ended up staying in Europe for three months, trying to bail out Ringling's disastrous showing there.

Just as the circus kicked off its European tour in Lille, Concello flew to Florida to oversee the creation of the Continental Circus's tent and substructure.[103] He told North he'd be back to get the European show closed up.[104] John was furious about his departure, but Arthur stood firm, explaining, "Shit, if I don't leave, there ain't gonna be no tent up at that damn World's Fair, I'll tell you that right now."[105]

There was more going on with Concello in Europe. On October 12, Henry North wrote his older brother a strongly worded advisory. He wrote, "Because of AMC's deluded machinations and mismanagement followed by his present physical collapse you have suddenly found the European Operation, which you had trustingly placed under his direction and supervision, in such an ill-planned, badly-staffed state of jeopardy that you must forthwith suspend its operation."[106] Henry advised his brother to cancel the rest of the European tour and regroup. He stated, "I suggest that you must devote immediate effort to the reorganization of your show in the States which I feel must have suffered tremendously from AMC's recent neglect with his preoccupation with extra curricular affairs."

It's difficult to determine exactly what happened, but speculation can be offered. First, there was the money. By the time the show reached Paris, the daily expense for the show was $12,000, and box office receipts rarely covered that.[107] Certified public accountants reviewed the books in early 1965 and reported a loss in Europe of $174,664 for the three months of 1964 and a loss of another $431,464 from September 18 through December 31, 1963—combined, that's just over $5 million in 2022. Their report stated, in part: ". . . the former executive director [meaning Concello] who handled the tour for the Company was not available for explanations and needed supporting documentation could not be obtained."[108] Yet two years later, records show that Rotterdam had the best receipts, but expenses still outweighed them by more than $2,000.[109]

The "recent neglect" and "preoccupation with extracurricular affairs" Henry wrote of suggests that Concello was either somehow overwhelmed by the foreign European culture and details for operating there, or he was involved with more women. Art's girlfriend, Maggie Smith, was not always at his side overseas.[110]

The "physical collapse" is even more mysterious. Concello had visited Europe over thirty times in three years,[111] and he'd made many other trips besides. This collapse Buddy wrote of has not been corroborated by other sources.

What is known is that a late October 1963 press release changed everything. It simply stated, "John Ringling North announced that Arthur M. Concello is no longer affiliated with Ringling Bros. Barnum & Bailey Combined Shows, Inc."[112] As for Concello, he got the message after his plane, inbound from Tampa, touched down in New York.[113]

North gave Concello thirty days to vacate his Venice office but neglected to assign anyone to watch over his former executive director during that time.[114] North next issued the directive to his Florida staff to find Concello's railcar, which served as both his home and office, and secure it so that he wouldn't be able to use it.[115] Art's half-sister, Grace Killian, who Arthur had installed into the front office of Ringling-Barnum, "So [the] Circus office should be all right now" in 1961,[116] got her two weeks' notice on October 27, 1963. The next day, Concello's American Express card, airline card, and telephone card were cancelled.[117]

The Sarasota Herald-Tribune caught up with Concello on October 31, 1963. He stated, "I left here in 1943 and again in 1953. What year is this?" intimating that North developed a pattern of releasing him from his Ringling obligations every ten years.[118] "No comment" was his response as to whether formal ties had been severed from Ringling Bros. and Barnum & Bailey. As for his railcar, *The Randy*, he moved it with no trouble from Venice back to Sarasota.

Like before, rumors ran rampant about why Concello was cut loose from Ringling-Barnum. *Variety* stated that he was dismissed because of deficit income from the European show, even though its reports from Paris now touted a spectacular circus, worthy of accolades.[119] Europeans just didn't buy enough tickets.

The Pantagraph, his hometown newspaper, informed its readers that Concello's position was taken over by North's former Yale classmate McCormick Steele.[120] On November 22, Mac Steele told his boss about the mess he found while trying to clean up the corporate office space Concello had used in Venice. "What files and memos (Concello and Perry) didn't take with them from the two offices . . . were just dumped on the floor."[121] Others said he threw things around in his former office, tossing files around "like a kid."[122]

Other clues exist that might explain Concello's dismissal. The Ringling Bros. and Barnum & Bailey legal adjuster at the time, Noyelles Burkhart, suggested North's personality may have had something to do with it. "I am surprised that Concello stayed this long with Mr. Big. John R. North is the toughest man that I ever had any dealings with. It is almost impossible to please the gentleman, and the best description that I have of him is that he is a beast without a heart or conscious [*sic*]."[123] Gone were the days when North and Concello dined out with their girlfriends, Dodie Heath and Margaret Smith, respectively, at 21 Club or Billy Gwon's. No more late nights were spent drinking too much,[124] and there were no more frank conversations between the Norths and Concello about investment opportunities like gold, coins, and a Swiss investment banking business.[125] Their relationship was morphing yet again.

With Concello fired, Ringling's Barnum & Bailey closed in Stuttgart on March 3, 1964, after presenting its three-ringed circus in ten European cities. Zurich, West Berlin, Cologne, Essen, Milan, Geneva, and London, which would have been the four-weeks' closing engagement ending on July 5, were dropped.

North wanted a circus in Europe, and he wanted another one at the 1964 New York World's Fair. Concello wanted neither but was informed he would bring both into reality. Art's recollection of the Fair's Continental Circus diverges from established fact. In 1973 Concello told a circus historian that he left Europe to ". . . come down here to Sarasota," where he "minded his own business" after telling "John, do it yourself. Screw you."[126] Yet shortly before the premiere performance, elephant presenter Barbara Woodcock recalled having heated words with Concello about getting enough dirt inside the structure for the elephants under her direction to safely perform on.[127] He acquiesced to Barbara's demands. Further, An *Amusement Business* photographer captured the elusive Concello on film with Fay Alexander and Al Dobritch shortly before the circus opened on May 8.[128] Arthur was at the World's Fair.

The World's Fair circus story began in early February 1962, when Robert Moses, president of New York World's Fair Corporation, announced that a circus would be featured at the 1964 fair. Sitting in the administrative building in Flushing Meadows Park, he signed the contract to bring in a one-ring, European-style circus. John Ringling North, president of Continental Circus, Inc., proclaimed that the "greatest acts obtainable from all corners of the world" would be signed to perform.[129] With Arthur M. Concello as executive vice president and Harry S. Dube as the treasurer, the newly formed company would produce the show where all the acts would be depicted as members of one big family.[130] *The Sarasota Herald Tribune* reported that 50 percent of the stock in the Continental Circus was owned by North, 25 percent by Concello,[131] and the other 25 percent by the Ringling-Barnum Corporation.[132]

Not surprisingly, Continental Circus, Inc. contracted with G & G Metals in Venice to produce a structure that would be created in Florida, disassembled to transport, and reassembled in New York. This million-dollar structure, 273 feet in circumference, seated five thousand with 60,000 square feet of floor space. It had an all-steel framework covered by fabric.[133] The canvas was a special kind of flame-proof, plastic-coated cloth[134] produced by DuPont and sewn together by a Sarasota firm, Leaf Tent and Sales Co., which was headed by the circus's former in-house tent maker.[135] When finished, it was "the largest coated cloth tent" ever made to be draped over a steel frame: Over twenty thousand yards of vinyl coated, eight-ounce army duck was designed to cover 153,000 square feet.[136] Concello assigned Lloyd Morgan, "the only man who knows canvas well enough to do this," to oversee the project.[137]

Russian-born talent manager and impresario Sol Hurok tried for years to bring a Russian circus to the United States but was repeatedly stymied. Morris Chalfen, another impresario, made it happen. After successfully touring Holiday on Ice behind the Iron Curtain during the Cold War, Chalfen brought the Moscow Circus to the United States as part of the State Department's Cultural Exchange program. With assistance from Concello, Chalfen produced both the American Circus that toured Russia and the Moscow Circus that toured America.

Just as Chalfen booked the European dates for Ringling's Barnum & Bailey, Concello booked the dates for the Soviet circus, starting in Philadelphia in September 1963 and extending into November after playing six more American cities: New York, Boston, Pittsburgh, Chicago, Minneapolis, and Milwaukee. A long-standing and unwritten agreement existed between Ringling-Barnum and Madison Square Garden. Its facilities would never be used for another circus as long as Ringling Bros. and Barnum & Bailey Circus didn't play in a different venue in New York City. The Garden felt Ringling-Barnum broke that agreement when North contracted with the World's Fair in Queens, opening the door for the Moscow Circus, routed by Concello, to play the venue.[138] By November, Concello's actions further infuriated North when the latter learned that his three-ring, forty-five-act Greatest Show on Earth lost its Pittsburgh date to the one-ringed, fifteen-act Moscow Circus.[139]

The Moscow Circus's gross revenues topped $1.5 million at the end of their seven-city run. Chalfen proclaimed the tour highly successful while venturing that the gross figure could have been even higher but for the national mourning period for President John F. Kennedy, who was assassinated on November 22. The show's top spot was Madison Square Garden, which garnered a gross of $600,000 for the fifteen days spent performing there.[140] No doubt, Concello was equally satisfied.

When Concello and North parted company in 1963, the circus owed Concello money, and he'd be damned if he wasn't going to get it. On January 13, 1964, his attorney filed a five-count suit in Tampa's Circuit Court against the Ringling Bros. and Barnum & Bailey Combined Circus for $40,589 ($335,702.45 in today's dollars), an amount Concello said he was owed. The five counts broke down this way: $25,000 of his 1963 salary, which was $31,250; $6,250 of his 1962 salary; $5,000 he paid to Helen Steinwachs, the circus's general auditor "on or about February 22, 1962;"[141] and two other counts for occasions when he advanced money to pay certain individuals, totaling $4,339. Art went to Venice twice to speak to Bundy about this debt. Bundy acknowledged that these debts were on the books, but North had explicitly directed him not to pay Concello "because I'm still sore at him."[142] Eventually, the case was settled out of court.

Though North had made it clear he no longer wanted Concello with him in the Ringling-Barnum Circus, the two were still inextricably tied early in 1964. Concello still owned 10 percent of the Ringling-Barnum Circus, 10 percent of North's other assets, and 25 percent of the Continental Circus at the World's Fair. Concello remained open to business opportunities after his circus obligations to John Ringling North dissolved. He knew he still had 10 percent of North—"oil, real estate, everything."[143] Unafraid of failure, he looked ahead for yet more opportunities.

Chapter 9

Diversification

1965–1984

"She is to circus 'flying' what Caruso was to opera."[1]

—Lubbock Avalanche-Journal

When Art separated from the Ringling's Barnum & Bailey, his longtime girlfriend and aerial choreographer for the circus, Maggie Smith, also disappeared from the circus scene. John North now turned to the other Concello for help. He called Antoinette on Halloween night to entice her back to help his circus as its aerial director, wiring her airfare to meet him in Paris to work out the details of her return.[2] Only then did he send a telegram to Pat Valdo confirming that she was back in charge of girls as aerial director.[3]

Antoinette got down to business immediately, training the showgirls throughout the 1964 tour. By the first week of December, she was back home, delighted to spend the downtime relaxing and fishing again.[4] But her respite didn't last long. Practice for the 1965 season started December 12, and for the first time in Venice, admission was charged for watching acts rehearse in its arena (designed by her ex-husband). Three weeks later, she oversaw a black-tie preview performance there for the benefit of New College of Sarasota. The star of the show, LaToria (Victoria Unus), performed as part of the "Swan Lake" ballet which featured twenty-eight aerialists.[5]

Antoinette had spent more than thirty-five years in show business and was currently teaching a corps of women how to perform in a circus, along with its traditions and culture. The American circus scene now included more girls from locations like France, Germany, England, Australia, and Spain.[6] The press took notice and asked her what it felt like to teach them.

She responded that she felt like she had a young United Nations under her care. Of the challenges communicating with them, she said, "I speak a little French, a little German and a little Indian sign language. I do, and they watch. It's amazing how quickly they learn."[7] Her charges enjoyed visiting American supermarkets, and some were eating cream cheese by the block, a fact which displeased their weight-conscious coach.[8] A mere glance, laden with meaning, was all it took for some of them to know they needed to cut back their calories.[9]

Back with the Big Show, Antoinette felt the tug of the audience. A series of operations on her arms, shoulders, and spine corrected conditions brought about by strenuous work that trapped her on earth after she retired in 1953. "For years, I could hardly put a dress on, or a coat,"[10] but nearly fifteen years later, when injuries sidelined the regulars, she began to fill in on the pedestal board by dropping the bar for others. Initially, she was struck by the difficulty of being up there after so long away. "By the end of the fifth show," she said while laughing, "I felt like I'd been through a world war."[11] Perhaps inspired by the applause, she began to add in simple tricks she had learned almost forty years earlier, "nothing fancy . . . a plange, a layout back dive to the net. I worked up there till the other flyer got well. It was a thrill. You walk in that arena and forget everything but the audience."[12] She said later, "It brings back a lot of memories. Of course I get a kick out of it, I'd be a liar if I said I didn't."[13] She may have gotten a kick out of her salary at this time, too—she was making a good salary for the time, $1,082.42 a month.[14]

The Ringling Bros. and Barnum & Bailey Circus debuted a new aerial ballet in 1967. Suspended from perches fit onto a monorail track, the showgirls performed ballet moves set to eight-count music, choreographed by Richard Barstow and Antoinette.[15] Members of the press speculated that courage must be the most sought-after trait. Antoinette refuted that. "A girl needs more sense than nerve . . ." she said. "I work with them until they acquire strength. Then up they go! And they love every minute of it!"[16]

When pressed, she talked about her experience with circuses decades ago: "I remember when we used to have to put on tights in a cornfield when it was so cold there was ice in the water buckets, and I remember the top of the canvas tent being so smoldering my makeup ran. But we didn't complain because we didn't know the difference air conditioning could make."[17] She didn't miss the tent but had to adjust to performing in arenas. She mused, "It would be hard to go back to tents. We'd miss the comfort of the warmth and the showers."[18]

As for Antoinette's ex-husband, Arthur, he did what he always did. Till now, whenever he left—or was asked to leave—The Greatest Show on Earth, he regrouped for a while and eventually partnered with Clyde

Beatty. Late in December 1965 (Beatty died in July), Concello purchased Walter Kernan's interest in the Clyde Beatty-Cole Bros. Circus from his widow, Bonnie, to help his friend Frank McClosky.[19] Doing so put him in a partnership with McClosky and Jerry Collins. It also made him part owner of King Bros. Circus with McClosky and Sells & Gray Circus with McClosky and Bill English.[20] One of the first things Concello did was to get to work with G & G Metal & Co. to build new seat wagons, which were now folding metal platforms raised and lowered by cables, pulleys, and electric motors. The new ones took even fewer men and less time to set up,[21] though they had to be reinforced before touring. He also improved the lighting and ordered a larger cage for the cat act.[22]

In April 1966, Concello, McClosky, and Collins were looking for more arenas to book the Beatty-Cole Circus into.[23] As was to be expected, Concello put loyalists in key positions with the circus. For instance, he installed Grace into the ticket wagon to get the first count of the money.[24] By August, Collins and McClosky purchased Concello's interest in the three tented shows,[25] but Art's people weren't run off until after the September 7 circus performance in Kankakee, Illinois. McClosky told the young general manager, John Pugh, "You need to run these people [Art's people] off before they destroy it. They'll destroy it before they leave."[26] Shortly after, Concello resigned as a corporate director of Acme Circus Operating Co.[27] He spun things by suggesting the daily grind was too much. He said, ". . . these things are all fine when you're thirty years old, or twenty-five, or eighteen or forty; but when you get to be my age, shit, you don't want no grief."[28] Not surprisingly, Pugh's recollection is rife with Concello's use of thug-like intimidation tactics not released in the trade publications or newspapers.

Maybe he saw a more lucrative opportunity on the horizon. In September 1966, Morris Chalfen approached Fred Podesta, president of Madison Square Garden (MSG) Attractions, a wholly owned Garden subsidiary, with a proposition. Irving M. Felt, the president of Madison Square Garden, Inc., and Art Concello were carbon-copied. Chalfen pitched a presentation to MSG-ABC Productions, Inc. for "Creating, Organizing, and Operating a New Full-Scale Arena Circus—Spectacular in Concept—to Play the Major Arenas of Europe Fall through Spring."[29] Because Chalfen's Holiday on Ice was now an MSG-ABC Productions, Inc. property and was successfully operating throughout Europe, Chalfen believed that it would be advantageous for MSG-ABC to increase their presence there with a circus. In his opinion, the time was right. He saw little competition in Europe for this type of family entertainment and knew there was a sufficient number of good arenas to play in. Further, he believed that the right man could make it all happen, and Arthur M. Concello was the right man.

In his proposal Chalfen included the receipts from dates played by Ringling's Barnum & Bailey in Europe. He laid it all out for Podesta, including reasons "pro and con" for bringing a circus to Europe. He suggested that a one-ring show, with its lower nut, could tour there from fall through spring and then play the Forum as "the Continental Circus" in New York City during the summer months. The most notable reason against it was that it might take a few years to realize significant profits. It was well known that MSG Attractions wanted to have its own circus, and with this proposal, Chalfen gave them the opportunity to have one, but Podesta never swung for it.

Not dissuaded, Chalfen and Concello teamed up once more in 1967. The cultural agreement between the world's superpowers—negotiated again between Chalfen and the State Department—renewed the opportunity for both countries to swap circuses. This time, Chalfen hired Concello, who reported directly to him as the president of Holiday on Ice Co. Arthur headed the "five companies of *Holiday on Ice* which toured the United States, Europe, South America, Africa and the Far East."[30] He also oversaw the Russian tour of an American Circus. As had happened in 1963, the American Circus went to the Soviet Union before the Moscow Circus came to the United States.

Concello lined up the American portion of the circus-exchange program, handling all the technical, mechanical, and personnel details. The American Circus was a one-ringer with about eighteen acts chosen by him and Maggie Smith. Included in the roster were three former Sailor Circus girls, along with circus standouts Elvin Bale, Johnny Yong, the Flying Palacios, and the Ferronis.[31] The State Department thought Moscow might delay the visa requests for the sixty-five-member circus troupe because of the tensions created by the Vietnam and Middle East wars,[32] but that didn't happen. When the Americans left on Pan Am Airways for Russia to start their fifteen-week engagement, the press advertised the American Circus as produced by Chalfen, directed by Concello, and managed by Jake Mills, who also served as its equestrian director.[33] Mills, raised as Jake Milinsky by Russian Jewish parents, had long been part owner of the Mills Bros. Circus with his brothers Jack and Harry until it closed the year before.

The opening three-hour performance in Moscow's Gorky Park on August 7 got off to a rocky start in front of a full house of 2,100 people, mostly adults. The single day budgeted for rehearsals had the cigar-chomping Concello working frantically polishing the show. He scoffed at the title of the show by echoing Antoinette's sentiments, "You can't have an 'American Circus.' All circuses are international. We've got people from all over—Germany, Argentina, Mexico, Holland . . ."[34] Sounding a bit like an ugly American, he went on, "We told them to give us some towns where it's warm this time. Our people didn't like those snowdrifts in Leningrad," he said, comparing this trip with the one in 1963. He got what he wanted. The American Circus tour went from Moscow to Tbilisi, the sunny capital of Soviet Georgia, then to Yerevan, the capital of Soviet Armenia on the Turkish border, spending about five weeks in each location. The Russians loved the American Circus, particularly the showmanship, slick production, and the speed and smoothness with which one act followed another.[35] One hundred ten performances were given in the USSR. Altogether, roughly two hundred thousand people attended.

With the American Circus touring the Soviet Union, Concello flew to Montreal to help the Moscow Circus get established. That done, he flew back to Yerevan to accompany the American Circus performers home. His frenetic pace left no time to visit his dying father in Bloomington. Papa Vas died December 14, 1967.

As Art flew back and forth across the Atlantic, a deal was being hammered out so that John Ringling North could sell the Ringling Bros and Barnum & Bailey Circus. The new owner was Hoffeld Corp., made up of Judge Roy Hofheinz and the Feld brothers. Before the $8 million deal was consummated in November 1967, North called Concello to tell him of his plan. "You ain't got no problem," Art told him. "Make me an offer what you'll give me for my ten percent."[36] They agreed on an undisclosed amount. Though he still retained his percentage of John's other assets, Art no longer had a stake in The Greatest Show on Earth.

Sometime between transatlantic flights and shortly after Ringling-Barnum was sold, Concello telephoned corporate headquarters to say he was ready to get back in the saddle. He spoke with Allen Bloom, director of routes and tours, who politely declined Art's offer. Art snarled a brusque "You'll be sorry" and slammed the receiver into its cradle.[37]

Moscow State Circus was the real moneymaker in the circus swap between world powers. The show opened its three-month tour[38] at Madison Square Garden on October 4 and featured bears, horseback juggling, and an illusionist who transformed a woman into a lion.[39] Well reviewed, it visited thirteen cities where it often broke box office records. In Oakland, California, for example, receipts were $201,185 ($1,579,536 in today's dollars).[40] Its program listed Concello as general manager, Bill Perry as a liaison, Gene Vercheski as the materials consultant, and Laz Rosen as the advance man.[41]

Fred Podesta of MSG Attractions remained intrigued by a circus's income potential, and he had an idea for one. First, he negotiated a one-year, non-baseball lease on New York's Shea Stadium, ending in October 1969.[42] His idea featured only aerial and high acts, and he asked Concello, as its general manager, to create and manage it. Concello chose Paul V. Kaye as the announcer and his assistant. Concello's friends Jake Mills and

Laz Rosen were on the show's staff, and Don Francisco was the talent manager.

Madison Square Garden's Thrill Circus, as it was known, nearly failed to open due to union troubles. Concello attempted to circumvent the American Guild of Variety Artists' demands by signing acts through Kaye, who also recruited them.[43] When that didn't satisfy the union, he joined with other circus producers to form the Circus Producers Association to combat the union's "unrealistic pay demands."[44] Gone were the days when Concello could make deals and "take care of" union problems with greenbacks as he did in 1961 with AGVA's Jackie Bright.[45]

However it happened, the union issues were resolved shortly before the opening.[46] The show received positive reviews during its stand at the New York Mets' home field, August 2–11, 1968.[47] Podesta watched the financials closely because if this one was successful, he believed he could extend the run to other ballparks across the country.[48] The lavish show pleased the public, but the stadium, which sat fifty-five thousand people, seemed empty with only five thousand people in it during each of the twelve performances.[49] Those optics were hard to overcome. The Thrill Circus had that one ten-day stand and closed.

With the Thrill Circus shuttered, Arthur took another break from the circus. He shot a lot of pool with friends Harold Voise, Willis Lawson, and others. He and Maggie enjoyed a weekly dinner date—Zinn's and Chang's were two of their favorite Sarasota spots—with Merle and Nena Evans. Sometimes, they dined at each other's houses and retired to the living room to watch television together if there was a circus special on it. They were all getting older. Once, Merle recalled, after dinner Art fell over a chair and broke a rib, which laid him up for five weeks.[50]

Occasionally, he helped circus people like impresario Tommy Hanneford. Art served as a director for his Circus Classics, Inc., the parent company formed in April 1968 to tour the Royal Hanneford Circus. During their nearly ten-year association, his involvement with Hanneford remained minimal and was likely only financial.

Three years passed before Concello tried to get back into the circus business. His day planner—once filled with appointments, birth and death dates of friends and family, reminders to watch his weight, sketches of (usually) riggings, and always the weather conditions, along with distances daily travelled—now was almost empty. Friends and associates—people like bandmaster Merle Evans and program seller Red Sonnenberg—reported the circus itch was returning to Little Caesar in 1971.[51] Yet circumstances were never quite right for the little man with the big cigar. That year Concello and Jake Mills tried to buy the Bartok Circus, "but when Lil' Artha found out that the show had a lot of mortgages on just about everything," he gave that up.[52] Without a circus to run, Concello busied himself in the periphery by attending a Circus Fans Association function honoring Bob Dover[53] and making a net for Radio City Music Hall's Christmas show.[54] A rumor reported that Concello, Jake Mills, Willis Lawson, and tent man, W. Novotny, were framing a circus to go out the next year,[55] but nothing came of this, either.

Concello's attention swayed now to what many saw as a wildly different company: taxicabs. In 1970 he bought the Yellow Cab Company from Sarasotan Cecil Brammer. He believed running it gave him and his girlfriend, Maggie, something to do.[56] He left Cecil Brammer in as manager, installed Maggie as operator and dispatcher, and tasked Grace Killian as bookkeeper. He also employed loyalists Bill Perry, Laz Rosen, and Marion Siefert,[57] who once graced the cover of *Cosmopolitan* magazine when she was Ringling-Barnum's star equestrienne. Grace's question for her brother—be it in circuses or the cab company—was always, "How much do we pay them?" Art's response was equally consistent. "As little as possible."[58]

Faced with rising fuel prices in the early 1970s and an anticipated shutdown of local bus service, he increased fares and asked the city for a permit to grow the number of cabs from fifteen to twenty.[59] He also formed the B & C Oil Company with locals Carl V. Funk Jr. and Robert Sokol. It supplied filling stations with the fuel his vehicles needed and was headquartered where Randy had his law practice, at the Palmer Bank Building in Sarasota. B & C Co. dissolved in October 1974,[60] around the time Art added Randy as a joint owner of Yellow Cab Company.[61]

Five years after a Yellow Cab driver was shot to death picking up a fare late on a Sunday night in April 1975, Arthur transferred the company entirely to his son. He had increased profits and efficiency and decided that he had had enough of that,[62] and so he got out.

Concello tracked numbers incessantly, including the 155 he usually found on his scale. But in the summer of 1972, his weight fell precipitously to 135. After a surgeon extracted a sludgy gall bladder, he slowly started regaining weight.[63] Mickey King remembered visiting the man she considered more a brother than a former brother-in-law shortly after his surgery. Mickey, Art, and Maggie sat down for dinner at his house. She recalled a big order of fish and chips with slaw and other fixings. "Well anyway, he sat beside me and reached over my plate and got a great big bun and cut into it, buttered it, and put it on my plate and said, 'Damn it, EAT!' What a wonderful sense of humor!"[64]

Once recovered, Art loved tooling around Sarasota in his Jeep, much like Brad Braden in *The Greatest Show on Earth* had rammed around the circus backyard two decades earlier on the big screen. His nineteen-years-younger girlfriend drove a Camaro. But if they went "someplace nice," they took his Cadillac.[65]

In the late 1960s, they took the Caddy to the invitation-only grand opening of the Old Heidelberg Castle restaurant. Shortly after they left their recently completed 4,522 square foot home (with four bedrooms and bathrooms, a four-car garage, a guest house, and a Concello-designed indoor-outdoor pool with a four-foot tunnel connecting both of them), burglars broke in and ransacked it. Maggie recalled the Jeep was stolen, along with her fur coats and all of Art's diamond rings. "Oh, it was terrible. I cried my eyes out. And Art said, 'They didn't bother us. We can replace what they've stolen.' He was so calm when everything goes wrong."[66] From that point forward, he usually drove a pickup truck. One of his two dogs rode shotgun: Bum, a German Shepard who loved to bum scraps from the table, or Villain, a pit bull Randy gave him one Christmas.

With his house on Desoto Road completed, he no longer called his railroad car home. It was still an office and a beloved hangout, which he kept at the airport through the mid-1970s. Concello feuded with the Sarasota Airport Authority for nearly a year over his railroad car's parking spot. Eventually, both parties reached an amicable settlement. Concello agreed to pay about $1,000 of the $7,000 it took to have his car moved[67]—undoubtedly still too much for Concello, but he knew when to walk away.

As the 1970s drew to a close, the desire to return to the circus, perhaps to recoup some of the assets lost in that house burglary, became overwhelming for Concello. In October 1978 he and his son formed VASCON, Inc. with Art as president and Randy as director. The company directed the tour of the Moscow Circus, headed by Concello and Carlos Vasques in 1979, which started in San Juan, Puerto Rico, on February 15,[68] and it visited eight states before concluding in Charlotte, South Carolina, on the third of June. Even though the show had good talent and was well promoted, it didn't draw well.[69] Frank B. Hall & Co., a financial services company, filed suit against VASCON, Inc. in 1980.[70] No details of the suit could be found, but it may well have been the reason the company—named using the first six letters of Arthur's surname at birth—dissolved in December 1980.

The details of how Arthur and John Ringling North reunited in business remains unknown. But on January 23, 1981, they partnered to form Nortart in Delaware,[71] with a goal to build rentable mini warehouses. For one reason, then another, Nortart built nothing in 1981. Nevertheless, Concello kept Bill Perry on his payroll to write city officials on their behalf, urging approval of the plan. Arthur had a soft spot for Perry, a deeply closeted gay man, and periodically allowed him to live in his railroad car, even though his health left him feeble, at least in Concello's judgmental eyes. In his daily record book, he acknowledged ". . . will half [*sic*] to get some one else for office if we build storage rooms."[72]

Contrary to whispered circus tradition, Arthur did not bury all his money in coffee cans by his railroad car or in his yard. While waiting for the city's approval to build, Art busied himself by investing and reinvesting $100,000 in short-term CDs with rates in the double-digits. He spent time with Laz Rosen, Wayne Larey, Tuffy Genders, Sam Stern, Harold and Eileen Voise—all friends from his Bloomington days. Sometimes they haunted the local Steak & Shake, the restaurant chain founded in their hometown. He continued his weekly meals with the Evanses and welcomed out-of-town visitors like Connie Clausen and Henry Ringling North and his son, John Ringling North II, whenever they came to town.

Now seventy, he often started his days around noon. On Saturday evenings, he made the short drive over to the Showfolks Club, where he would cut up jackpots and shoot pool.[73] Other evenings he watched television. He chose sporting events—from tennis to boxing, baseball to gymnastics—in the early evening, television shows like *Hogan's Heroes* and *M*A*S*H* later, and movies like John Wayne westerns into the wee hours of the morning. In 1981 he made sure to catch the highlights of the royal wedding, noted when Egyptian president Sadat was shot, and delighted when the baseball strike was over. He watched a lot of television. When he visited Antoinette, he often fell asleep in the chair she had in front of her set.[74]

In his daily secretary, Concello now documented the many times Maggie had friends over, like Patty Kirby and fellow Brit Brenda McClosky, Frank's second wife. He also made note that he sent John Ringling North a birthday card on August 4, 1981.

Though he interacted infrequently with his son Randy, he spent considerable time with his young granddaughter, who regularly crossed her backyard to Grandpa and Nanny's for dinner or to be taken to a nearby park to swing. Some of the energy he needed to keep up with the rambunctious child came from the cases of Coca-Cola he bought and the ten boxes of Robert Burns's cigars, purchased from Tampa's Eli Witt smoke shop.

Not all the games he played were child's play, however. "Process server was by the lot," he wrote in his day planner for March 6, 1981. "He caught me but I said I was not who I was,"[75] and three months later, he wrote, "Denver is trying to serve me again."[76] Typically, he never provided more details about this lawsuit and no further information could be found, but it may be that something happened in Denver during the Moscow Circus's visit there from March 31 to April 8, 1979.

Art woke his longtime girlfriend at 11:45 p.m. on December 31, 1983, so they could watch the televised ball drop in New York City's Times Square together. He couldn't predict the exact nature of the next year's events in his life and the lives of those around him, but he knew that some of those closest to him needed his help. Grace had suffered a stroke the previous year,[77] and his brother, a lifelong alcoholic, was also unwell. Art initially paid for an in-home nurse to be with Grace but then decided to move his half-brother Joe from the houseboat he had purchased and had docked for him in Tampa Bay's marina[78] to her home at Circus City Trailer Park. The two siblings looked after one another for years.

When Ringling-Barnum played nearby Champaign, *The Pantagraph* ran a story with show executives who, years before, called Bloomington home. A photo of Antoinette, Billy Ward, and Elden Day was nestled on page five. The accompanying caption informed readers that they were three of the six former Bloomingtonians employed by the circus giant. The other three were Eddie Ward, train supervisor; Tuffy Genders, general manager; and Wayne Larey, purchasing agent. All of these people the article said, had lived and worked in all corners of the world—Kiev, Leningrad, Moscow, Copenhagen, Berlin, Paris, and of course Australia, where Larey worked as a Concello flyer and act manager for years.[79] A fellow longtime trouper said that Antoinette, Tuffy, and Elden watched the flying act every time the net went up. "They never miss watching it. It is a ritual with them," he said.[80]

Antoinette undoubtedly remembered the first days of learning her craft when she transferred the barn at 1201 E. Emerson in Bloomington to a local man in 1965.[81] When Circus World Museum in Baraboo, Wisconsin—the home of the original Ringling brothers—learned the property was being sold, Tom Parkinson, University of Illinois Assembly Hall director and circus historian, visited the site on the museum's behalf. He found a building filled with rigging boxes, a pedestal board, rolled and rotted net, six trunks in various stages of disrepair, and the pipe necessary for erecting a flying-return frame. He also noted two dressing rooms packed with papers, files, and photographs strewn everywhere. He discovered the financial papers for Russell Bros.' tour of Canada, which was, as he correctly summed up, "one of the most profitable [tours] ever made by a show."[82] Parkinson's report, which accompanied the material he brought to Baraboo's museum, aptly concluded, "Mr. Concello would flat pass out if he knew we had this material."[83] He knew Arthur was a private man.

By the time Antoinette worked with Barstow, Feld, and others to create two versions of Ringling-Barnum (known as the red and blue units) in 1969, Randy had graduated with a business degree from the College of Emporia, Kansas, and was on his way toward completing his law degree there. He was admitted to the Florida bar in 1970.

Mrs. Arthur Concello, as she still referred to herself, was often asked about her time in circuses—both her accomplishments and her challenges. Of her earliest years, she said, "It involved a lot of hard work and practice. I just kept my ears open and my mouth shut."[84] She noted that everything she learned—iron jaw, cloud swing, rings, web, horizontal bars, and wire walking—gave her the strength to do the triple,[85] though she was also proud of completing the double full twister and the double cutaway, feats not accomplished by any other woman of the time.[86]

She spoke fondly of her family's home and disputed birthplace. One time she was awoken by a customs inspector, who informed her the train was in Sutton, Quebec. "I quickly put on my clothes and went out to talk to the stationmaster. I hadn't been there in years but he remembered my family. My aunt lived just around the corner. She and others came to the train, and where they had something of a family reunion."[87] The circus had been her sister Mickey's and her salvation. They made it their lives.

Though only 5 feet 2 inches—down two inches from her tallest—but still 102 pounds,[88] Antoinette even now carried herself elegantly and with dignity.[89] She quietly commanded attention and got it, along with respect. Whenever the circus played large cities and she was with it, an ad ran in the local paper, calling on girls to audition. Antoinette chose those who won a spot with the circus and described what she looked for in potential hires: "If a girl talks to me and she's fidgety, I know right away she's too nervous and high-strung for this work. I can tell by her speech, her gestures . . . We want no dopies and no drinkers; those things don't mix with circus work."[90]

When not on the pedestal board dropping bars, she stood just beyond the spotlight's reach, looking up, foot tapping, moving gently to the music while drawing on her omnipresent cigarette with the elegance of Marlene Dietrich. A reporter, obviously taken with the former Camel Cigarette girl, wrote, "she's slim and good looking, and carries an extra pair of tights with her just in case . . ."[91] Others who had been with the show a while described watching Tony in winter quarters: "It was amazing. She's in her sixties . . . her physical condition remains superb, just as it was, old-timers tell me, when she was young. She is to circus 'flying' what Caruso was to opera."[92]

She also had plenty to say about the new circus, the one which played inside buildings and not under a canvas. She wondered if the younger generation of performers could handle the hardships she once regularly endured. "When I started we worked under a big tent. The rain leaked through the canvas, the heat caused us to perspire so much it was dangerous, and the brutally cold weather . . . I remember times the bar was so cold it was like grabbing a piece of ice. But what worried me most was the high winds that would blow up under the tent, upsetting our split-second timing. It was very dangerous. It's a lot easier now working indoors."[93]

It was the triple somersault that got her the most questions and gave her the opportunity to reflect back on what it took to do it. When she started flying under Eddie Ward, it had been a time when female aerialists were mainly employed as flashy decoration on the pedestal board. Some did simple tricks. But Antoinette was different from the very beginning. She said it best: "I wanted to fly higher and better."[94] She tried explaining why she was so driven to another reporter this way: "A lot of people think it's all for the applause, but it's something you've got to set your mind on doing. If you don't accomplish [it], you aren't going to get the hand—or the money."[95]

The woman's determination was only surpassed by her desire to overcome any challenge. Now seventy, she had a perspective on her career and her accomplishments. "I didn't realize the value of it [the triple] back in those days. Few men can do it. There was a superstition that you would black out. I think they said that just to keep women from doing it [but] I knew that wasn't true because I'd already been doing a triple into the net at the finish. At first, I did a two-and-a-half, and there was a lot of publicity. Then I did the triple, and there was more publicity . . . Every time I did the triple, I'd say to myself, 'Don't come up too soon. Stay in it, stay in it.'"[96] That trick was like others she mastered—a matter of strength and confidence, grace and showmanship, and practice, practice, practice.

Only once did the woman most often described as regal share her greatest regret. The interviewer Dean Jensen, a seasoned newspaperman and circus enthusiast, asked her about it over dinner when the Big Show was playing in Kansas City. He heard her voice catch and saw her eyes well with tears. "It was only because of my silly pride. I was scheduled to graduate in a few weeks but I just couldn't bring myself to attend the graduation ceremonies," she started. "I knew it would be a time when all the other girls would be there with their parents and they would be wearing pretty store-bought dresses. One of the nuns would surely have made me a dress, but I knew it wouldn't be as pretty as the store-bought ones and people would take pity on me. One of the things I regret most in my life is that I didn't go back for my diploma."[97]

On the thirtieth anniversary of the release of the movie *The Greatest Show on Earth*, a reporter asked Antoinette what her impressions were of working on it. She said of DeMille, "He'd ask me to come in after rehearsals and read the script and see if it was authentic. He was one of the most humble, great men I've ever known." Once started on the topic, she didn't (or perhaps couldn't) stop. "I like Cornel Wilde, too. He called me 'Legs Concello.' And I helped Dorothy Lamour with the part where she hung from her teeth. She had beautiful teeth. The one I really like was Charlton Heston. He was down to earth, like an old shoe. He once drew a picture of me and autographed it. I've still got it in my circus trunk."[98] She also treasured the pendant from Betty Hutton, fittingly engraved with the words: "To the greatest from the most grateful."[99]

Just as every great athlete gets asked about their injuries, the past, and the future, so too was Antoinette. Her body had endured innumerable injuries, bladder trouble,[100] and surgeries; she admitted as late as 1981, when she was seventy-one years old, that her passion for flying was insatiable: "Every now and then I go up there, not during any performance, but when nobody's around—just to prove to myself I can still do it. I don't do any triple somersaults, but I can still fly."[101] When asked if she ever thought of retiring, she said, "Oh no. I take each day and each year as it comes. I want to continue as long as I feel good and I'm needed and wanted. When I'm not, I'll quit."[102]

A few years after Circus World, the circus-themed amusement park opened in Haines City, Florida, it featured a circular web number performed by young women trained by Antoinette.[103] She continued work as the aerial director for both the red and the blue units. But as the 1970s turned into the 1980s, the number of days she spent feeling good were dwindling.

Antoinette resigned as aerial director for the Ringling Bros. and Barnum & Bailey Circus in 1983. Her last published words came in her description of Miguel Vazquez, the man who successfully performed the first quadruple somersault from the flying trapeze during a performance in Tucson in July 1982. Antoinette praised Vasquez's work ethic and form, saying, "In one year's time he has improved so much. His form is real nice now. I take my hat off to him."[104] He earned the praise. The seventeen-year-old Miguel soon started consistently catching the unimaginable trick, the quadruple somersault.

When journalist Gene Plowden was gathering material for a book he was writing about the women of circus, he wrote Randy to get responses from his mother, who by this time lived with him, next door to Art and Maggie. Plowden understood where Antoinette's star was in the constellation of circus greats and believed his book would be incomplete without her in it. His typewritten questions asked, "Are you proud of your accomplishments? Would you do it again?"[105] In a shaky hand, she wrote her response on his letter, "Proud & yes, I'd do it all again but even Better!"[106]

Always a heavy smoker, Antoinette was being killed by lung cancer. Treatment for it included radiation therapy, which left her weak and sick. Merle Evans, her friend since the days of the Syracuse Shrine Circus in 1930, recalled how she used a bandanna to cover her balding head. Eventually, she decided she could not stand the treatments.[107] She was dead twelve days later.

Art's datebook entry for February 4, 1984, includes the only words he circled that year: "Antoinette passed away last night."[108] Art picked Mickey King up at Sarasota's airport that evening and drove her to his railcar apartment, where she stayed. Randy didn't tell him about the death of his mother, the woman who often proclaimed herself to be "the only Mrs. Concello." The news came from Bill Perry, whose ambulance driving friend had been called to pick up her body next door. "So this is how I know she passed away," Art wrote.[109] One can only imagine the range of emotions he felt both at that time and when Randy brought her ashes to Art in a box five days later. He gave some of them to her sister Mickey, who had them buried in Bloomington.[110]

The most extensive obituary for Marie Antoinette Concello appeared in Bloomington's *The Pantagraph*, which reported her death at seventy-three on February 5, 1984. The article reviewed her career, including her humble beginnings under the tutelage of Eddie Ward and her trajectory to circus superstardom. Of her, Kenneth Feld of the Ringling Brothers and Barnum & Bailey Circus said, "She was the greatest female trapeze artist who ever lived, but more importantly, her real contribution was her devotion to her art, which she passed on to countless young women who wanted to become aerialists."[111]

Chapter 10

Closing the Circle

1984–2001

"A showman is someone who gives the audience what it wants. The audience is the unconscious genius. It doesn't always want today what it wanted yesterday and is going to want tomorrow. But it knows what it wants when it wants it. The secret of showmanship is timing."[1]

—Mike Todd

Former circus reporter for *The Billboard* Tom Parkinson once asked Concello to reflect upon what he perceived as his greatest accomplishment. Parkinson wanted to know if Little Caesar believed his biggest contribution was in the ring as a flyer or in the ticket wagon as a circus owner and executive. Concello deflected the limelight yet again. "Oh, I don't know, Tom; I don't know. I was never too interested in flying. I did it for money, for the circus. Management, I seen more money. Owning a circus—strictly with me it was like going to the office, but you make money doing it."[2]

Art still visited the Showfolks' Club on Saturdays. But now in the twilight of his life, he sometimes went there midweek, too. In the club, he could listen to the stories of the circus that were such an integral part of his identity. There was some satisfaction in hearing the episodes he witnessed from a different perspective. Rarely did he correct another person or offer his view.

Nortart, Inc., the company created in 1981 by Concello and John Ringling North, finally finished building ten stores on Thirteenth Street, six more on Twelfth Street, and a warehouse property on Fifteenth Street, all in Sarasota in 1983.[3] There he parked his railroad cars, *The Randy*, and two others, the biggest reminder of his heyday on the circus. He called the property the lot, a nod to the role circus played in his life, and visited it daily. After the robbery at his home in the late 1960s, he kept two dogs at his house and another two, Lady and Bandit, at the lot.[4]

As Concello grew older, his experience with death grew more intimate. Mayme Ward, the wife of his mentor, Eddie, and the seasoned professional he once trouped with as a teenager, died in her home at the Circus City Trailer Park, the property once owned by Concello but now owned by a member from one of his acts, the Flying Palacios.[5] He attended her funeral service in January 1973,[6] but did not return to Bloomington for her interment.

Over the next few years, there were more funerals. In 1974, he was pall bearer for his circus dressage rider turned Yellow Cab driver Marion Siefert.[7] His fellow former circus owner and Maggie's former boss, Jake Mills, died late in December 1974. Morris Chalfen, Art's partner for the American and Moscow circuses, died November 4, 1979. If he were a sentimental man, perhaps Frank McClosky's passing would have hit him hardest. His life was very similar to Art's. Young Francis Mieczinkoski ran away from home to join a circus when he was fifteen, working his way up from rigger to general manager of Ringling-Barnum in 1954 and ending his career as part owner of the Clyde Beatty-Cole Bros. Circus, Sells & Gray Circus, and King Bros. Circus. He fell to cancer on November 8, 1979, at the age of seventy-two. Three years later he again served as a pall bearer for Merle Evans's wife and his longtime booster, Nena.[8] Eileen Voise, Harold's wife, died January 13, 1983.

Art became a twenty-miler in his seventh decade,[9] meaning he never strayed far from home. He still preferred life in the shadows, so his birthday celebrations were quiet ones. On March 26, he took Maggie and Merle to dinner at Zinn's, a fancy restaurant in Sarasota featuring an indoor-outdoor waterfall. Merle remembered the evening and his quirky friend this way: "He didn't want everyone to know. He is funny. Never registers, never votes, and he don't want to do jury duty."[10]

Concello's daily chores ran the gamut from doctor's appointments—he picked up three pairs of glasses one summer day in 1984—to mowing the lawn with blades he sharpened himself. He frequently sought help to fix his indoor-outdoor pool, and he watched television, especially the Winter and Summer Olympics. He rarely attended circuses. When he did, he noted the date, time, and the show's title, but never a review. Only once in 1984 did he venture away from Sarasota to visit New York City, where he met with Henry Ringling North and the attorneys at Hodges, Reavis-McGraff—likely to review oil property matters.[11] He still retained 10 percent of John North's oil assets in Oklahoma.

He lived humbly and often dressed like a bum. He took his son's discarded golf shoes, removed the cleats, and wore them around town. "The joke was that Art wouldn't have shoes if his son didn't golf," recalled one of his younger friends.[12] When he went to his old railcar hangout on Fifteenth Street, he took the time to take a few swings on the trapeze bar he had hanging nearby. He continued this habit up through his eighties.

Driven by a lifetime's desire to acquire money, in his later years, he used some of it to help those he liked. He never advertised that his wallet was fat, but people knew. His friends understood they could count on him if needed. "If I hit a rut today or tomorrow, I'd call on him. He'd be there," said Mickey King, his former sister-in-law, who notified him when a niece got into trouble in 1984.[13] He sent funds to get the girl out of the jam.[14]

After Antoinette passed away, he reworked his will. He encouraged his girlfriend, Maggie Smith; his half-sister, Grace Killian; and his on-again, off-again employee and devotee, Bill Perry, to do the same.[15] It was a good thing, too. Grace died of lung cancer August 24, 1985, less than three months after his former boss, enabler, partner, mentor, adversary, and friend, John Ringling North, took his last breath in Brussels, Belgium. Before those two deaths, though, he had a wedding to plan.

Arthur had eyed the pretty Brit Margaret Smith in Ringling-Barnum in 1952. He finally made Maggie (as he called her) his wife thirty-two years later on June 29, 1984. Art waited until Antoinette passed before making another woman his wife. He always loved the girl he grew up with in his own complicated way. Of his waiting to marry another woman, a fellow performer explained, "He didn't want to hurt her [Antoinette] any more than he had already hurt her,"[16] which reflected a sensitivity Art would never acknowledge.

In 2016, Margaret, who had—and still—adored Arthur for years, recalled her wedding: "Yeah, we waited and waited and waited, and one day all out of the blue . . . this lady comes in, and I said, 'Who's this?' It was the notary public. She came in and he said, 'We're getting married . . . did you forget the ring?' I said, 'Yeah, I went and got a ring. You told me to get a ring a long time ago. It's probably got lost by now.' But we found it . . . and his sister Grace and Harold Voise were our two stand-ins . . . I always thought I'd be in a beautiful white gown, you know. There I was in a dirty old dress, a house dress and he was in his shorts . . ."[17] Maggie made sandwiches and tea for—as she termed it—her "wedding feast."[18]

After writing "I got married to Maggie" in his desk diary, he filed his will, leaving most of everything to his new wife. Two notable exceptions were his railcars and his Swiss bank account, bequeathed to his son, whose name was misspelled throughout as Randolph, not Randall. Like his nuptials, his will was witnessed by one of his best pals from his teenaged days in Bloomington, Harold Voise.

Concello visited with Voise regularly, both on the phone and in person. By September 1984, Art noted his friend had "brain trouble—not good."[19]

Harold's doctor gave him a brochure on Alzheimer's disease. He handed it to his driver and buddy, who read it and decided to step up his visits. By the next July, Art took Voise for daily drives to get him milk shakes, "but poor Harold has lost his mind—has the same thing as Nena had."[20] After Voise had a stroke, Art "got a man that stayed at his house 24 hrs a day and took good care of him."[21] When he suffered another stroke a month before he passed away, Concello put his friend in a nursing home where he received around-the-clock care. Art noted, "He was luckey [*sic*] he never had any pain."[22] A short while later, he tracked down contact information for Harold's brother and nephew in Michigan. He called to tell them he possessed Voise's circus treasures. He gave them a short time frame to come get the stuff and said that he would destroy it all after that date. They left immediately and retrieved the material from Art's garage.

Concello's generosity extended to the family of friends and more. George Voise, a performer like his brother Harold, also lived in Sarasota. Concello paid for his hospitalization when he suffered a stroke later in 1986. After his release, Art took care of his finances and bought air conditioners for George's home so "he will be comfortable."[23] He invited German Manfred Fritsch, "Doval the Great" (also billed as the "Matchless Maestro of the Silver Strand"), to live on his property and hosted many British friends of Maggie for dinners with them.

Art remained an intensely private person. Often when invited to dinner, he'd say to Maggie, "No, I don't want to go with them people."[24] Nevertheless, he maintained his loyalty to his friends, and Merle Evans was one of his oldest and closest. The Concellos now had him over on Thanksgivings and Christmases until his last in 1987, when they brought the meal to his house because he felt too ill to make it to theirs. He called Merle every day after Nena died and continued doing so until the old bandmaster passed away on New Year's Eve 1987 at the age of ninety-three.

By the late 1980s, his most trusted friends were Willis Lawson, Wayne Larey, and Tuffy Genders. He saw more of Lawson and Larey than Genders because the latter lived in Venice, about a half-hour's drive away. Fellow Bloomington native Laz Rosen might once have been counted as a friend, but something had changed. By 1981, when Concello referenced him in his day planner, he often used the word "idiot" when describing Rosen's poor abilities with mathematics and money. He relegated him to the status of an errand runner, something he'd been doing since the 1950s. There were plenty of opportunities for Rosen to get him stuff like cigars—especially when it got him out of Concello's place.

Art maintained his creed right up to the end. He "had the yes or no. [It was] never I'll see what I can do," Maggie explained.[25] This was part of the secret to his managerial success. He let his managers manage. If they couldn't take care of the problem, whatever it was, he replaced them. He told them, "You're in charge of that. I don't want to hear nothing about it. When I put you in charge of something, you take care of it. Don't bring me stories."[26] The man tapped to manage the strip mall storefronts enjoyed the same liberties and responsibilities.

Sometimes trouble came from next door at Randy's house. In Maggie's eyes, Randy was a tough, hard-hearted man. "I don't think Randy gave love to anybody, really . . . He didn't show his love to anybody or anything, period."[27] Doors were kicked in and sometimes, when the screaming got particularly loud, Maggie called for Art to come home early. He always did. She felt his presence ensured her and their property's safety.[28]

At some point in the late 1980s or early 1990s, Concello was assaulted while he was on the lot at the Fifteenth Street strip mall. To mere acquaintances, he was a changed man afterwards; some even said he'd been brought to his knees by it.[29] Retired aerialist Norma Fox remembered Art frequently shooting pool at the Showfolks Club and noted that his billiards games stopped after he was mugged. "He didn't even talk. He just sat there and stared you know. He got hurt . . . nobody knew what the reason was."[30] Just like the house robbery in the late 1960s, the conjecture was that the perpetrator could have been someone who knew Concello and believed he still carried around a fat bankroll in his pocket. In reality, a homeless man Art had put up in his railcar did it.[31]

Till the end, Concello rewarded loyalty and understood the need to care for his family. In August 1985, he paid for Grace's interment at Park Hill Cemetery back home in Bloomington. Likewise, when Joe Snort passed away, he coordinated his graveside services there in December 1989.[32] Ed Raycraft, the Bloomington friend who had sold Cadillacs to Concello, Evans, the North brothers, and so many others over the years, passed away around the same time. Arthur did not go back to Illinois for any of these services.

The mid-1990s took more of his circus friends. Bill Perry died August 6, 1990. Henry Ringling North departed this life in Geneva, Switzerland, on October 2, 1993. Former fellow flyer Wayne Larey died July 22, 1996. Harold D. "Tuffy" Genders, the boy who perfected truancy with Concello, passed away on December 1, 1997. Willis Lawson was the only friend to outlive Concello. He did so by just twenty-six days.

His days of thinking clearly diminished in his late eighties. Car keys were taken from him when he was found in a ditch, confused.[33] Breathing got to be his most difficult trick in the early summer days of 2001. The reluctant showman battled a hacking cough that wracked his shriveled frame. Though he smoked cigars up to the end, it wasn't lung cancer that killed him. It was pneumonia. He didn't want to go to the hospital, for fear of dying there. Yet that's where he took his last breath on July 5,

2001. As per wishes outlined in his will, no funeral or memorial service were scheduled.

Obituaries varied widely. In Sarasota, his death earned a few paragraphs. Overseas, in both England and Australia, obituaries ran much longer. In *The Times* of London, the headline read: "Arthur Concello: Acrobat who changed the working methods of the circus and made a fortune from it." The piece noted the Concellos' 1934 triumphant return to Great Britain, when they performed the triple for the Prince of Wales.[34]

The Sydney, Australia, obituary veered toward salaciousness. "Concello sailed close to the wind and earned the nickname, 'Little Caesar' in part because of the cut he took from all the petty criminal rackets which attended the affairs of the show," it stated, adding, "Life on the road was also marked by Concello's frequent rows with Antoinette, sparked by his many infidelities."[35] Concello's seat wagons were highlighted, as well as his cunning to profitably maneuver the show from under canvas into arenas. The nearly half-page obituary summarized him by stating that one of the greatest trapeze artists of the twentieth century who transformed himself into "the most important and forceful circus manager of his time" was dead.[36]

A few lines from his boyhood paper recorded his death nearly three weeks later. Of all the death notices, he would have liked the brief and easy-to-miss one from *The Pantagraph* most.[37]

When asked to sum up her husband, Maggie, the woman who literally took a bullet for him, took her time answering. The man who never asked her opinion on anything[38] earned a one-word response: "Love." Arthur M. Concello was as complicated a man as that word. Decades earlier, he had married Antoinette for love but pretty quickly became the poster boy for philandering. He gave his son opportunities that he never had, but he couldn't understand why the boy he sent away emotionally and literally time and again showed such little respect or loyalty. He could have been a nicer man, a more considerate one, and definitely a less feared one, but he likely would not have been so successful if he had.

He had had a much less complicated relationship with money. He wanted it—lots of it. He earned it first by being a star above the ring. Looking around him, he realized that flying wouldn't last forever. Even the greats like Alfredo Codona got hurt, and those injuries could ruin a career and the phenomenal income stream that went with it. So he began training and supplying acts to circuses big and small. When he later transitioned to ownership and big-show management, he increased efficiencies, show profits, and his own income, as well as used people as tools for doing so. By his cunning and unscrupulousness, he made himself invaluable by providing loans when people, John and Henry Ringling North included, needed funds to keep their lives under control. In fact, he could provide everything needed or wanted, including women. While he perfected the rackets that lined his pockets, he emptied his soul.

From a very early age, he saw everything in his world as an opportunity to increase his personal wealth and power. Those closest to him said he never took time to look back. Yet on a different level, he did. Every time he climbed the rope ladder to a pedestal board and took the bar in his hands, a part of him reconnected to the thrill of learning trapeze as a youngster. With each swing, he took comfort in knowing his muscle memory would always help him land safely in the net. As his time on earth wound down, the size and scope of his world diminished, but he still ruled it. He went out on his terms, in his way, and likely with a smuggled stogie in his hand.

Notes

INTRODUCTION

1. Zack Terrell to P. N. Branson, February 11, 1947, Fred D. Pfening III Collection.

CHAPTER 1

1. Tom Parkinson, "A 1973 Interview with Art Concello," *Bandwagon* 45, no. 5 (September–October 2001): 8.
2. "City Offers Inducements to Trade," *Pantagraph*, March 14, 1914, 20.
3. Frank Parker Stockbridge, "Today and Tomorrow," *Kerrville (TX) Times*, February 26, 1931, 2.
4. "Muscle Magnifiers," *Pantagraph*, October 4, 1875, 3.
5. "Muscle Magnifiers," *Pantagraph*, February 25, 1876, 4.
6. "Dexter Fellows—the Greatest Ballyhoo Man on Earth," *New England Historical Society*, August 5, 2020, http://NewEnglandHistoricalSociety.com.
7. Howard M. Vasconcellos, "Circus Man from Starbuck," *Spokesman-Review* (Spokane, WA), December 12, 1956, 4.
8. Robert Lewis Taylor, *Center Ring: The People of the Circus* (Garden City, NY: Doubleday, 1956), 167.
9. "Honor Students," *Pantagraph*, February 6, 1925, 15.
10. Taylor, *Center Ring*, 167–168.
11. "Circus Will Unload at Alton Yards at 5 A.M.," *Pantagraph*, July 7, 1926, 7.
12. Earl Chapin May, "Only the Daring Work for Him," *Popular Science Monthly* 105, no. 5 (May 1926): 32.
13. May, *Popular Science Monthly*, 133.
14. US Department of Labor, Bureau of Labor Statistics, 1927–1928, Bulletin Number 476, Table 1, 3.

15. Treasury Department, Bureau of Internal Revenue, "Statistics of Income for 1927," published by Government Publishing Office, 1929, 3.

16. "Local Man Is Rated Art's Best Teacher," *Pantagraph*, December 4, 1927, 25.

17. "Circus Greets Kenosha Today for Two Shows," *Kenosha (WI) News*, July 12, 1927, 3. Figures in press stories like this were often grossly exaggerated.

18. "Hagenbeck-Wallace Circus," *The Billboard* 39, no. 9 (September 24, 1927): 71.

19. Parkinson, *Bandwagon*, 7.

20. Earl Chapin May, "Grab It," *American Magazine* 106, no. 1 (July 1928): 158.

21. Antoinette Concello, September 1978, CWM Audio 74, 25 October 2020, https://circus.pastperfectonline.com.

22. "Certificate of Incorporation," *Pantagraph*, March 7, 1923, 6.

23. May, *Popular Science Monthly*, 31.

24. May, *Popular Science Monthly*, 133.

25. May, *American Magazine*, 158.

26. "All Play, Aerial Stars Say of Daring Stunts," *Pantagraph*, January 8, 1928, 17.

27. "All Play," *Pantagraph*, 17.

28. "Hearing in Alleged Smuggling Case," *St. Albans (VT) Daily Messenger*, June 21, 1906, 2.

29. Sag Kash, "Father of Circus Aerialists Recalls Days of Prohibition," *Sarasota News*, November 15, 1959, 34.

30. Julie Cappiello, telephone interview with Special Collections Specialist at Milner Library, Illinois State University, Mark Schmitt, September 1, 2020.

31. Census of Canada, 1901, https://www.bac-lac.gc.ca (August 6, 2020).

32. George Emery, "The Only Little Girl Who Ever Ran Away from Home to Join the Circus and Became a Big Star," *Yankee* 30, no. 6 (June 1971): 84.

33. Emery, *Yankee*, 83.

34. Mickey King interview by Steve Gossard, no date, Audio File: GOS _Mickey_King _b_Streaming.mp3; SPC, ISU.

35. Emery, *Yankee*, 83–84.

36. Emery, *Yankee*, 145.

37. "Father of 21 Children is Arraigned for Non-Support," *Rutland (VT) Daily Herald*, August 9, 1924, 1.

38. Josephine L. Webster, "Report of the General Secretary, Vermont Children's Aid Society," *Sixth Annual Report, 1925*, 9.

39. Mickey King, Audio File: GOS_Mickey_King_b_Streaming.mp3.

40. Mickey King, Audio file: GOS_Mickey_King_1_b_Streaming.mp3.

41. Kevin Dann, "From Degeneration to Regeneration: The Eugenics Survey of Vermont, 1925–1926," *Proceedings of the Vermont Historical Society* 59, no. 1 (Winter 1991): 15.

42. "She Flies," *Barre (VT) Daily Times*, June 1, 1949, 11.

43. "Mt. St. Mary Seniors Beat Freshmen 12–6," *Burlington (VT) Free Press*, November 21, 1924, 13.

44. Mickey King interview by Steve Gossard, no date, Audio File: Mickey_King audio.mp3, SPC, ISU.

45. Dean Jensen, "Antoinette Concello: Circus Legend," *Milwaukee Sentinel*, August 29, 1980, 10.

46. Mickey_King, audio.mp3.
47. Mickey King, interview notes by Steve Gossard, October 17, 1988, SPC, ISU.
48. Taylor, *Center Ring*, 170.
49. Joy Stilley, "Trapeze Artist Teaches Troupe Now," *El Paso Times*, May 2, 1972, 2(B).
50. Antoinette Concello, September 1978, CWM Audio 74.
51. Mickey King, October 17, 1988, interview notes by Steve Gossard.
52. Antoinette Concello, September 1978, CWM Audio 74.
53. Eddie Ward, letter to Zack Terrell, from Fred D. Pfening III Collection.
54. Mickey King, Audio File: Mickey_King_audio.mp3, SPC, ISU.
55. Parkinson, *Bandwagon*, 7.
56. Parkinson, *Bandwagon*, 7.
57. Antoinette Concello, September 1978, CWM Audio 74.

CHAPTER 2

1. Margaret Lane, "The Girl on the Flying Trapeze," *Vancouver (B.C.) Sun*, March 23, 1935, 31.
2. "Fred Buchanan Rises from Printer's Devil to Circus Proprietor," *Chillicothe (MO) Constitution-Tribune*, September 2, 1927, 13.
3. "Succeeds Geo. Jabour," *Argus-Leader* (Sioux Falls, SD), August 4, 1903, 5.
4. "Fred Buchanan Circus Magnate," *Argus-Leader* (Sioux Falls, SD), July 31, 1913, 5.
5. Joseph T. Bradbury, "The Fred Buchanan Railroad Circuses 1923–1931, Part VII—1930 Season," *Bandwagon* 27, no. 2 (March–April 1983): 5.
6. "Robbins Circus Will Present Cannon Act," *Argus-Leader* (Sioux Falls, SD), May 25, 1930, 7. Press releases rarely reported factual numbers; usually, numbers of performers or employees were exaggerated.
7. "Robbins' Bros. Circus Has Auspicious Opening," *The Billboard* 42, no. 19 (May 10, 1930): 52.
8. Tom Parkinson, "A 1973 Interview with Art Concello," *Bandwagon* 45, no. 5 (September–October 2001): 8.
9. 1930 Contract, Art Concello Papers, 1930–1982, Series 1: Business Records, Box 3, Folder 1, SPC, ISU.
10. "4000 Gape at Death Defys (sic) in Zuhrah Winter Circus," *Minneapolis Star*, January 28, 1930, 14.
11. "President Wagner Visits Robbins," *White Tops* 3, no. 1 (April 1930): 1, 5.
12. "Circus Robbers Still Free, Police Continue Search," *Burlington Hawk-Eye* (Burlington, IA), May 8, 1930, 2.
13. Mickey King, interview by Steve Gossard, no date, Audio File: Mickey _King audio.mp3; SPC, ISU.
14. "Robbins Bros.' Circus," *The Billboard* 42, no. 24 (June 14, 1930): 75.
15. Bradbury, *Bandwagon*, 13.
16. Mickey King, interview by Steve Gossard, November 14, 1991, Audio File: GOS_Mickey_King_2_a_11-14-91.mp3; SPC, ISU.

17. Antoinette Concello, September 1978, CWM Audio 74, https://circus.pastperfectonline.com.
18. Parkinson, *Bandwagon*, 8.
19. Johnnie Schmidt, "My Tour with the Sells-Floto Circus in 1930," *Bandwagon* 24, no. 2 (March–April 1980): 24.
20. Charles Graves, "The Circus Comes to Town," *Sphere* (London, England), December 23, 1933, 472.
21. Alfredo Codona, letter to Pat Valdo, October 8, 1931, CWM MSS 15, Box 1, File 8.
22. 1931 Contract, Art Concello Papers, 1930–1982, SPC, ISU.
23. "General Outdoor News, Sells-Floto Circus," *The Billboard* 43, no. 29 (July 18, 1931): 72.
24. 1932 Contract, Art Concello Papers, 1930–1982, SPC, ISU.
25. 1932 Contract, Art Concello Papers, SPC, ISU.
26. "1933 Ringling-Barnum Big Show Performer Salary List," Fred D. Pfening III Collection.
27. Charles Graves, "Signing Them Up for the Circus," *Sphere* (London, England), December 22, 1934, 484.
28. "Berlin Remembers Fun and Frolics at the Scala," DW.com, accessed September 22, 2020, https://www.dw.com/en/berlin-remembers-fun-and-frolics-at-the-scala/a-44809270.
29. Robert E. Handley Concello Collection, SPC, ISU.
30. Virginia Gardiner, "Bloomington, Home of the Stars of the Flying Trapeze," *Chicago Tribune*, April 11, 1937, 109.
31. "Big Saturday Night for R-B in Boston," *The Billboard* 45, no. 20 (May 20, 1933): 55, 63.
32. Antoinette Concello, September 1978, CWM Audio 74.
33. "Circuses Are All the Same!" *Daily Mirror* (London, England), December 21, 1934, 8.
34. "Circus Returns to Olympia," *Acton Gazette* (London, England), December 28, 1934, 4.
35. "Royalty and the Circus," *Western Mail* (Glamorgan, Wales), January 7, 1935, 6.
36. "Just their Job," *Daily Mirror* (London, England), January 30, 1935, 9.
37. 1934 Diary, CWM MSS 12, Concello, Arthur Papers.
38. 1931 and 1934 Diaries, CWM MSS 12, Concello, Arthur Papers.
39. 1934 Diary, CWM MSS 12, Concello, Arthur Papers.
40. Contracts, Art Concello Papers, SPC, ISU.
41. "Flying Concellos Correspondences with Europe and Shrines," SC-2015-02, Folder 19, SPC, ISU.
42. Robert Carothers, "Big Day with a Big Show," *The Billboard* 47, no. 41 (October 12, 1935): 35–36.
43. "Fred Bradna to Direct Santos & Antigas Show," *The Billboard* 48, no. 31 (August 1, 1936): 34.
44. Arthur Concello, letter to Sverre Braathen, December 18, 1935, SPC, ISU.
45. "Concellos Buys Famous Ward Estate for Training Aerialists," *Pantagraph*, August 4, 1935, 9.

46. Frederick Woltman, "Daring Young Man on the Flying Trapeze is from Bloomington, Ill," *New York World Telegram*, April 13, 1939, 3.

47. Parkinson, *Bandwagon*, 9.

48. "Under the Marquee," *The Billboard* 47, no. 51 (December 21, 1935): 36.

49. "Financial Records, 1937, RBBB," SC-2015-02, Folder 3, SPC, ISU.

50. "They All Need Energy . . . So They 'Get a Life with a Camel,'" *Kansas City (MO) Star*, October 15, 1934, 8.

51. "Adventures of the Hill Top Gang in Boyville," advertisement, *Cincinnati Enquirer*, October 25, 1936, 125.

52. "Canadian Girl Aerial Artist Tops Circus Bill—Is Very Attractive," *Lethbridge Herald* (Alberta, Canada), August 17, 1939, 64.

53. Raymond Toole Stott, "That Daring Young Girl on the Flying Trapeze," *Sawdust Ring* 2, no. 4 (January–March 1935): 9.

54. Toole Stott, *Sawdust Ring*, 9.

55. Parkinson, *Bandwagon*, 28.

56. Toole Stott, *Sawdust Ring*, 9.

57. The first woman to complete a triple somersault on the flying trapeze was Russian-born Lena Jordan, who first accomplished the trick in 1897. "The Triple," *Truth* (Sydney, Australia) May 23, 1897, 2.

58. Gardiner, *Chicago Tribune*, 109.

59. "Circus Girl," *Detroit Free Press*, February 6, 1937, 28.

60. Antoinette Concello, September 1978, CWM Audio 74.

61. Mickey King, interview by Steve Gossard, undated interview notes, SPC, ISU.

62. Blair Bolles, "Tony Concello Does Difficult Stunts on Flying Trapeze," *Evening Star* (Washington, DC), May 19, 1936, 21.

63. "Daring Women of the Trapeze," *Hope (AR) Star*, April 19, 1941, 3.

64. Mickey King, interview notes by Steve Gossard, December 15, 1987, SPC, ISU.

65. Bolles, *Evening Star*, 21.

66. "Under the Marquee," *The Billboard* 50, no. 16 (April 16, 1938): 38.

67. "Around the Lot with R-B," *The Billboard* 50, no. 24 (June 11, 1938): 31.

68. Jack Pulaski, "Ringling Bros., Barnum & Bailey," *Variety* 130, no. 5 (April 13, 1938): 55.

69. Henry Ringling North and Alden Hatch, *Circus Kings: Our Ringling Family Story*, (Garden City, New York: Doubleday, 1960), 240.

70. Fred Bradna, *Big Top: My Forty Years with the Greatest Show on Earth* (New York: Simon & Schuster, 1952), 317.

71. "R-B Bows to Near Capacity," *The Billboard* 50, no. 16 (April 16, 1938): 74–75.

72. "Strike Called, but Circus Goes On," *Variety* 130, no. 5 (April 13, 1938): 1, 53.

73. "Compromise Ends Walkout of R-B Circus Employees,"*The Billboard* 50, no. 17 (April 23, 1938): 3, 69.

74. "Circus' Fold Saves Ringling Money," *Variety* 131, no. 4 (July 6, 1938): 55.

75. "Circuses: Strike on Ringling-Barnum," *The Billboard* 50, no. 27 (June 25, 1938): 32.

76. Fred Bradna, *Big Top*, 144.

77. "Fire Fears Halt Circus Removal," *Reading (PA) Times*, June 27, 1938, 13.

78. Ringling Bros and Barnum & Bailey Circus 1938 Anti-Strike scroll, SPC, ISU.
79. "Strike Closes 'Big Show,'" *The Billboard* 50, no. 27 (July 2, 1938): 3, 65–66.
80. Helen Wallenda letter, July 3, 1938, Sverre Braathen Correspondence Files, SPC, ISU.
81. "Packing of Circus Begun in Rain as Stars Threaten Union Head," *New York Times*, June 28, 1938, 21.
82. "Wet Canvas Delayed Circus Packing for Shipment to Winter Quarters," *Standard-Sentinel* (Hazelton, PA), June 27, 1938, 7.
83. "Packing of Circus Begun," *New York Times*, 21.
84. Tom Parkinson and Charles Philip Fox, *Circus Moves by Rail* (Boulder, CO: Pruett Publishing Co., 1978), 43.
85. Contracts from Fred D. Pfening III Collection.
86. Forbes telegram to Concello, July 7, 1938, Robert E. Handley Collection, Concello Box 2, SPC, ISU.
87. "Under the Marquee," *The Billboard* 50, no. 37 (September 10, 1938): 30.
88. Eleanor Clarage, "Main Street Meditations," *Cleveland Plain Dealer*, February 10, 1939, 9.
89. Gladwin A. Hill, "Hard Acts Look Easy as Circus Performers Go through Routine," *Arizona Republic* (Phoenix), September 25, 1938, 7.
90. Hill, *Arizona Republic* (Phoenix), 7.
91. "Circus Days Numbered, Say Outdoor Showmen, Blaming Radio and Films," *Variety* 131, no. 9 (August 10, 1938): 1, 55.
92. Frederic Denver Pfening III, "The American Circus and the Great Depression: 1929–1939," (master's thesis, Ohio State University, 1976).

CHAPTER 3

1. George Brinton Beal, *Through the Back Door of the Circus with George Brinton Beal* (Springfield, MA: McLoughlin Bros. Inc, 1938), 106–107.
2. "Circus Aerialist, Visiting Relatives Here, Boasts of Breaking Big Top Bad Luck Rules," *Democrat and Chronicle* (Rochester, NY), March 10, 1939, 24.
3. Parkinson, *Bandwagon*, 11.
4. Parkinson, *Bandwagon*, 11.
5. Henry Ringing North Collection, "Engineer's Report," March 15, 1939, Box 8, Folder 83, SPC, ISU
6. "New Era in R-B Presentation," *The Billboard* 51, no. 15 (April 15, 1939): 3, 36.
7. "Ringling Sarasota Quarters Tax Free," *The Billboard* 51, no. 17 (April 29, 1939): 27.
8. "Ringling Grosses Zoom; Air Conditioning Helps," *Variety* 135, no. 2 (June 21, 1939): 55. Results on the air conditioning were modest at best. The idea was dropped in subsequent seasons.
9. "R-B Show Pulls Three Fine Houses in Cincy," *The Billboard* 51, no. 25 (June 24, 1939): 33.
10. "Ringling Executors Must Post Bond," *The Billboard* 51, no. 25 (June 24, 1939): 32.
11. "Big One Breaks in New Lot," *The Billboard* 51, no. 20 (May 20, 1939): 32, 68.

12. "N.Y. Expo Attractions—Cavalcade of Centaurs," *Variety* 134, no. 11 (May 24, 1939): 46.

13. Henry Ringling North and Alden Hatch, *Circus Kings: Our Ringling Family Story* (Garden City, NY: Doubleday, 1960), 246.

14. North and Hatch, *Circus Kings*, 261.

15. "Canadian Girl Aerial Artist Tops Circus Bill—Is Very Attractive," *Lethbridge Herald* (Alberta, Canada), August 17, 1939, 6.

16. Beal, *Through the Back Door of the Circus*, 107

17. Beal, *Through the Back Door of the Circus*, 106–107.

18. "World's Greatest Trainer of Circus Aerialists but 29," *Oshkosh Daily Northwestern*, April 6, 1940, 5.

19. Art Concello Papers, 1930–1982, Box 1, Folder 3: Financial Record, 1937—RBB&B Combined Show, SPC, ISU.

20. Virginia Gardiner, "Bloomington, Home of the Stars of the Flying Trapeze," *Chicago Tribune*, April 11, 1937, 5.

21. Hubbard Keavy, "He Ran Away with a Circus Now Art Concello Owns One," *Pantagraph*, June 23, 1944, 3.

22. "Glamor of Circus Blamed," *Nebraska State Journal* (Lincoln, NE), May 25, 1922, 7.

23. *Tavlinsky v. Ringling Bros. Circus Co.*, 113 Neb. 632, 204 N.W. 388, 1925 Neb. LEXIS 164 (Supreme Court of Nebraska June 12, 1925, Filed), accessed June 5 2020, https://advance-lexiscom.libproxy.lib.ilstu.edu/api/document?collection=cases&id=urn:contentItem:3YGC-M750-00KR-D3D2-00000-00&context=1516831.

24. John M. Staley, "Circus Steward," *Bandwagon* 40, no. 6 (November—December 1996): 63.

25. "In Municipal Court," *Nebraska State Journal* (Lincoln, NE), December 1, 1936, 13.

26. Jack Tavlin, letter to George Smith, from Fred D. Pfening III Collection.

27. "New York's World's Fair—Special Events," *The Billboard* 51, no. 22 (June 3, 1939): 30–31.

28. Tavlin telegram to Concello, July 14, 1939, Robert E. Handley Concello Collection, SPC, ISU.

29. Tavlin telegram to Concello, March 20, 1940, CWM MSS 12, Concello, Arthur Papers, CWM.

30. Tavlin telegram to Concello, March 22, 1940, CWM MSS 12, Concello, Arthur Papers, CWM.

31. Concello telegram to Tavlin, March 23, 1940, CWM MSS 12, Concello, Arthur Papers, CWM.

32. "R.-B. & B. Circus Near Capacity Easter Week," *Variety* 142, no. 7 (April 23, 1941): 55.

33. Art Concello Papers, 1930–1982, Box 1, Folder 12—Loss and Gain Statement, 1942, SPC, ISU.

34. CWM MSS 12, Concello, Arthur Papers, CWM.

35. Lew Rosen, letter to Concello, CWM MSS 12, Concello, Arthur Papers, CWM.

36. Contract in Fred D. Pfening III Collection.

37. North and Hatch, *Circus Kings*, 316.

38. Parkinson, *Bandwagon*, 11.

39. "Art Concellos Named Manager of Big Circus," *Pantagraph* (Bloomington, IL), April 15, 1942, 12.

40. "Loan Refinancing—Correspondence," Ida Ringling North letter to Newman & Bisco, May 8, 1942, State Archives of Florida.

41. Jack Pulaski, "Ringling Show this Year Actually Lives up to 'Greatest Show' Billing," *Variety* 146, no. 6 (April 15, 1942): 55.

42. Parkinson, *Bandwagon*, 11.

43. Henry Ringling North, letter to Concello, April 14, 1942, CWM MSS 12, Concello, Arthur Papers, CWM.

44. "Loading Lists—New York and Road," CWM MSS 12, Concello, Arthur Papers, CWM.

45. "RB Big in Philly Sans Musicians; Band Picketing," *The Billboard* 54, no. 25 (June 20, 1942): 38.

46. Stuart O'Nan, *Circus Fire: A True Story of an American Tragedy* (New York: Doubleday, 2000), 4.

47. Robert Hasson, "Circus Tragedy," *Bandwagon* 27, no. 2 (March–April 1983): 18.

48. O'Nan, *Circus Fire*, 15.

49. "Over 40 RB Animals Burn," *The Billboard* 54, no. 33 (August 15, 1942): 38, 46.

50. O'Nan, *Circus Fire*, 14.

51. Hassan, *Bandwagon*, 18.

52. John Ringling North, handwritten note, August 8, 1942, CWM MSS 12 Concello, Arthur Papers, CWM.

53. F. DeWolfe letter to William P. Dunn, Jr., January 29, 1943, CWM MSS 36, Ringling Family Papers, "North, John Business Correspondence, 1943, 1944," CWM.

54. Mattie Vasconcellos, letter to Concello, December 15, 1942, CWM MSS 12, Concello, Arthur Papers, CWM.

55. C. A. "Red" Sonnenberg, unpublished manuscript, SPC, ISU.

56. Concello, letter to H. Dube, October 2, 1942, CWM MSS 12, Concello, Arthur Papers, CWM.

57. "Circus to Be Here 5 Days in October," *St. Louis Post-Dispatch*, September 20, 1942, 43.

58. North and Hatch, *Circus Kings*, 263.

59. Jimmy Gurnett, "RB Big in Philly, Sans Musicians, Band Picketing," *The Billboard* 54, no. 25 (June 20, 1942): 38.

60. Concello, memo to North brothers, November 5, 1942, CWM MSS 12, Concello, Arthur Papers, CWM.

61. 1942 Income Tax Return for Concello, CWM MSS 12, Concello, Arthur, Papers, CWM.

62. Parkinson, *Bandwagon*, 12.

CHAPTER 4

1. Antoinette Concello, letter to Grace Killian, not dated, CWM MSS 12, Concello, Arthur Papers, CWM.

2. *Ringling Bros and Barnum & Bailey Route Book* (Sarasota, FL: J.C. Johnson, 1942), 4–5.

3. "Robert Ringling Heads RB," *The Billboard* 55, no. 4 (January 23, 1943): 36.

4. David Hammarstrom, *Big Top Boss: John Ringling North and the Circus* (Urbana: University of Illinois Press, 1992), 98.

5. Minutes, Board of Director RBBB Shows, Inc., 1937–1939, CWM MSS 36, Box 43, Folder 34, CWM.

6. "Robert Ringling Heads RB," *The Billboard*, 49.

7. Dick Anderson, "Ringling Brothers and Barnum & Bailey Official Illustrated Souvenir Guide to the Sarasota, Florida Winter Quarters of the Greatest Show on Earth," *Bandwagon* 58, no. 4 (October–December 2014), 65.

8. Herb Sicks, "Confidential (Report)," January 19, 1942, CWM MSS 36, Box 10, Folder 28, "Concello, Arthur Correspondence, North, John and Henry," CWM.

9. Anderson, *Bandwagon*, 69.

10. Jack Pulaski, "Ringling Circus Revives Parade, Show Combo of B'way and Big Top," *Variety* 150, no. 5 (April 14, 1943): 55.

11. "RB Pulls War-Bond, 14,000," *The Billboard* 55 no. 16 (April 17, 1943): 3.

12. Pulaski, "Ringling Circus Revives Parade," 55.

13. Hubbard Keavy, "Daring Young Man on Flying Trapeze Now Manages Circus," *Daily Press* (Newport News, VA), June 11, 1944, 25.

14. Robert Lewis Taylor, *Center Ring: The People of the Circus* (Garden City, New York: Doubleday, 1956), 179.

15. "Ringling Biz, Over Million, Again Phenom," *The Billboard* 55, no. 18 (May 1, 1943): 38.

16. Personal check, February 23, 1943, CWM MSS 12, Concello, Arthur Papers, CWM.

17. Dick Anderson, "Reflections," copy of unsourced, not dated, newspaper article, SPC, ISU.

18. Counter check, February 4, 1943, CWM MSS 12, Concello, Arthur Papers, CWM.

19. Eddie Kohl, letter to Concello, May 9, 1943, CWM MSS 12, Concello, Arthur Papers, CWM.

20. Willie Kraus, letter to Concello, April 6, 1943, CWM MSS 12, Concello, Arthur Papers, CWM.

21. Concello, letter to Kraus, April 29, 1943, CWM MSS 12, Concello, Arthur Papers, CWM.

22. J. D. Newman, letter to Concello, March 4, 1943, CWM MSS 12, Concello, Arthur Papers.

23. Concello, letter to James McElwee, April 29, 1943, CWM MSS 12, Concello, Arthur Papers, CWM.

24. Frank McClosky, letter to Concello, May 4, 1943, CWM MSS 12, Concello, Arthur Papers, CWM.

25. Roger Getty, letter to Concello, January 27, 1943, CWM MSS 12, Concello, Arthur Papers, CWM.

26. Mattie Vasconcellos, letter to Art and Antoinette Concello, March 5, 1943, CWM MSS 12, Concello, Arthur Papers, CWM.

27. Vasconcellos, letter to Art and Antoinette Concello, March 5, 1943.

28. Concello, letter to McElwee, April 29, 1943.

29. "Circus Defends Sales of Liquor," *South Bend Tribune* (South Bend, IN), July 27, 1955, 38.

30. Blue rooms were known as the privilege car on railroad shows. Art equated privilege cars to pie cars.

31. Joe McKennon, *Circus Lingo* (Sarasota, FL: Carnival Publishers of Sarasota, 1980), 72.

32. Frank McClosky, letter to Concello, not dated, CWM MSS 12, Concello, Arthur Papers, CWM.

33. Concello, letter to Frank McClosky, April 29, 1943, CWM MSS 12, Concello, Arthur Papers, CWM.

34. Concello, letter to Frank McClosky, April 29, 1943.

35. Concello letter to Willie Kraus, April 29, 1943, CWM MSS 12, Concello, Arthur Papers, CWM.

36. Arthur Marshal Concellos, National Personnel Records Center, St. Louis, MO.

37. "Certificates of War Necessity, 1943," Art Concello Papers, 1930–1982, Box 1, Folder 7, SPC, ISU.

38. Henry Ringling North and Alden Hatch, *Circus Kings: Our Ringling Family Story* (Garden City, NY: Doubleday, 1960), 365.

39. Henry North, letter to John North, July 29, 1943, HRN Collection, Box 8, Folder 105, "Correspondence, 1942–1990), SPC, ISU.

40. North, letter to John North, July 29, 1943.

41. "RB Pulls War-Bond," *The Billboard*, 53.

42. Concello, letter to McElwee, July 26, 1943, CWM MSS 12, Concello, Arthur Papers.

43. Keith Webb and Joseph F. Laredo, *Russell Bros. Circus Scrapbook* (US: Webb and Laredo, 2017), 3.

44. Webb and Laredo, *Russell Bros. Circus Scrapbook*, 4.

45. "For Sale, Russell Bros Circus," advertisement, *The Billboard* 51, no. 2 (January 14, 1939): 35.

46. J. D. Newman, letter to Mr. Stevenson at Loeb & Loeb, June 16, 1943, CWM MSS 12, Concello, Arthur Papers, CWM.

47. J. D. Newman, telegram to Pauline Webb, May 10, 1943, CWM MSS 12, Concello, Arthur Papers, CWM.

48. Pauline Webb, telegram to J. D. Newman, May 10, 1943, CWM MSS 12, Concello, Arthur Papers, May 10, 1943, CWM.

49. Concello, telegram to John Ringling North, May 11, 1943, CWM MSS 12, Concello, Arthur Papers, CWM.

50. J. D. Newman, telegram to Pauline Webb, May 22, 1943, CWM MSS 12, Concello, Arthur Papers, CWM.

51. Pauline Webb telegram to J. D. Newman, May 28, 1943, CWM MSS 12, Concello, Arthur Papers, CWM.

52. Concello v. C. W. Webb et al., No. 486296, CWM MSS 12, Concello, Arthur Papers, CWM.

53. Concello, telegram to J. D. Newman, June 26, 1943, CWM MSS 12, Concello, Arthur Papers, CWM.

54. Stuart Thayer, "C. W. Webb's Russell Brothers Circus," *Bandwagon* 13, no. 2 (March–April 1969): 19.

55. Cancelled checks, CWM MSS 12, Concello, Arthur Papers.

56. Tom Parkinson, "A 1973 Interview with Art Concello," *Bandwagon* 45, no. 5 (September–October 2001): 13.

57. Concello, telegram to Frank or Paul Miller, not dated, CWM MSS 12, Concello, Arthur Papers, CWM.

58. "Circus Partners in Legal Tangle," *Los Angeles Evening Citizen News*, December 8, 1943, 9.

59. "Russell Partners in Fight over Profits, Sue for Dissolution," *Variety* 153, no. 1 (December 15, 1943): 45.

60. Parkinson, *Bandwagon*, 17.

61. Anderson, *Bandwagon*, 68.

62. Frank McClosky, letter to Concello, June 29, 1943, CWM MSS 12, Concello, Arthur Papers, CWM.

63. Concello, letter to James F. McElwee, July 26, 1943, CWM MSS 12, Concello, Arthur Papers, CWM.

64. Concello's bank statements, CWM MSS 12, Concello, Arthur Papers, CWM.

65. Concello, letter to Roger Getty, Corn Belt Bank, July 17, 1943, CWM MSS 12, Concello, Arthur Papers, CWM.

66. Concello, letter to Frank McClosky, July 12, 1943, CWM MSS 12, Concello, Arthur Papers, CWM.

67. Jack Tavlin, letter to Concello, July 16, 1943, CWM MSS 12, Concello, Arthur Papers, CWM.

68. Concello, letter to Jack Tavlin, July 26, 1943, CWM MSS 12, Concello, Arthur Papers, CWM.

69. Jack Tavlin, letter to Concello, July 28, 1943, CWM MSS 12, Concello, Arthur Papers, CWM.

70. Jack Tavlin, letter to Concello, October 12, 1943, CWM MSS 12, Concello, Arthur Papers, CWM.

71. "Tavlin's Dept. Store Show Gets Big Play," *The Billboard* 55, no. 1 (December 18, 1943): 37.

72. Walter Kernan, V-mail to Frank McClosky, December 10, 1943, CWM MSS 12, Concello, Arthur Papers, CWM.

73. Concello, letter to Walter Kernan, July 13, 1943, CWM MSS 12, Concello, Arthur Papers, CWM.

74. Walter Kernan, letter to Concello, not dated, CWM MSS 12, Concello, Arthur Papers, CWM.

75. Parkinson, *Bandwagon*, 13.

76. Noyelles Burkart, letter to Everett W. Ritchey, August 21, 1943, Ritchey Collection, SPC, ISU.

77. Bill Antes, letter to Sverre Braathen, September 9, 1943, Braathen Correspondence Files, SPC, ISU.

78. Art Concello Deposition, Case 489,775, December 31, 1943, 46, CWM MSS 12, Concello, Arthur Papers, CWM.

79. "Russell to Barn," *The Billboard* 55, no. 39 (September 25, 1943): 38.

80. "Concello at Selig Zoo," *The Billboard* 55, no. 49 (December 4, 1943): 55.

81. Antes, letter to Braathen, September 9, 1943.

82. Elden Day, letter to Concello, November 12, 1943, CWM MSS 12, Concello, Arthur Papers, CWM.

83. Concello, letter to Frank McClosky, November 29, 1943, CWM MSS 12, Concello, Arthur Papers, CWM.

84. Concello, letter to Allen King, January 1, 1944, CWM MSS 12, Concello, Arthur Papers, CWM.

85. Concello, telegram to Jack Tavlin, December 24, 1943, CWM MSS 12, Concello, Arthur Papers, CWM.

86. Concello, letter to Tex Copeland, February 28, 1944, CWM MSS 12, Concello, Arthur Papers, CWM.

87. Concello, letter to Merle Evans February 14, 1944, CWM MSS 12, Concello, Arthur Papers, CWM.

88. Chang Reynolds, "Clyde Beatty in Person, Season of 1944," *Bandwagon* 13, no. 3 (May–June 1969): 10.

89. Dude Rhodus, letter to Concello, not dated, CWM MSS 12, Concello, Arthur Papers, CWM.

90. Concello, letter to C.D. Curtis, January 13, 1944, CWM MSS 12, Concello, Arthur Papers, CWM.

91. Concello, letter to Lew Rosen, February 1, 1944, CWM MSS 12, Concello, Arthur Papers, CWM.

92. Mooney, letter to Concello, January 13, 1944, CWM MSS 12, Concello, Arthur Papers, CWM.

93. Concello, letter to C.D. Curtis, CWM.

94. Parkinson, *Bandwagon*, 13.

95. Reynolds, *Bandwagon*, 12.

96. Reynolds, *Bandwagon*, 10.

97. Keavy, "Daring Young Man," 25.

98. Antoinette Concello, letter to Grace Killian, January 25, 1944, CWM MSS 12, Concello, Arthur Papers, CWM.

99. Bill Antes, letter to Braathen, February 11, 1944, Braathen Correspondence Files, SPC, ISU.

100. Eddie Jackson, letter to Sverre Braathen, March 4, 1944, Braathen Correspondence Files, SPC, ISU.

101. Reynolds, *Bandwagon*, 12.

102. "Clyde Beatty-Russell Bros. Route Book, 1944," accessed April 18, 2022, https://digital.library.illinoisstate.edu/digital/collection/p15990coll5/id/14293.

103. Artoney Co., Inc., registered February 4, 1944, in California, accessed September 22, 2021, https://businesssearch.sos.ca.gov/.

104. Reynolds, *Bandwagon*, 13.

105. Bill Antes letter to Sverre Braathen, May 18, 1944, Braathen Correspondence Files, SPC, ISU.

106. Antes, letter to Sverre Braathen, May 18, 1944.

107. Art Concello Papers, 1930–1982, Box 1, File 6, SPC, ISU.

108. C. A. Sonnenberg, "Almost Fifty Years Under the Big Top, But Still Only Fifty Feet Ahead of the Sheriff," *Bandwagon* 48, no. 4 (July–August 2004): 24.

109. "Good Week-end Crowd for B-R and S.L. Cronin," *The Billboard* 56, no. 18 (April 29, 1944): 40.

110. "Good Week-end Crowd for B-R and S.L. Cronin," *The Billboard,* 58.

111. Susie Hasselbrink, email message to author, January 28, 2019.

112. Reynolds, *Bandwagon,* 17.

113. Parkinson, *Bandwagon,* 14.

114. Parkinson, *Bandwagon,* 13.

115. *Clyde Beatty-Russell Bros. Combined Circus Souvenir Program and Season Route,* 1944, from Circus Route Book Collection, 1859–2002, SPC, ISU.

116. Parkinson, *Bandwagon,* 14.

117. Parkinson, *Bandwagon,* 15.

118. Parkinson, *Bandwagon,* 14.

119. William L. Elbirn, "Russell Bros Great Pan-Pacific Circus Season of 1945," *Bandwagon* 7, no. 3 (May–June 1963): 14.

120. McKennon, *Circus Lingo,* 68.

121. Elbirn, *Bandwagon,* 15.

122. Concello, letter to Ed Raycraft, January 15, 1944, CWM MSS 12, Concello, Arthur Papers, CWM.

123. Chattel Mortgage, December 14, 1944, Art Concello Papers, 1930–1982, Box 1, Folder 2, SPC, ISU.

124. "Russell Bros.' Circus," advertisement in *The Billboard* 56, no. 51 (December 16, 1944): 43.

125. Parkinson, *Bandwagon,* 14.

126. Waldo Tupper, letter to Concello, July 30, 1944, CWM MSS 12, Concello, Arthur Papers, CWM.

127. Dee Hunt, letter to Sverre Braathen, October 15, 1944, Braathen Correspondence Files, SPC, ISU.

128. Evans-Couls correspondence, Fred D. Pfening III Collection.

129. "Vasconcellos' Rites to be Held Friday," *Pantagraph* (Bloomington, IL), February 20, 1945, 3.

130. C. A. Sonnenberg, unpublished manuscript, n.p., SPC, ISU.

131. Elbirn, *Bandwagon,* 16.

132. "Russell Heavy with Top Acts," *The Billboard* 57, no. 14 (April 7, 1945): 44.

133. Dan Judge, letter to Aubrey Haley, September 18, 1945, CWM MSS 36, General Files, Box 66, File 64, "Russell Bros. And RBPP," CWM.

134. "Tomorrow Is Circus Day in Corvallis," *Corvallis (OR) Gazette-Times,* May 21, 1945, 2.

135. Bill Antes, letter to Sverre Braathen, May 24, 1945, Braathen Correspondence Files, SPC, ISU.

136. Parkinson, *Bandwagon,* 14.

137. B. Wilson, letter from Non-Ringling Archive Material, Box 1, Folder 1, "Arthur Bros. Circus," SPC, ISU.

138. "Arthur Granted Injunction to Halt "Smear" Campaign," *The Billboard* 57, no. 32 (August 11, 1945): 42.

139. William L. Elbirn, "Arthur Bros. Circus," *Bandwagon* 6, no. 6 (November–December 1962): 7.

140. Elbirn, "Russell Bros," *Bandwagon*, 18.

141. Wallace R. Love, letter to H.C. Millsap, November 2, 1945, CWM MSS 12, Concello, Arthur Papers, CWM.

142. H. C. Millsap, letter to Sol Friedman, November 8, 1945, CWM MSS 12, Concello, Arthur Papers, CWM.

CHAPTER 5

1. Tom Parkinson, "A 1973 Interview with Art Concello," *Bandwagon* 45, no. 5 (September–October 2001): 17.

2. D. R. Carson, W. Matthie and G. Borders, "Clyde Beatty Trained Wild Animal Railroad Circus," *Bandwagon* 14, no. 3 (May–June 1970): 25.

3. Wallace Love, letter to California Department of Employment, January 1946, CWM MSS 12, Concello, Arthur Papers, CWM.

4. Stan Windhorn, "Blow Torch Haircuts," *Pantagraph*, December 9, 1945, 3.

5. Carson et al., *Bandwagon*, 26.

6. Parkinson, *Bandwagon*, 15.

7. Parkinson, *Bandwagon*, 15.

8. Carson et al., *Bandwagon*, 28.

9. Parkinson, *Bandwagon*, 15.

10. John Sealock, "Eurekan at Work, Builds Circus Wagons," *Pantagraph* (Bloomington, IL), February 10, 1946, 9.

11. Elfriede Friedersdorf, letter to Sverre Braathen, October 27, 1947, Braathen Correspondence Files, SPC, ISU.

12. McLean County Recorder, January 7, 1946, Index of Deeds, September 1941–March 1948, 21.

13. "Dummy Robinson," accessed 19 August 2020, https://boxrec.com/en/proboxer/332566.

14. Concello, letter to Charles Siegrist, February 23, 1946, CWM MSS 12, Concello, Arthur Papers, CWM.

15. Earl Chapin May, *Circus from Rome to Ringling* (New York: Duffield and Green, 1932), 322.

16. "Hard-Working Ira Watts Spans Two Circus Eras in Key Posts," *The Billboard* 62, no. 39 (September 30, 1950): 53, 59.

17. "New Manager of Emporia Circus Is Seasoned Vet," *Emporia (KS) Daily Gazette*, November 11, 1937, 8.

18. Concello, telegram to Ira Watts, February 8, 1946, CWM MSS 12, Concello, Arthur Papers, CWM.

19. "Beatty Piles Up 205G in L.A.," *The Billboard* 58, no. 19 (May 11, 1946): 72.

20. Waldo Tupper, letter to Concello, April 29, 1946, CWM MSS 12, Concello, Arthur Papers, CWM.

21. Parkinson, *Bandwagon,* 15.

22. Bill Antes, letter to Sverre Braathen, July 26, 1946, Braathen Correspondence Files, SPC, ISU.

23. Fred D. Pfening III, telephone interview with author, September 8, 2017.

24. Carson et al., *Bandwagon,* 31.

25. Buckles Woodcock, *Buckles Blog,* September 7, 2004, accessed April 24, 2017, http://www.bucklesw.blogspot.com.

26. CWM MSS 36, Concello, Arthur, Box 10, File 27, "Correspondence, Millsap, H.C. Attorney," CWM.

27. Wallace Love, letter to Ira Watts, May 13, 1947, CWM MSS 12, Concello, Arthur Papers, CWM.

28. "Robt. Ringling Fights Ouster," *The Billboard* 58, no. 16 (April 20, 1946): 72.

29. "Ringling Estate Interests Purchased for $1,250,000," *The Billboard* 59, no. 34 (August 30, 1947): 55.

30. Henry Ringling North and Alden Hatch, *Circus Kings: Our Ringling Family Story* (Garden City, NY: Doubleday, 1960), 282.

31. Leonard Bisco, letter to Art Concello, September 29, 1947, CWM MSS 36, Box 179, Folder "Ringling, John (Estate of)," CWM.

32. North and Hatch, *Circus Kings,* 278.

33. "Under the Marquee," *The Billboard* 59, no. 25 (June 28, 1947): 76.

34. Elfride Friedersdorf, letter to Braathen, October 27, 1947, SPC.

35. "Personals," *Sarasota Herald-Tribune,* October 31, 1947, 5.

36. Stan Windhorn, "Central Illinois Air News, Hops to New York," *Pantagraph,* May 10, 1947, 3.

37. "Arthur M. Concello Pilot's License," Federal Aviation Administration, accessed February 18, 2017, http://amsrvs.registry.faa.gov.

38. "AMC Flying Act on Polack Bros 1947–1948," Harold "Tuffy" Genders Collection, Box 1, Folder 3, Estes, 1920–1992, SPC, ISU.

39. "Dressing Room Gossip—Cole Bros.," *The Billboard* 60, no. 24 (June 12, 1948): 63.

40. "Dressing Room Gossip—Cole Bros.," *The Billboard* 59, no. 29 (July 26, 1947): 78.

41. Windhorn, "Central Illinois Air News," 3.

42. Parkinson, *Bandwagon,* 16.

43. "Dressing Room Gossip—Ringling-Barnum," *The Billboard* 59, no. 38 (September 27, 1947): 49.

44. 'Dressing Room Gossip—Ringling-Barnum," *The Billboard* 59, no. 43 (November 1, 1947): 54.

45. "Former Mattoon Boy with Sells-Floto Circus," *Journal Gazette* (Mattoon, IL), August 23, 1923, 4.

46. "Thomas with Circus in South America," *Journal Gazette* (Mattoon, IL), October 13, 1928, 6.

47. "Aerial Troupes Return to City After Tours," *Pantagraph* (Bloomington, IL), November 3, 1929, 3.

48. "Wire Walker Invents New Device That Eliminates Bothersome Guys," *Pantagraph* (Bloomington, IL), January 22, 1939, 3.

49. "Kaiser Van Leer Co," advertisement, *Pantagraph* (Bloomington, IL), April 19, 1937, 40.

50. "Only One in World, Makes the Ropes They Swing On," *Pantagraph* (Bloomington, IL), April 14, 1946, 6.

51. "Dressing Room Gossip—Russell Bros.," *The Billboard* 57, no. 35 (September 8, 1945): 52.

52. Parkinson, *Bandwagon*, 17.

53. "Concello Now General Manager," *The Billboard* 59, no. 69 (November 29, 1947): 69.

54. Concello, letter to E. Womble, October 2, 1947, CWM MSS 36, Concello, Arthur Papers, Box 11, Folder 10–11 "Seat Wagons," CWM.

55. E. Womble, letter to Concello, September 13, 1947, CWM MSS 36, Concello, Arthur Papers, Box 11, Folder 10–11, CWM.

56. "Circus Hall of Fame Gets Wagon Replica," *Tampa Bay Times* (St. Petersburg, FL), April 16, 1960, 19.

57. "Dressing Room Gossip—Ringling-Barnum," *The Billboard* 59, no. 38 (September 27, 1947): 49.

58. Parkinson, *Bandwagon*, 17.

59. C.A. "Red" Sonnenberg, unpublished manuscript, n.p., SPC, ISU.

60. "Top Ringling Job in Muddle," *The Billboard* 59, no. 44 (November 8, 1947): 50.

61. "J. R. North Back at R-B Helm," *The Billboard* 59, no. 46 (November 22, 1947): 67.

62. J. R. Griffin, letter to Concello, November 17, 1947, CWM MSS 12, Concello, Arthur Papers, CWM.

63. William Taggart, interview with author, January 9, 2016.

64. Taggart, interview, January 9, 2016.

65. "Covering Sarasota with the Main Street Reporter," *Sarasota Herald-Tribune*, July 14, 1948, 4.

66. "R-B Staff Changes Confirmed," *The Billboard* 60, no. 1 (January 3, 1948): 50.

67. David Lewis Hammarstrom, *Behind the Big Top* (South Brunswick, NJ: A.S. Barnes, 1980), 146.

68. Taggart, interview, January 9, 2016.

69. Frank McClosky, letter to Charlie Campbell, January 9, 1948, CWM MSS 36, General Files, Box 63, Folder 49, CWM.

70. J. R. Griffin, inter-office communication to Concello, August 11, 1948, CWM MSS 36, General Files, Box 60, Folder 53, "Griffin, J. R.," CWM.

71. CWM MSS 36, General Files, Box 38, Folder 19, "Artony Co, Art Concello, Antoinette Concello & Grace Killian, RBB&B Seat Wagon Manufacture," CWM.

72. North and Hatch, *Circus Kings*, 285.

73. Hammarstrom, *Behind the Big Top*, 145.

74. Paul R. Reeve, letter to Concello, February 15, 1949, CWM MSS, Concello, Arthur Papers, Box 10, Folders 9–11, "Correspondence, General, 1949," CWM.

75. Concello, letter to E. Womble, May 28, 1949, CWM MSS 36, Concello, Arthur Papers, Box 11, Folders 10–11 "Seat Wagons," CWM.

76. E. Womble, letter to Concello, May 30, 1949, CWM MSS 36, Concello, Arthur Papers, Box 11, Folders 10–11 "Seat Wagons," CWM.

77. Bill Curtis, letter to Tom Parkinson, December 2, 1951, CWM MSS 34 Parkinson, Tom Papers, Box 11, Folders 4–16, CWM.

78. Bill Curtis, letter to Tom Parkinson, February 2, 1952, CWM MSS 34 Parkinson, Tom Papers, Box 11, Folders 4–16, CWM.
79. Parkinson, *Bandwagon*, 18.
80. Hammarstrom, *Behind the Big Top*, 146.
81. "Ex-Trapezist Now Head Man of Ringling's Show, Invents Seating Plan," *Ogdensburg (NY) Advance News*, April 25, 1948, 3.
82. "Two Men Killed in Pittsburgh," *The Billboard* 60, no. 24 (June 12, 1948): 62.
83. Beverly Kelley, "The Wonder City That Moves by Night," *National Geographic* 93, no. 3 (March 1948): 296.
84. "Ringling's First California Showing in 7 Years Rings Bell," *The Billboard* 60, no. 39 (September 24, 1948): 53.
85. "Filmdom Names Join RB to Put Over Hospital Benefit," *The Billboard* 60, no. 37 (September 11, 1948): 65.
86. "Straws at Phoenix for R-B," *The Billboard* 60, no. 40 (October 2, 1948): 42.
87. "Concello Forfeits Bail at San Diego," *The Billboard* 60, no. 49 (December 4, 1948): 55.
88. "Circus Season Most Successful in Many Years," *Boston Globe*, August 29, 1948, 40.
89. John Ringling North II, telephone interview with author, November 26, 2019.
90. Ernest J. Albrecht, "Miles White, the Little Eccentric with the Big Talent," *Bandwagon* 37, no. 6 (November–December 1993), 50–60.
91. Mary Jane Miller, interview with Mort Gamble and author, January 11, 2016.
92. Edward Hoagland, interview with author, April 8, 2019.
93. "Large Storage Barn for Rent," advertisement, *Pantagraph* (Bloomington, IL), October 6, 1948, 15.
94. George Grim, "Circus Boss Sends Passes to Pal of 25 Years Ago," *Star Tribune* (Minneapolis, MN), July 29, 1948, 11.
95. David Lewis Hammarstrom, *Big Top Boss: John Ringling North and the Circus* (Urbana: University of Illinois Press, 1992), 143.

CHAPTER 6

1. Nena Thomas Evans, letter to Helen Steinwachs, June 16, 1963, CWM MSS 36, Box 58, Folder "Corresp. Inter Office—Misc. RBB&B 1963," CWM.
2. Tom O'Connell, "Art Flew thru the Air to Come Top Ringling Exec.," *The Billboard* 62, no. 25 (June 24, 1950): 53, 88.
3. Edwin Schallert, "Selznick, North Reveal Plans for Circus Epic," *Los Angeles Times*, April 16, 1948, 23.
4. Tom Parkinson, "A 1973 Interview with Art Concello," *Bandwagon* 45, no. 5 (September–October 2001): 19.
5. David Lewis Hammarstrom, *Behind the Big Top* (South Brunswick, NY: A. S. Barnes, 1980), 147.
6. "AFI Catalog of Feature Films: The Greatest Show on Earth (1952)," accessed May 22, 2020, https://catalog.afi.com/Catalog/moviedetails/50496.

7. CWM 36, Box 43, File 34, "Minutes, Board of Directors RBB&B Shows, 1937–1959 and other relevant papers." CWM.

8. Scott Eyman, *Empire of Dreams* (New York, NY: Simon & Schuster, 2010), 423.

9. Jerry Digney, "Cecil B. DeMille's Greatest Show on Earth Film Epic Forty Years Ago," *Bandwagon* 35, no. 6 (November–December 1991): 48.

10. Concello, letter to John Ringling North, July 1, 1950, CWM MSS 36, Concello, Arthur Papers, Box 10, Folders 28–29, "North, John & Henry," CWM.

11. "AFI Catalog." https://aficatalog.afi.com/.

12. Concello, memo to Henry Ringling North, October 21, 1950, CWM MSS 36, Box 69, Folder 57, CWM.

13. Henry Ringling North, letter to John North, August 12, 1949, CWM 36, Henry Ringling North Personal Papers, CWM.

14. Eyman, *Empire of Dreams,* 428.

15. Eyman, *Empire of Dreams,* 429.

16. "Personality," *Time Magazine* 59, no. 19 (May 12, 1952): 43.

17. Frank Braden, letter to Henry Ringling North, April 25, 1952, HRN Collection, Special Collections, Box 6, Folder 73, SPC, ISU.

18. John Kobal, *Lost World of DeMille* (Jackson: University Press of Mississippi, 2019), 196.

19. Kobal, *Lost World of DeMille,* 196.

20. Transcription of Concello-Burns discussion, March 25, 1950, CWM MSS 36, Box 65, Folder 6, CWM.

21. CWM MSS 36, General Files, Box 65, File 6, Paramount Pictures, Inc. "Greatest Show on Earth" Movie—1950, CWM.

22. Parkinson, *Bandwagon,* 19.

23. Jackie LeClaire, interview with David Lewis Hammarstrom, April 1986, available at Special Collections, Milner Library, ISU.

24. CWM MSS 36, General Files, Box 65, File 6, Paramount Pictures, Inc. "Greatest Show on Earth" Movie—1950, CWM.

25. CWM MSS 36, General Files, Box 65, File 5, Paramount Pictures, Inc. "Greatest Show on Earth" Movie—1950, CWM.

26. CWM MSS 36, General Files, Box 65, File 5, Paramount Pictures, Inc. "Greatest Show on Earth" Movie—1950, CWM.

27. Betty Hutton, "I Was Really the Girl on the Flying Trapeze," *Times Union* (Albany, NY), January 27, 1952, 12.

28. Gladwin Hill, "She Floats Through the Air," *New York Times,* January 21, 1951, 85.

29. Hutton, "I Was Really the Girl," 12.

30. Thomas Allen, "Girl on the Flying Trapeze," *Maclean's Magazine,* May 1, 1953, 68.

31. "AFI Catalog." https://aficatalog.afi.com/.

32. CWM MSS 36, General Files, Box 65, Folder 5, Paramount Pictures, Inc. "Greatest Show on Earth" Movie—1950, CWM.

33. Eyman, *Empire of Dreams,* 430.

34. "Impact of DeMille Lasts Long Time," *Sarasota Herald Tribune,* January 7, 1962, 18.

35. Robert Lewis Taylor, *Center Ring: The People of the Circus* (Garden City, New York: Doubleday), 161.

36. Norma Fox, interview with Mort Gamble and author, Sarasota, FL, January 7, 2016.

37. CWM MSS 36, General Files, Box 65, Folder 5, Paramount Pictures, Inc. "Greatest Show on Earth" Movie—1950, CWM.

38. Concello, letter to Henry North, December 1, 1951, CWM MSS 36, Box 188, Folder "North (J. R. N.–H. R. N.)," CWM.

39. "AFI Catalog." https://aficatalog.afi.com/.

40. "R-B Movie May Set New Gross Mark," *The Billboard* 65, no. 16 (April 18, 1953): 57.

41. Joe Guzman, telephone interview with author, October 29, 2019.

42. Edward Hoagland, telephone interview with author, April 8, 2019.

43. Concello letter to Art Carnahan, August 18, 1953, Art Concello Papers, 1930–1982, "Art Carnahan Materials," SPC, ISU.

44. Mickey_King_audio.mp3, from Special Collections, SPC, ISU.

45. Allen, *Maclean's Magazine*, 19.

46. "Living with the Circus," *Woman's Home Companion* 77, no. 8 (August 12, 1950): 113–128.

47. "Circus Jots," *Greater Show World* 33, no. 9 (September 1950): 20.

48. C. A. "Red" Sonnenberg, Unpublished manuscript, n.p., SPC, ISU.

49. Guzman, interview, October 29, 2019.

50. Ernest J. Albrecht, "Miles White, The Little Eccentric with the Big Talent," *Bandwagon* 37, no. 6 (November–December 1993): 57.

51. Bambi Burnes, interview with author, May 12, 2016.

52. Guzman, interview, October 29, 2019.

53. Mary Jane Miller, interview with Mort Gamble and author, Sarasota, Florida, January 11, 2016.

54. The Flying Harolds, anchored by Art's friend, Harold Voise, rotated with the Comets during their Madison Square Garden dates.

55. "Is Big Top Disappearing? New Season to Bring More Indoor Circus Operations," *The Billboard* 62, no. 14 (April 8, 1950): 151.

56. Concello, letter to John North, July 1, 1950.

57. Henry North, letter to John North, August 7, 1949, CWM MSS 36, Henry Ringling North Personal Papers, CWM.

58. Jim McHugh, "R-B Canvas Trek Starts Big," *The Billboard* 62, no. 21 (May 27, 1950): 70.

59. CWM MSS 36, General Files, Box 58, File 58 "Dube, Harry S., Program Book Dept. RBB&B," CWM.

60. Concello, letter to John Ringling North, October 6, 1951, CWM MSS 36, Concello, Arthur Papers, Box 10, Folders 28–29, CWM.

61. "Ringling Scores Capacities as Washington Skies Clear," *The Billboard* 64, no. 13 (May 31, 1952): 56, 74.

62. John Ringling North, letter to Concello, September 20, 1950, CWM MSS 36, Concello, Arthur Papers, Box 10, Folders 28–29, CWM.

63. Concello, letter to John Ringling North, July 24, 1950, CWM 36, Concello, Arthur Papers, Box 10, Folders 28–29, CWM.

64. Concello, letter to John Ringling North, September 5, 1950, CWM MSS 36, Concello, Arthur Papers, Box 10, Folders 28–29, CWM.

65. North, letter to Concello, September 20, 1950.

66. Concello, letter to John Ringling North, July 28, 1950, CWM MSS 36, Concello, Arthur Papers, Box 10, Folders 28–29, CWM.

67. George Woods, letter to Concello, August 1, 1950, CWM MSS 36 General Files, Box 69, Folder 73, "Woods, George," CWM.

68. Henry Ringling North, letter to John Ringling North, August 9, 1949, CWM MSS 36, Henry Ringling North Personal Papers, CWM.

69. "Ringling's Cuban Biz Exceeding '49 Level," *The Billboard* 62, no. 51 (December 23, 1950): 48.

70. Concello, letter to John Ringling North, October 14, 1950, CWM MSS 36, Box 185, JRN Business, Folder, "North, John Ringling 1950 Correspondence," CWM.

71. Concello, memo to John Ringling North, November 18, 1950, CWM MSS 36, Box 185, JRN Business, Folder, "North, John Ringling 1950 Correspondence," CWM.

72. Concello, letter to John Ringling North, December 20, 1950, CWM MSS 36, Box 185 JRN Business, Folder "North, John Ringling 1948 Correspondence," CWM.

73. CWM MSS 36, Rockland Oil Co, Box 1, CWM.

74. Concello, letter to John Ringling North, March 20, 1950, CWM MSS 36, Box 185, JRN Business, Folder "North, John Ringling 1950 Correspondence," CWM.

75. Concello, letter to John Ringling North, March 24, 1950, CWM MSS 36, Box 185, JRN Business, Folder "North, John Ringling 1950 Correspondence," CWM.

76. "Sarasota Nitery to Use R-B Acts; Concello in Deal," *The Billboard* 62, no. 43 (October 28, 1950): 63.

77. Concello, letter to North, October 14, 1950.

78. Bill Ballantine, *Wild Tigers and Tame Fleas* (New York: Rinehart, 1958), 100.

79. Concello, letter to John Ringling North, April 16, 1950, CWM MSS 36, Concello, Arthur Papers, Box 10, Folders 28–29, CWM.

80. CWM MSS 36 General Files, Box 62, Folder 34 "Kirk & Pinkerton and Kirt-Pinkerton Sparrow, etc.," CWM.

81. Eddie Billetti, letter to Concello, August 15, 1952, CWM MSS 36 General Files, Box 42, Folder 4, "Hebeler's Shop, Sarasota, FL, Edward S. Hebeler, Eddie Billetti," CWM.

82. "North-Concello-Dube Combine Imports Rotor, German Device," *The Billboard* 62, no. 35 (September 2, 1950): 53.

83. Concello, letter to John Ringling North, February 16, 1951, CWM MSS 36, Ringling Family Papers, John Ringling North "Personal" unsourced Papers, "Rotor (Carl Friese)," CWM.

84. Concello, letter to John Ringling North, April 22, 1958, CWM MSS, 36, Ringling Family Papers, John Ringling North "Personal" Unsourced Papers, "Rotor (Carl Friese)," CWM.

85. Concello, letter to John Ringling North, July 24, 1950, CWM MSS 36, Box 185 JRN Business, Folder "North, John Ringling 1950 Correspondence," CWM.

86. Concello, letter to John Ringling North, October 14, 1950.

87. "City Life," *Sarasota Herald Tribune*, December 3, 1950, 7.

88. John Ringling North, letter to Concello, undated, CWM MSS 36, Box 188, Folder "Personal Misc," CWM.

89. Concello, memo dated January 2, 1951, CWM MSS 36, Box 188, Folder "North JRN–HRN," CWM.

90. "Ringling Adds Week to Cuban Run; Biz Good," *The Billboard* 63, no. 2 (January 13, 1951): 56.

91. "Waldo T. Tupper Dies," *White Tops* 24, no. 1–2 (January–February 1951): 15.

92. Concello, letter to John Ringling North, February 10, 1951, CWM MSS 36, Box 188, Folder "Personal Misc," CWM.

93. Concello, letter to John Ringling North, October 6, 1951, CWM MSS 36, Box 188, Folder "Personal Misc," CWM.

94. Bones Brown, letter to Concello, November 25, 1951, CWM MSS 36, Concello, Arthur Papers, Box 10, Folder 30 "Performer Solicitations," CWM.

95. Concello, letter to Judge Duval, September 13, 1952, CWM MSS 36, General Files, Box 58, Folder 65–67, CWM.

96. Nena Thomas, letter to Henry Ringling North, November 25, 1951, HRN Collection, Box 6, Folder 5, SPC, ISU.

97. "Youngster Gets House for Christmas," *Sarasota Herald Tribune*, December 25, 1951, 3.

98. Gloria Norris, letter to Concello, June 15, 1951, CWM MSS 36, Box 188, Folder "Personal Misc. JRN," CWM.

99. Steinbeck material in CWM MSS 36, JRN/HRN Boxes, CWM.

100. Concello, letter to John North, December 27, 1951, CWM MSS 36, Box 184, Folder "North, John Ringling 1951 Correspondence," CWM.

101. Nena Thomas, letter to Henry Ringling North, January 31, 1952, HRN Collection, Box 6, Folder 1, SPC, ISU.

102. Nena Thomas, letter to Henry Ringling North, February 26, 1952, HRN Collection, Box 6, Folder 1, SPC, ISU.

103. Allen, *Maclean's Magazine*, 68.

104. "Moriturus Keeps Mind on Work," *Evening Sun* (Baltimore, MD), June 2, 1951, 10.

105. Will Jones, "'Greatest Show' Goes Hollywood," *Star Tribune* (Minneapolis, MN), July 27, 1951, 35.

106. Nena Thomas, letter to Henry Ringling North, January 31, 1952, HRN Collection Box 6, Folder 73, SPC, ISU.

107. Nena Thomas, letter to Henry Ringling North, February 19, 1952, HRN Collection, Box 6, Folder 73, SPC, ISU.

108. "Out-of-Door School Holds Annual Horse Show," *Sarasota Herald Tribune*, April 27, 1952, 17.

109. Concello, letter to Henry North, January 12, 1952, CWM MSS 36, Henry Ringling North Personal Papers, CWM.

110. "RB Gotham Advance Sales Way Ahead," *The Billboard* 64, no. 14 (April 5, 1952): 71, 80.

111. Concello, letter to John Ringling North, August 1, 1952, CWM MSS 36, Box 184, Folder "North, John Ringling 1952 Correspondence," CWM.

112. Concello, letter to J.R. Griffin, August 9, 1952, CWM MSS 36, Box 10, Folder 14, CWM.

113. Concello, letter to John Ringling North, August 23, 1952, CWM MSS 36, General Files, Box 69, Folder 8 "Venezuela, South America," CWM.

114. "R-B Rehearses Spec; Flag, Indian Scenes," *The Billboard* 65, no. 11 (March 14, 1953): 62.

115. Concello, letter to John North, November 5, 1952, CWM MSS 36, Box 184, Folder "North, John Ringling 1952 Correspondence," CWM.

116. Sverre Braathen, letter to Pat Valdo, December 25, 1952, Braathen Correspondence Files, SPC, ISU.

117. Concello, letter to John Ringling North, October 4, 1952, CWM MSS 36, General Files, Box 41, Folder 23 "Greatest Show on Earth" Movie, CWM.

118. "North, John Ringling; Alfred of New York," the Sandra and Gary Baden Collection of Celebrity Endorsements in Advertising, 1897–1979, Archives Center, National Museum of American History, Washington, DC.

119. Concello, letter to Henry Ringling North, May 14, 1953, HRN Collection, Box 6, Folder 1, SPC, ISU.

120. Earl Wilson, "Betty to Take Circus Trapeze Act to London," undated clipping from unknown newspaper, SPC, ISU.

121. F. J. McKenna, memo to Concello, June 3, 1953, and Concello, response to McKenna, July 13, 1953, CWM MSS 36, Box 10, Folder 14, CWM.

122. Concello, letter to Roland Butler, June 11, 1953, CWM MSS 26, Caldwell, Paul N. Papers, CWM.

123. Concello, letter to Antoinette Concello, September 3, 1953, CWM MSS 36, Concello, Arthur Papers, Box 10, Folder 14 General, 1953, CWM.

124. Concello, list of things for Joe "Snort" Killian to do, September 4, 1953, CWM MSS 36, Box 10, Folder "Concello, Arthur Correspondence 1953," CWM.

125. Concello, list of things for Joe "Snort" Killian to do, September 4, 1953.

126. Concello, letter to Antoinette Concello, September 3, 1953.

127. "Ballet Star Calls Tune for Circus Aerialists," *Statesville Record and Landmark* (Statesville, NC), January 31, 1961, 3.

128. "Ringling Circus Girl Shot in RR Car," *El Paso Herald-Post*, October 10, 1953, 7.

129. "Woman Sought in Shooting of Circus Acrobat," *El Paso Herald-Post*, October 12, 1953, 1.

130. "Circus Superintendent Says Girl Aerialist Was Shot Accidentally," *El Paso Herald-Post*, October 13, 1953, 1.

131. "Shooting of Circus Girl Acrobat in El Paso Probed," *Albuquerque Journal*, October 19, 1953, 1.

132. Allen, *Maclean's Magazine*, 68.

133. Allen, *Maclean's Magazine*, 70.

134. Clyde Noble, letter to Harold Ramage, January 31, 1954, Box 1, Local Collection, SPC, ISU.

135. Fred D. Pfening III, interview with author, September 17, 2020.

136. Concello, handwritten note to John Ringling North, December 2, 1953, CWM 36, Concello, Arthur Papers, Box 11, Folder 6, "Resignation letter," CWM.

CHAPTER 7

1. Tom Parkinson, "A 1973 Interview with Art Concello," *Bandwagon* 45, no. 5 (September–October 2001): 24.

2. Clyde Noble, letter to Harold Ramage, January 31, 1954, Box 1 Local Collection, Special Collections, Milner Library, ISU.

3. "Beatty Denies Talking of Pact with Concello," *The Billboard* 66, no. 7 (February 13, 1954): 63.

4. "Royal American Set for Memphis Opener," *The Billboard* 66, no. 18 (May 1, 1954): 56, 62.

5. "No Action Seen after Beatty, Concello Talks," *The Billboard* 66, no. 13 (March 27, 1954): 1, 44.

6. "Concello Buys Control of Clyde Beatty Circus," *The Billboard* 67, no. 3 (January 15, 1955): 63, 74.

7. "Beatty Show Flashes Color as Los Angeles Run Starts," *The Billboard* 67, no. 15 (April 9, 1955): 112.

8. "Beatty Show Orders Five Seat Wagons," *The Billboard* 67, no. 7 (February 12, 1955): 72.

9. "Beatty Business Continues High," *The Billboard* 67, no. 18 (April 30, 1955): 56.

10. "North Names Burke Ringling Executive," *The Billboard* 67, no. 13 (March 26, 1955): 24.

11. Bob Hasson, "The 1955 Tour of Ringling Bros. and Barnum & Bailey Circus," *Bandwagon* 31, no. 6 (November–December 1987): 16.

12. Michael Burke, *Outrageous Good Fortune* (Boston: Little, Brown, 1984), 182.

13. Phil Santora, "Circus Folk Blast Owner North," *Daily News* (New York, NY), August 7, 1956, 27.

14. Phil Santora, "Big Top Flop?" *Daily News* (New York, NY), August 9, 1956, 32.

15. Kenneth D. Hull, "I Had to Join the Circus," *Bandwagon* 26, no. 3 (May–June 1982): 15.

16. Burke, *Outrageous Good Fortune*, 183–184.

17. Burke, *Outrageous Good Fortune*, 184.

18. Burke, *Outrageous Good Fortune*, 186.

19. Their letters of resignation, which are part of the Ringling Archive in Circus World's Library, are dated between July 23 and July 25. But *The Billboard* reported their departure as happening August 4, after the St. Paul date (see next note for *Billboard*'s citation).

20. "Ringling Drops Managers, Lose 1 Show as Men Idle," *The Billboard* 67, no. 33 (August 13, 1955): 72.

21. Hasson, *Bandwagon*, 16.

22. US Congress, Senate, *Interim Report, Hearings on S. Res 44 and 249, Select Comm. on Improper Activities in the Labor and Management Field*, 86th Cong. (1959).

23. Burke, *Outrageous Good Fortune*, 188.

24. "Speculation Grows on R-B Quitting Madison Square Garden," *The Billboard* 67, no. 24 (June 11, 1955): 66, 68.

25. "Ringling Plans Latest Closing, Cuba Run; Loses Day to Mud," *The Billboard* 67, no. 43 (October 22, 1955): 64.

26. Miss Gerry, letter to Henry North, May 8, 1956, HRN Collection, Box 6, Folder 1, SPC, ISU.

27. "Boston Fair for R-B; AGVA Weak," *The Billboard* 68, no. 1 (May 26, 1956): 66.

28. Miss Gerry, letter to Henry North, May 8, 1956.

29. Joe Taggert, letter to Sverre Braathen, June 5, 1956, Braathen Correspondence Files, SPC, ISU.

30. "List Staff Posts for Ringling's 1956 Tour," *The Billboard* 68, no. 1 (May 19, 1956): 54.

31. On the last day, 150 tickets were sold for the big top that sat 4,000. Lane Talburt, "From Deming to Deland," *Bandwagon* 54, no. 2 (March–April 2010): 33.

32. "Beatty Firm Files Bankruptcy Petition," *The Billboard* 68, no. 1 (May 26, 1956): 66.

33. "It's All Off," *Deming (NM) Headlight*, July 17, 1956, 1.

34. Talburt, *Bandwagon*, 35.

35. Merle Evans, letter to Sverre Braathen, January 7, 1957, Braathen Correspondence Files, SPC, ISU.

36. Eddie Jackson, letter to Sverre Braathen, October 6, 1955, Braathen Correspondence Files, SPC, ISU.

37. Santora, "Circus Folk Blast North," *Daily News*.

38. CWM MSS 36, General Files, Box 61, Folder 3, Hatch, Alden, CWM.

39. "John Ringling North's statement to the press." Copy in Fred D. Pfening III Collection.

40. Bill Ballantine, "Concello Story," *Bandwagon* 55, no. 2 (March–April 2011): 8.

41. Michael Burke, memo to managers, July 21, 1956, CWM MSS 36, General Files, Box 55, Folder 71, CWM.

42. Ballantine, *Bandwagon*, 7.

43. "Why the Ringling Circus Closed: from the Horse's Mouth, J.R. North," *Variety* 203, no. 12 (August 22, 1956): 2, 50.

44. Ballantine, *Bandwagon*, 6.

45. "Concello-North Talks Start Circus Rumors," *Orlando Sentinel*, July 26, 1956, 10.

46. Lawrence Dame, "Henry North Tells Ringling Tale," *Sarasota Herald-Tribune*, March 27, 1960, 56.

47. Document dated July 31, 1956, CWM MSS 36, Concello, Arthur Papers, Box 10, Folder 17, General, 1956, CWM.

48. Ballantine, *Bandwagon*, 8.

49. David Lewis Hammarstrom, *Big Top Boss: John Ringling North and the Circus* (Urbana: University of Illinois Press, 1992), 287.

50. Ballantine, *Bandwagon*, 8.

51. "Concello Back with Circus; Indoor Tour Planned," *Tampa Tribune*, October 17, 1956, 19

52. Ballantine, *Bandwagon*, 8.

53. Westbrook Pegler, "Circus Reorganized for Non-Canvas Run," *News-Herald* (Franklin, PA), December 7, 1956, 4.

54. "Why the Ringling Circus Closed," *Variety*, 2, 50.

55. Concello, memo to Genders and Morgan, April 7, 1957, CWM MSS 36, Concello, Arthur Papers, Box 10, Folder 18, General, 1957, CWM.

56. Umberto Bedini, letter to Henry Ringling North, November 2, 1956, HRN Collection, Box 6, Accordion File "Northbrook—1960," "Umberto Bedini," SPC, ISU.

57. "R-B Contracts Arenas: Pacts Not Signed Yet," *The Billboard* 68, no. 44 (November 3, 1956): 60.

58. Concello, memo to managers, December 20, 1956, CWM MSS 36, Concello, Arthur Papers, Box 10, Folder 17, General, 1956, CWM.

59. William Moore, "Hoffa's Teamster Aid Denies Hiring of Goons," *Chicago Tribune*, September 3, 1958, A3.

60. Ballantine, *Bandwagon*, 12.

61. "Billers Sign with R-B, Set for 3 Others," *The Billboard* 69, no. 1 (February 23, 1957): 90.

62. Ballantine, *Bandwagon*, 12.

63. Ballantine, *Bandwagon*, 11.

64. Ballantine, *Bandwagon*, 12.

65. Gene Plowden, "Concello Builds a New Circus," *Tallahassee Democrat*, March 27, 1957, 19.

66. "8000 Nut Aim of R-B, Ink Teamsters 'No Strike' Pact," *The Billboard* 69, no. 19 (May 6, 1957): 80.

67. Tom Parkinson, "A 1973 Interview with Art Concello," *Bandwagon* 45, no. 5 (September–October 2001): 21.

68. "Circus is Facing Fight to Survive," *New York Times*, March 24, 1957, 75.

69. Pegler, *News-Herald*.

70. "Rules in Selling Sponsored Dates," CWM MSS 36, Box 47, Folder 39, "Financial Records & Misc, RBB&B 1956–1959," CWM.

71. "8000 Nut," *The Billboard*, 80.

72. "Circuses, Ringling Brothers and Barnum & Bailey," *The Billboard* 70, no. 10 (April 21, 1958): 66.

73. Ballantine, *Bandwagon*, 8.

74. Harry S. Dube, memo, April 7, 1948, to Concello, CWM MSS 36, Concello, Arthur Papers, Box 10, Folder 7 General, 1948, CWM.

75. Concello memo, April 11, 1958, CWM MSS 36, Concello, Arthur Papers, Box 10, Folder 19 General, 1958, CWM.

76. "Ringling Big in Mexico City," *The Billboard* 69, no. 52 (December 23, 1957): 51.

77. Parkinson, *Bandwagon*, 23.

78. Ballantine, *Bandwagon*, 12.

79. Ballantine, *Bandwagon*, 12.

80. Ballantine, *Bandwagon*, 11.

81. Ballantine, *Bandwagon*, 6.

82. "How Ringling Barnum Circus Fits into Arena Operation," *The Billboard* 69, no 16 (April 20, 1957): 65.

83. Green Bay architect, letter to Concello, October 10, 1957, CWM MSS 36, Concello, Arthur Papers, Box 10, Folder 18 General, 1957, CWM.

84. Rudy Bundy, memo to Tuffy Genders, August 14, 1962, CWM MSS 26, Caldwell, Paul N., Papers, CWM.

85. 1961 Concello Diary, March 1.

86. Architect, letter to Concello, August 20, 1958, CWM 36, Concello, Arthur Papers, Box 10, Folder 19 General, 1958, CWM.

87. Concello, memo to Werner Buck, October 16, 1957, CWM 36, Concello, Arthur Papers, Box 10, Folder 18 General, 1957, CWM.

88. Ballantine, *Bandwagon*, 15.

89. "Seek to Bar Ringling Auction, Car Sales," *The Billboard* 70, no. 1 (February 24, 1958): 47.

90. Charles Duble, letter to Sverre Braathen, March 26, 1958, Braathen Correspondence Files, SPC, ISU.

91. "Under the Marquee," *The Billboard* 68, no. 6 (February 11, 1956): 51.

92. Grace Killian & M. Antoinette Concello v. Arthur M. Concello, Case 10,967, Cir. Ct. 12th Judicial Circuit, Sarasota County, 557.

93. M. Antoinette Concello v. Arthur M. Concello, Case 10,966, Cir. Ct. 12th Judicial Circuit, Sarasota County, 619.

94. M. Antoinette Concello v. Arthur M. Concello, Case 10,966, 619.

95. Mickey King, interview notes by Steve Gossard, undated, SPC, ISU.

96. "Rockland Oil Co," CWM MSS 36, Rockland Oil, Box 2, "Hodges, Reavis & McGraff, Statement for JRN," CWM.

97. "R-B Board Meets," *The Billboard* 69, no. 2 (June 17, 1957): 76.

98. "$20 Million Circus Mismanagement Suit Filed Against Norths, Concello," *Sarasota News*, 6 September 1957, 1.

99. Concello, letter to Henry Ringling North, June 18, 1958, CWM MSS 36, Concello, Arthur Box 10, Folders 28–29 North, John & Henry, CWM.

100. Merle Evans, letter to Concello, September 20, 1957, CWM MSS 36, Concello, Arthur Papers, Box 10, Folder 18, General, 1957, CWM.

101. Concello, letter to Merle Evans, September 28, 1957, CWM MSS 36, Concello, Arthur Papers, Box 10, Folder 18, General, 1957, CWM.

102. "Ringling Timetable," *The Billboard* 70, no. 9 (March 3, 1958): 62.

103. "Surplus Animals, Equipment to be Sold," *Sarasota Herald-Tribune*, February 25, 1958, 1.

104. Stuart Lancaster, letter dated February 25, 1958, CWM MSS 36, General Files, Box 62, Folder 47, CWM.

105. "Timely Comment," *Sarasota Herald-Tribune*, February 26, 1958, 9.

106. "Concello Denies Norths Willing to Sell Ringling Stock or Winter Quarters," *Tampa Tribune*, February 28, 1958, 12.

107. "North Said Willing to Sell Interest," *Sarasota Herald-Tribune*, February 28, 1958, 3.

108. "Concello Denies Norths" *Tampa Tribune*, 12.

109. Concello, letter to Norths, March 10, 1958, CWM MSS 36, Concello, Arthur Papers, Box 10, Folder 19 General, 1958, CWM.

110. "Wide Action Continues for Ringling, Estate," *The Billboard* 70, no. 12 (March 24, 1958): 77, 82.

111. Ward Cannel, "Big Year for Circuses, Trouble Pursues Big One," *Kenosha (WI) News*, April 3, 1958, 23.

112. Hugh R. Dowling letter to Concello, March 14, 1958, CWM MSS 36, Concello, Arthur Papers, Box 10, Folder 19 General, 1958, CWM.

113. Document from CWM MSS 36, Concello, Arthur Papers, Box 10, Folder 15 General, 1954, CWM.

114. Concello, letter to Fred McKenna, May 1, 1958, CWM MSS 36, Concello, Arthur Papers, Box 10, Folder 19 General, 1958, CWM.

115. Grace Killian, letter to Concello, March 27, 1958, CWM MSS 36, Concello, Arthur, Box 10, Folder 19 General 1958, CWM.

116. "Inside Stuff," *Variety* 210, no. 4 (March 26, 1958): 69.

117. Concello, letter to Grace Killian, March 27, 1958, CWM MSS 36, Concello, Arthur Papers, Box 10, Folder 19 General, 1958, CWM.

118. Concello, letter to Grace Killian, April 28, 1958, CWM MSS 36, Concello, Arthur, Box 10, Folder 19 General, 1958, CWM.

119. Concello, letter to Antoinette Concello, May 29, 1958, CWM MSS 36, Concello, Arthur Papers, Box 10, Folder 19, General, 1958, CWM.

120. "Starlight Musical Names Leading Male Performers," *Indianapolis Star*, June 10, 1958, 22.

121. "Under the Marquee," *The Billboard* 70, no. 27 (July 7, 1958): 46–47.

122. Concello, letter to John Ringling North, July 29, 1958, CWM MSS 36, Concello, Arthur Papers, Box 10, Folder 19 General, 1958, CWM.

123. "Eagles Joins Ringling Show," *The Billboard* 70, no. 45 (November 10, 1958): 53.

124. Concello, letter to John Ringling North, October 14, 1959, CWM MSS 36, Concello, Arthur Papers, Box 10, Folders 28–19 North, John & Henry, CWM.

125. Concello, letter to John Ringling North, October 14, 1959, CWM MSS 36, Concello, Arthur Papers, Box 10, Folders 28–29 North, John & Henry, CWM.

126. Sag Kash, "Hall of Fame Aerial Pixie Once Put Peter Pan to Shame," *Sarasota News*, August 24, 1959, 9.

127. Kash, "Hall of Fame Aerial Pixie," *Sarasota News*, 9.

128. Sag Kash, "Father of Circus Aerialists Recalls Days of Prohibition," *Sarasota News*, November 15, 1959, 34.

129. "Arvida Buys Ringling Properties," *News Tribune* (Fort Pierce, FL), May 18, 1959, Newspapers.com.

130. Concello, letter to John North, October 14, 1959, CWM MSS 36, North, Henry Ringling Papers, CWM.

131. "Ringling's Winter Quarters Purchased by Arvida Corp.," *Palm Beach Post*, November 4, 1959, 20.

132. Concello, letter to John North, October 14, 1959, CWM MSS 36, North, Henry Ringling Papers, CWM.

133. Concello, letter to John Seawell, June 17, 1959, CWM MSS 36, General Files, Box 65, Folder 24 "Perry, Wm," CWM.

134. 1961 Concello Diary, March 18, SPC, ISU.

135. Concello, memo to Bill Perry, November 10, 1959, CWM MSS 36, General Files, Box 65, Folder 25, CWM.

136. "Perry Seeks State Post," *Tampa Bay Times*, January 2, 1940, 13.

137. Bill Perry, letter to Henry North, July 19, 1960, HRN Collection, Box 6, Accordion folder "Northbrook—1960" File "P–Q," SPC, ISU.

138. Concello, letter to Henry North, June 23, 1959, HRN Collection, Box 6, Folder 1, SPC, ISU.

139. Henry North, letter to Concello, July 2, 1959, CWM MSS 36, North, Henry Ringling Papers, CWM.

140. Concello, letter to Tuffy Genders, CWM MSS 36, General Files, Box 60, Folder 20, Genders, Harold, CWM.

141. Concello, letter to Rudy Bundy, CWM MSS 36, General Files, Box 55, Folder 69 Bundy, Rudy, CWM.

142. Concello, letter to Bundy, April 16, 1959, CWM MSS 36, General Folders, Box 55, File 69 Bundy, Rudy, CWM.

143. Concello, letter to Henry North, May 4, 1959, HRN Collection, Box 6, Folder 1, SPC, ISU.

144. Concello, letter to Henry North, May 4, 1959, HRN Collection, Box 6, Folder 1, SPC, ISU. "The circus is a jealous wench . . . She is a ravening hag who sucks your vitality as a vampire drinks blood—who kills the brightest stars in her crown and who will allow no private life to those who serve her; wrecking homes, ruining their bodies, and destroying the happiness of their loved ones by her insatiable demands." Henry Ringling North and Alden Hatch, *Circus Kings*, 11.

145. "Concello to see Europe's Arenas for 2d R-B Unit," *The Billboard* 71, no. 30 (July 27, 1959): 52.

146. John North, letter to Michael Burke, June 12, 1956, CWM MSS 36, General Files, Box 63, Folder 27 Management Corp. of America (Umberto Bedini—Italy), CWM.

147. "Circus Ponders Shifting Winter Home Elsewhere," *Sarasota News*, November 17, 1959, 1.

148. "Mayor Reports on Conference," *Sarasota News*, April 15, 1960, 1.

149. "Venice Site Being Eyed by Ringling," *Sarasota Herald-Tribune*, December 20, 1959, 1.

150. "Circus Days Back as Big Top Train Returns to Venice," *Sarasota News*, November 29, 1960, 16.

151. "Ringling Bros. Sinks Deep Roots in Venice," *Sarasota Herald-Tribune*, December 4, 1960, 17.

152. "At New Home Today, Venice Welcomes Ringling Circus," *Sarasota Herald-Tribune*, November 29, 1960, 1.

153. "Ringling Renews Its Historic Circus Train," *Post-Crescent* (Appleton, WI), October 24, 1960, 40.

154. Al Kuettner, "One of the 'Flying Concellos' Puts Circus Back on Paying Basis," *Shamokin (PA) News-Dispatch*, April 18, 1960, 9.

155. "Circus Back on Rails, Venice Plans Revealed," *Sarasota Herald-Tribune*, January 28, 1960, 4.

156. Kuettner, *Shamokin (PA) News-Dispatch*, 9.

157. "Circus Back on Rails," *Sarasota Herald-Tribune*, 4.

158. "Recap," *Sarasota News*, June 7, 1960, 2.

159. Lewis Rosen, letter to Concello, December 17, 1959, CWM MSS 36, Box 66, General Files, Folder 53 Rosen, Lewis RBB&B Agent, CWM.

160. Lewis Rosen, letter to Concello, December 22, 1959, CWM MSS 36, General Files, Box 66, File 53 Rosen, Lewis RBB&B Agent, CWM.

161. "4 Years Under Roofs, Ringling Circus Now More Solvent than in Decade," *Variety* 218, no. 10 (May 4, 1960): 53.

162. Concello, letter to Lewis Rosen, June 8, 1960, CWM MSS 36, General Files, Box 66, File 53 Rosen, Lewis RBB&B Agent, CWM.

163. C. A. "Red" Sonnenberg, Unpublished manuscript, n.p., SPC, ISU.

164. "Ringling Show in Top Financial Shape as 1960 Tour Moves into Last Half," *Variety* 219, no. 12 (August 17, 1960): 47, 50.

165. Concello, letter to Irvin Feld, June 6, 1960, CWM MSS 36, General Files, Box 69, File 33 Feld, Irvin, CWM.

166. "Shorter N.Y. Run No $ Bar for Ringling Show," *Amusement Business* 74, no. 19 (May 12, 1962): 46.

167. Concello, letter to John Ringling North, April 10, 1960, CWM MSS 36, Concello, Arthur Papers, Box 10, Folder 21 General, 1960, CWM.

168. Parkinson, *Bandwagon*, 22.

169. John Mather, letter to Henry North, August 31, 1960, HRN Collections, Box 6, Folder 74, SPC, ISU.

170. Henry North, letter to Dick Conovor, August 13, 1960, CWM MSS 36 North, Henry Ringling Papers, CWM.

171. John North, letter to Concello, December 10, 1960, CWM MSS 36, Concello, Arthur Papers, Box 10, Folders 28–29 North, John & Henry, CWM.

CHAPTER 8

1. Tom Parkinson, "A 1973 Interview with Art Concello," *Bandwagon* 45, no. 5 (September–October 2001): 24.

2. 1961 Diary, 18 February, Art Concello Diaries, SPC, ISU.

3. Antoinette Concello's Scrapbook, SPC, ISU.

4. Antoinette Concello's Scrapbook, SPC, ISU.

5. 1961 Diary, June 26, Art Concello Diaries, SPC, ISU.

6. 1961 Diary, September 3, Art Concello Diaries.

7. 1961 Diary, February 20, Art Concello Diaries.

8. 1961 Diary, March 20, Art Concello Diaries.

9. 1961 Diary, April 7, Art Concello Diaries.

10. 1961 Diary, October 2, Art Concello Diaries.

11. "Lots of Action for Sailor Circus," *Sarasota Herald-Tribune*, November 7, 1961, 4.

12. "Color Spreads in Comeau Family from Daughters to Father, 101," *Sarasota News*, June 7, 1962, 3.

13. 1961 Diary, December 23, Art Concello Diaries.

14. "Ringling Sues Over Slogan," *New York Times*, April 28, 1960, 27.

15. "Ringling Circus Sues Beatty Over Slogan," *Variety* 220, no. 5 (September 28, 1960): 63.

16. Ringling Bros.-Barnum & Bailey Combined Shows, Inc. v. Acme Circus Operating Co., 12 A.D.2d 894, 1961 N.Y. App. Div. LEXIS 12898 (Supreme Court of New York, Appellate Division, First Department, February 2, 1961), accessed April 19, 2022, https://advance.lexis.com/api/document?collection=cases&id=urn:contentItem:3RRT-37B0-003C-C23G-00000-00&context=1516831.

17. "Trailers to Success," *Amusement Business* 73, no. 13 (April 2, 1961): 30.

18. Gene Plowden, "New Kind of Glamor is Shown by Circus," *Sarasota Herald-Tribune*, January 29, 1962, 13.

19. 1961 Diary, February 25, Art Concello Diaries.

20. "Shorter N.Y. Run No $ Bar for Ringling Show," *Amusement Business* 74, no. 19 (May 12, 1962): 46.

21. Eddie Billetti, letter to Concello from CWM MSS 36, General Files, Box 42, File 4 Hebeler's Shop, Sarasota, FL, Edward S. Hebeler, Eddie Billetti, CWM.

22. 1961 Diary, April 12, Art Concello Diaries.

23. Concello, letter to Belmonte Cristiani, March 22, 1961, CWM MSS 36, Box 13, File "Cuba, Mexico and South America," CWM.

24. "Ringling Details South American Unit," *Amusement Business* 73, no. 5 (February 6, 1961): 7.

25. "Ringling Bros. And Barnum & Bailey Circus, Spring 1961" Bandwagon 8, no. 2 (March–April 1964): 24.

26. William Perry, letter to Richard B. Smith, February 24, 1961, CWM MSS 36, Box 13, File "Cuba, Mexico, S. America," CWM.

27. John Ek, letter to Concello, May 19, 1961 from CWM MSS 36, Box 13, File "Cuba, Mexico, S. America," CWM.

28. 1961 Diary, June 27, Art Concello Diaries.

29. 1961 Diary, June 27, Art Concello Diaries.

30. 1961 Diary, June 29, Art Concello Diaries.

31. 1961 Diary, June 30, Art Concello Diaries.

32. 1961 Diary, June 30, Art Concello Diaries.

33. Memorandum of Understanding, May 9, 1962, CWM MSS 36 Cuba, Mexico, and South America Series, Box 13, File 21, CWM.

34. Milton R. Bass, "Lively Arts," *Berkshire Eagle* (Pittsfield, MA), April 27, 1961, 6.

35. "Popcorn and Popeyes," *Newsweek* 55, no. 15 (April 11, 1960): 35–36.

36. "Letters: Circus Time, Again," *Newsweek* 55, no. 19 (May 9, 1960): 8.

37. "Circus Adds a New Performer—The First Female Press Agent," *Tampa Tribune*, January 20, 1963, 45.

38. "Circus Adds a New Performer," *Tampa Tribune*, 45.

39. "Ringling on ABC-TV," *Amusement Business* 72, no. 2 (January 12, 1963): 25.

40. "Film Stars Arrive in Venice to Begin Circus TV Series," *Tampa Tribune*, January 15, 1963, 11.

41. "Ringling on ABC-TV," *Amusement Business*, 25.

42. "Greatest Show on Earth," *Variety* 232, no. 5 (September 25, 1963): 35.

43. "Circus TV Series Slotted," *Amusement Business* 75, no. 17 (April 27, 1963): 29.

44. "Film Stars Arrive in Venice," *Tampa Tribune*, 11.

45. "Crowds Jam Rehearsals," *Sarasota News*, January 15, 1963, 1.

46. "TV Stars Flying on Circus Trapeze," *Sarasota Herald-Tribune*, October 15, 1963, 15.

47. Jim Peacock, "Canadian-born Woman Has Circus Job," *Ottawa (ON) Citizen*, April 8, 1963, 29.

48. CWM MSS, 36 General Files, Box 60, File 13, "C &G Metals Co," CWM.

49. "Film Stars Arrive in Venice," *Tampa Tribune*, 11.

50. Jack Briggs, "Circus Plugs Venice, U.S.A.," *Sarasota Herald-Tribune*, February 9, 1963, 15.

51. Concello, letter to Tuffy Genders, March 27, 1962, CWM MSS 36 General Files, Box 66, File 38 "Rigging, Aerial," CWM.

52. 1961 Diary, August 23, Art Concello Diaries.

53. Laurie Bishop, "Extravagant Genius Weaves Historical, Circus Magic," *Sarasota Herald-Tribune*, 27 June 1977, 31

54. Bishop, "Extravagant Genius," *Sarasota Herald-Tribune*, 31.

55. Parkinson, *Bandwagon*, 23.

56. Bishop, "Extravagant Genius," *Sarasota Herald-Tribune*, 31.

57. "New Attraction Selects Venice," *Tampa Bay Times*, November 3, 1962, 10.

58. "Morris Chalfen, 72, Impresario, is Dead," *New York Times*, November 6, 1979, D19.

59. "'Holiday on Ice'—to Use Rails," *Amusement Business* 74, no. 46 (November 17, 1962): 7.

60. Jack Briggs, "Holiday on Ice Equipment Is Christened in Ceremony," *Sarasota Herald-Tribune*, June 15, 1963, 13.

61. "2d Ice Show to Use Rails," *Amusement Business* 75, no. 29 (July 20, 1963): 8.

62. "A Surprise Party for Art Concello," *Amusement Business* 73, no. 17 (May 1, 1961): 17.

63. 1961 Diary, April 17, Art Concello Diaries.

64. 1961 Diary, various dates, Art Concello Diaries.

65. 1961 Diary, various dates, Art Concello Diaries.

66. 1961 Diary, October 10–12, Art Concello Diaries.

67. Mayo Clinic Reports on Employees, CWM MSS 36 Concello, Arthur Papers, Box 10, File 21, General, 1960, CWM.

68. Concello, letter to Bob Dover, September 10, 1961, CWM MSS 36 General Files, Box 58, File 52 Dover, Bob Supt. Perf. Personnel—RBB&B, CWM.

69. 1961 Diary, March 30, Art Concello Diaries.

70. Parkinson, *Bandwagon*, 24.

71. 1961 Diary, various dates, Art Concello Diaries.

72. 1961 Diary, March 5, Art Concello Diaries.

73. "G" memo to "Sam," June 11, 1963, AMC Papers, 1930–1982, Box 1, File 18, SPC, ISU.

74. 1961 Diary, May 17, Art Concello Diaries.

75. "Jack Tavlin: Ace of Many Trades," *New York Amsterdam News*, February 2, 1963, 26.

76. 1961 Diary, June 6–7, Art Concello Diaries.

77. Maggie Concello, interview with author, Sarasota, Florida, October 12, 2016.

78. 1961 Diary, 3 July. Author's punctuation retained.

79. Parkinson, *Bandwagon*, 24.

80. 1961 Diary, July 13, Art Concello Diaries.

81. 1961 Diary, July 27, Art Concello Diaries.

82. 1961 Diary, July 20, Art Concello Diaries.

83. 1961 Diary, December 1, Art Concello Diaries.

84. Concello, letter to John North, April 19, 1962, CWM MSS 36, Box 25, Folder 31, CWM.

85. "R-B Plan: A Permanent Show for Europe," *Amusement Business* 75, no. 20 (May 18, 1963): 34.

86. "Ringling Stars Will Go to Russia in Circus Exchange, European Version of Greatest Show also Planned," *Sarasota Herald-Tribune*, May 26, 1963, 12.

87. "R-B Plan," *Amusement Business*, 34.

88. Kathy Marti Sabino, telephone interview with author, October 23, 2019.

89. Marti Sabino, interview, October 23, 2019.

90. "Ringling Stars Will Go," *Sarasota Herald-Tribune*, 77.

91. Jackie LeClaire, interview with Mort Gamble and author, Sarasota, Florida, January 8, 2016.

92. "Promoter Chalfen Hails Circus Swap as Life to Soviet-American Relations," *Variety* 231, no. 6 (July 3, 1963): 51.

93. "Moscow Lauds U.S. Circus," *Amusement Business* 75, no. 29 (July 20, 1963): 23.

94. Advisory Committee on the Arts, US Department of State, International Information and Cultural Series, "Cultural Presentations USA, 1967–1968, Report to the Congress and the Public," volume 98, 7–8.

95. "Nyet to Clowns," *Amusement Business* 75, no. 30 (July 27, 1963): 30.

96. "Moscow Scalpers," *Amusement Business* 75, no. 33 (August 17, 1963): 26.

97. Marti Sabino, interview, October 23, 2019.

98. "R-B Plan," *Amusement Business*, 34.

99. "Route of European Show," July 26, 1963, CWM 36 European Tour 1963–1964, Box 25, File 31, CWM.

100. Marti Sabino, interview, October 23, 2019.

101. Merle Evans, letter to Paul Van Pool, September 25 (no year given), unprocessed Van Pool Collection, CWM.

102. Rudy Bundy, self-interview, circa 1980, CWM Audio 75, https://circus.pastperfectonline.com.

103. Jack Briggs, "Ringling Circus Due Back in Venice on November 26," *Sarasota Herald-Tribune*, October 15, 1963, 15.

104. Bundy, self-interview, circa 1980.

105. Parkinson, *Bandwagon*, 24.

106. Henry North, letter to John North, October 12, 1963 from HRN Collection Box 8, File 98, SPC, ISU.

107. "Ringling Circus Disappoints at Paris Boxoffice," *Variety* 232, no. 9 (October 23, 1963): 53.

108. Documentation, Fred D. Pfening III Collection

109. Morris Chalfen, "Presentation to MSG-ABC Productions, Inc.," Art Concello Papers, 1930–1982, Box 2, File 24b, SPC, ISU.

110. Jack Clary, "Blonde Takes Over Key Position of Pacing Ringling Circus Performance," *Morning Call* (Allentown, PA), April 17, 1963, 31.

111. "R-B Plan," *Amusement Business*, 34.

112. Mae Lyons press release, October 28, 1963 from CWM MSS 26, Caldwell, Paul N., Papers, CWM.

113. Rudy Bundy, memo to Helen Steinwachs, October 28, 1963 from CWM MSS 26, Caldwell, Paul N., Papers, CWM.

114. Chappie Fox report to Bob Parkinson, 8 January 1964 from CWM MSS 34, Box 33 Tom Parkinson Papers, File 2 RBBB Seasons of 1961–1974, CWM.

115. John North, letter to Rudy Bundy, October 27, 1963 from CWM MSS 26, Caldwell, Paul N., Papers, CWM.

116. 1961 Diary, February 16, Art Concello Diaries.

117. Rudy Bundy, memo, October 28, 1963, CWM MSS 26, Caldwell, Paul N., Papers, CWM.

118. Jack Briggs, "No Talk on Circus 'Shakeup'," *Sarasota Herald Tribune*, November 1, 1963, 21.

119. "Ringling Bros. And Barnum & Bailey Circus a Three-ring Click in Paris," *Variety* 232, no. 6 (October 2, 1963): 64.

120. "Art Concello Out as Ringling Chief," *Pantagraph*, November 19, 1963, 8.

121. Mac Steele, letter to Rudy Bundy, November 22, 1963, CWM MSS 26, Caldwell, Paul N., Papers, CWM.

122. Rudy Bundy, memo, October 28, 1963.

123. Noyelles Burkhart, letter to Everett Ritchie, November 20, 1963, Ritchie Correspondence Files, SPC, ISU.

124. 1961 Diary, January 5, 1962, Art Concello Diaries.

125. 1961 Diary, May 12 and April 9 respectively, Art Concello Diaries.

126. Parkinson, *Bandwagon*, 24.

127. Fred D. Pfening III, "Barbara Woodcock: The Last Empress," *White Tops* 94, no. 1 (January–February 2021): 47.

128. "AB Views Late Work at Fair's Circus," *Amusement Business* 76, no. 21 (May 30, 1964): 37.

129. "World's Fair to Have Continental Circus," *Williamsburg News* (Brooklyn, NY), February 9, 1962, 4.

130. "World's Fair Circus to be Ringling-Staffed 1-Ringer," *Amusement Business* 74, no. 7 (February 17, 1962): 7.

131. Jack Briggs, "No Talk on Circus 'Shakeup'," *Sarasota Herald-Tribune*, November 1, 1963, 21.

132. Jack Briggs, "Sarasota Real Estate Man New Ringling Circus Boss," *Sarasota Herald-Tribune*, November 5, 1963, 9.

133. "Ringling to Build Show Plant," *Sarasota Herald-Tribune*, November 3, 1962, 3.

134. "Ringling Stars Will Go," *Sarasota Herald-Tribune*, 34.

135. "New Attraction Selects Venice," *Tampa Bay Times*, 10.

136. "Social Call," *Amusement Business* 75, no. 30 (July 27, 1963): 29.

137. "Ringling Stars Will Go," *Sarasota Herald-Tribune*, 34.

138. "Two U.S. Circuses Head Overseas: Chalfen to USSR; Ringling to Europe," *Variety* 230, no. 6 (April 3, 1963): 95.

139. "Ringling Circus Fires Art Concello," *Variety* 232, no. 12 (November 13, 1963): 58.

140. "Gross for Moscow Circus Tops $1.5 Million in U.S." *Amusement Business* 75, no. 52 (December 28, 1963): 74.

141. "Art Concello Sues Circus for Wages, Cash Advances," *Sarasota Herald Tribune*, January 14, 1964, 15.

142. "Art Concello Sues Circus for Wages, Cash Advances," *Sarasota Herald-Tribune*, January 14, 1964, 77.

143. Parkinson, *Bandwagon*, 25.

CHAPTER 9

1. "The Plainsman," *Lubbock Avalanche-Journal*, May 31, 1972, 9.

2. Dean Jensen, "Antoinette Concello: Circus Legend," *Milwaukee Sentinel*, August 29, 1980, 52.

3. John North, telegram to Pat Valdo, October 23, 1963, CWM MSS 26, Caldwell, Paul N., Papers, CWM.

4. Helen Griffith, "Discotheque is Becoming Popular Word," *Sarasota Herald-Tribune*, December 11, 1964, 30.

5. Charlie Briggs, "International Flavored Circus Premiers for New College," *Tampa Tribune*, January 8, 1965, 34.

6. Jack Briggs, "Queen of Trapeze Returns as a Coach," *Sarasota Herald-Tribune*, December 13, 1963, 13.

7. Wilma Higginbotham, "Talented Backstage Workers Have Spent Lives with Circus," *Charleston (WV) Daily Mail*, February 25, 1966, 12.

8. "No Weight Problem for Busy Mrs. Concello," *Redlands (CA) Daily Facts*, May 9, 1966, 9.

9. Donna Skura, private message to author, March 3, 2021.

10. John Culhane, "Trapeze: The Quest for the 'Impossible' Quadruple Somersault," *New York Times*, March 19, 1978, SM6.

11. "No Weight Problem," *Redlands Daily Facts*, 9.

12. "Lady of Triple Can Still Fly," *Decatur (IL) Herald*, May 21, 1979, 2.

13. Joan Cook, "Ex-Circus Aerialist, Filling In, Goes Aloft Again," *New York Times*, April 1, 1967, 33.

14. Bank check dated 11/30/66. Bundy Collection, Fred D. Pfening III Collection.

15. Jack Briggs, "Problems Attacked as Circus Readies," *Sarasota Herald-Tribune*, December 12, 1967, 16.

16. "Cuisine Now Aerial Director's Fame," *Tennessean* (Nashville, TN), June 19, 1969, 44.

17. Mary Ann Lee, "Former Aerialist with No Regrets," *St. Louis Globe-Democrat*, August 30, 1967, 10D.

18. Higginbotham, *Charleston Daily Mail*, 12.

19. Tom Parkinson, "A 1973 Interview with Art Concello," *Bandwagon* 45, no. 5 (September–October 2001): 26.

20. "Concello on Beatty Team," *Amusement Business* 75, no. 5 (February 5, 1966): 30.

21. "Beatty-Cole Seat Wagons: Time Savers," *Amusement Business* 79, no. 1 (January 14, 1967): 33.

22. Lane Talburt, "John Pugh, Part III: A Lifetime with the Circus," *Bandwagon* 66, no. 1 (January–March 2022): 84.

23. "Beatty Eyes Bldg. Dates After L.I. Success," *Amusement Business* 78, no. 17 (April 30, 1966): 28.

24. Talburt, *Bandwagon*, 86.

25. "Circus Leader's Interests," *Miami News*, August 29, 1966, 5.

26. Talburt, *Bandwagon*, 88.

27. "ACME Revamps, Concello Out of 3 Shows," *Amusement Business* 78, no. 36 (September 10, 1966): 22.

28. Parkinson, *Bandwagon*, 26.

29. Morris Chalfen, "Presentation to MSG-ABC Productions, Inc.," Art Concello Papers, 1930–1982, Box 2, File 24b, SPC, ISU.

30. "Concello Joins Holiday on Ice," *Variety* 246, no. 5 (March 22, 1967): 70.

31. Dora Walters, "Circus Billed to Perform in Soviet Ring," *Tampa Bay Times* (St. Petersburg, FL), July 19, 1967, 38.

32. "U.S. Circus Leaves for Russia Tour," *Springfield (MO) News-Leader*, August 7, 1967, 18.

33. "U.S. Circus: Off to Russia," *Amusement Business* 79, no. 32 (August 19, 1967): 25.

34. "American Circus Opens Tour of Russian Cities," *Asbury (NJ) Park Press*, August 12, 1967, 6.

35. Advisory Committee on the Arts, US Department of State, International Information and Cultural Series, "Cultural Presentations USA, 1967–1968," Report to the Congress and the Public, volume 98, 7–8.

36. Parkinson, *Bandwagon*, 25.

37. Allen Bloom told Fred D. Pfening III this story. Fred D. Pfening III, interview with author, March 28, 2020.

38. Frank Starr, "Muscovites Cheer a Circus from the U.S.," *Chicago Tribune*, August 12, 1967, D12.

39. "Moscow's U.S. Show Told," *Amusement Business* 79, no. 33 (August 26, 1967): 28.

40. "Circus Scene: Looking Ahead to 1968," *Amusement Business* 79, no. 50 (December 23, 1967): 26.

41. "Soviet Circus Stars," *Amusement Business* 79, no. 42 (October 28, 1967): 22–23.

42. "Thrill Circus, 1969 Tour?," *Amusement Business* 80, no. 33 (August 29, 1968): 7.

43. "Zero Hour AGVA Pact Greenlights 'Thrill Circus'," *Variety* 251, no. 12 (August 7, 1968): 49.

44. "Circus Producers Form Assn. to Combat AGVA's 'Unrealistic' Pay Demands," *Variety* 251, no. 11 (July 31, 1968): 50.

45. 1961 Diary, April 28, September 28, Art Concello Diaries, SPC, ISU.

46. Joe Cohen, "See 'Thrill Circus' as Forerunner of New MSG Outdoor Amusement," *Variety* 251, no. 12 (August 7, 1968): 51.

47. "MSG to Promote Own 'Thrill' Show at Shea Stadium," *Variety* 251, no. 6 (June 26, 1968): 48.

48. "Shea Stadium Thrill Circus 'Pilot' for Possible Tour," *Amusement Business* 80, no. 26 (July 6, 1968): 25.

49. "Thrill Circus, 1969 Tour?," *Amusement Business*, 7.

50. Merle Evans, letter to Bob Good, October 23, 1971, Fred D. Pfening III Collection.

51. Evans, letter to Good, October 23, 1971.

52. C. A. Sonnenberg, letter to Tom Parkinson, February 8, 1971, CWM MSS 34 Parkinson, Thomas P. Papers, Box 13 Correspondence, File 29, "Sonnenberg, C. A.," CWM.

53. "Jackpots," *Amusement Business* 83, no. 26 (July 3, 1971): 31.

54. Evans, letter to Good, October 23, 1971.

55. "Jackpots," *Amusement Business* 84, no. 33 (August 12, 1972): 29.

56. Maggie Concello, interview with author, Sarasota, Florida, October 12, 2016.

57. C. A. Sonnenberg letter to Tom Parkinson, March 10, 1970, CWM MSS 34 Parkinson, Thomas P. Papers, Box 13, File 29, "Sonnenberg, C. A.," CWM.

58. Maggie Concello, interview with author, January 24, 2014.

59. Bruce Montgomery, "City to Hear Request for Taxicab Fare Hike," *Sarasota Herald-Tribune*, July 8, 1974, 13.

60. "B & C Oil Co," accessed September 9, 2020, https://search.sunbiz.org/Inquiry/CorporationSearch/SearchResultDetail?inquirytype=EntityName&directionType=Initial&searchNameOrder=BCOIL%203938700&aggregateId=domp-393870-2063cfcd-f70b-4e17-bde4-931f69b69023&searchTerm=b%20and%20c%20oil&listNameOrder=BCOIL%203938700.

61. John Dietz, "Reward Fund May be Established in Murder Case," *Sarasota Herald-Tribune*, April 21, 1975, 25.

62. Maggie Concello, interview, October 12, 2016.

63. Merle Evans, letter to Bob Good, July 26, 1972, Fred D. Pfening III Collection.

64. Mickey King, interview by Steve Gossard, no date, Audio File: GOS_Mickey_King_1_a_Streaming.mp3, Special Collections, Milner Library, ISU.

65. Maggie Concello, interview, October 12, 2016.

66. Maggie Concello, interview, October 12, 2016.

67. "Airport Authority to Try for New Rates Deals," *Sarasota Herald-Tribune*, January 30, 1975, 68.

68. "U.S. Tour Set," *Circus Report* 8, no. 7 (February 12, 1979): 1.

69. "Circus Year in Review," *Bandwagon* 24, no. 1 (January–February 1980): 18.

70. "News of Record—Suits Filed," *Sarasota Herald-Tribune*, February 28, 1980, 16.

71. "Nortart, Inc," accessed on April 17, 2020, https://icons.corp.delaware.gov/entitysearch/NameSearch.aspx.

72. 1981 Diary, September 30, Art Concello Diaries, SPC, ISU.

73. Norma Fox, interview with Mort Gamble and author, Sarasota, Florida, January 7, 2016.

74. 1981 Diary, various dates, Art Concello Diaries.

75. 1981 Diary, March 6, Art Concello Diaries.

76. 1981 Diary, June 4, Art Concello Diaries.

77. Merle Evans, letter to Mari Jo Couls, November 18, 1983, Fred D. Pfening III Collection.

78. Willie Edelston, interview with Mort Gamble and author, Sarasota, Florida, January 7, 2016.

79. June Simpson, "It's Still the Circus Life for Them," *Pantagraph*, September 20, 1969, 5.

80. C. A. Sonnenberg, unpublished manuscript, SPC, ISU.

81. Warranty Deed, August 3, 1965, McLean County (IL) Records.

82. Tom Parkinson, letter to C. P. Fox, October 12, 1965, CWM MSS 34, Parkinson, Thomas P Papers, Box 11 Folder 81.

83. Tom Parkinson, letter to C. P. Fox, October 12, 1965.

84. Kathy Clarey, "Circus Housemother: The Public Wants to See Youth," *Fresno Bee*, September 4, 1973, 10.

85. "Lady of Triple" *Decatur Herald*, 2.

86. Dorothy Stanich, "Color Spreads in Comeau Family from Daughters to Father, 101," *Sarasota News*, June 7, 1962, 3.

87. "For 30 Years, the Girl on the Flying Trapeze," *Tallahassee Democrat*, July 26, 1973, 6.

88. "Sequin-clad Showgirls Tell How They Keep Thin," *Van Nuys Valley News and Green Sheet*, August 1, 1976, 25.

89. Mary Jane Miller, interview with Mort Gamble and author, Sarasota, Florida, January 11, 2016.

90. "For 30 Years, the Girl on the Flying Trapeze," *Tallahassee Democrat*, July 26, 1973, 6.

91. Culhane, "Trapeze," *New York Times*, SM6.

92. "The Plainsman," *Lubbock Avalanche-Journal*, 9.

93. Patricia Leeds, "At 70, She Still Flies High with Circus," *Chicago Tribune*, November 11, 1981, C1.

94. "Cuisine Now Aerial Director's Fame," *Tennessean*, 44.

95. Terry Goodrich, "Circus Star Recalls Her Life as Swinger," *American Statesman* (Austin, TX), August 1, 1982, B1.

96. "For 30 Years," *Tallahassee Democrat*, 6.

97. Jensen, "Antoinette Concello, Circus Legend," 52.

98. Goodrich, "Circus Star Recalls," *American Statesman*, B1.

99. Jensen, "Antoinette Concello, Circus Legend," 52.

100. 1961 Diary, May 24, Art Concello Diaries.

101. Leeds, "At 70, She Still Flies," *Chicago Tribune*, C1.

102. Clarey, "Circus Housemother," *Fresno Bee*, 10.

103. "Billy Barton," *Circus Report* 6, no. 30 (July 25, 1977): 5.

104. Beverly Mills, "Spinning to Fame on a Flying Trapeze," *News and Observer* (Raleigh, NC), February 20, 1983, 125.

105. Gene Plowden, letter to Randy Concello, December 4, 1983, Art Concello Papers, 1930–1982, "Plowden–Concello, Antoinette Concello, 1983," SPC, ISU.

106. Gene Plowden, letter to Randy Concello, December 4, 1983.

107. Merle Evans, letter to Mari Jo Couls, January 23, 1984, Fred D. Pfening III Collection.

108. 1984 Diary, February 4, Art Concello Diaries, SPC, ISU.

109. 1984 Diary, February 5, Art Concello Diaries, SPC, ISU.

110. 1984 Diary, February 9, Art Concello Diaries.

111. Martha Sullivan, "Trapeze Queen Concello Dead," *Pantagraph*, February 8, 1984, 4.

CHAPTER 10

1. "Mike Todd: He Lost a Racetrack on a Horse," *Amusement Business* 85, no. 49, December 8, 1973, 26.

2. Tom Parkinson, "A 1973 Interview with Art Concello," *Bandwagon* 45, no. 5 (September–October 2001): 26.

3. Sarasota County Appraiser records, accessed on July 1, 2020, https://www.sc-pa.com.

4. Maggie Concello, interview with author, Sarasota, Florida, October 12, 2016.

5. Dorothy Stockbridge, "Flying Family Upholds Circus City Image," *Sarasota Journal*, January 6, 1977, 49.

6. Noyelles Burkhart, letter to Everett Ritchie, January 15, 1973, Ritchie Correspondence Collection, SPC, ISU.

7. "Circus Milestones: Marion B. Siefert," *White Tops* 47, no. 6 (November 30, 1974): 69.

8. Maggie Concello, interview, October 12, 2016.

9. Merle Evans, letter to Mari Jo Couls, October 12, 1983, Fred D. Pfening III Collection.

10. Merle Evans, letter to Mari Jo Couls, April 8, 1984, Fred D. Pfening III Collections.

11. 1984 Diary, May 30, Art Concello Diaries, SPC, ISU.

12. Bill Piltz, telephone interview with author, June 9, 2021.

13. Mickey King, interview by Steve Gossard, no date, Audio File: GOS_Mickey_King_1_a_Streaming.mp3, SPC, ISU.

14. 1984 Diary, July 2, Art Concello Diaries.

15. 1984 Diary, May 15, Art Concello Diaries.

16. Mary Jane Miller, interview with Mort Gamble and author, Sarasota, Florida, January 11, 2016.

17. Maggie Concello, interview, October 12, 2016.

18. Maggie Concello, interview, October 12, 2016.

19. 1984 Diary, September 25, Art Concello Diaries.

20. Merle Evans, letter to Evelyn Cook, July 29, 1985, Fred D. Pfening III Collection.

21. Concello, letter to Jack Voise, August 16, 1986, Harold and Eileen Voise Papers, 1941–2010, SPC, ISU.

22. Concello, letter to Jack Voise, August 16, 1986.

23. Concello, letter to Jack Voise, August 16, 1986.

24. Maggie Concello, interview, October 12, 2016.

25. Maggie Concello, interview, October 12, 2016.

26. Maggie Concello, interview, January 15, 2016.

27. Maggie Concello, interview, January 15, 2016.

28. 1984 Diary, various dates, Art Concello Diaries.

29. Miller, interview, January 11, 2016.

30. Norma Fox, interview with Mort Gamble and author, Sarasota, Florida, January 7, 2016.

31. Piltz, interview, June 9, 2021.

32. "Central Illinois Deaths: Joseph F. Killian," *Pantagraph*, December 10, 1989, 19.

33. Piltz, interview, June 9, 2021.

34. "Arthur Concello," *Times* (London), July 19, 2001, 21.

35. "Obituaries: Arthur Concello," *Sydney Morning Herald*, July 26, 2001, 32.

36. "Obituaries: Arthur Concello," *Daily Telegraph* (London), July 12, 2001, accessed on July 16, 2020, https://advance.lexis.com/api/document?collection=news&id=urn:contentItem :43GG-KRD0-010F-T3YT-00000-00&context=1516831.

37. Bill Flick, "On to the 'Big' Top," *Pantagraph*, July 22, 2001, 33.

38. Maggie Concello, interview, October 12, 2016.

Selected Bibliography

Archival Collections

Circus World Museum, Robert L. Parkinson Library & Research Center, Baraboo, WI.

Special Collections, Circus & Allied Arts Collection, Milner Library, Illinois State University. Normal, IL.

Books and Journal Articles

Beal, George Brinton. *Through the Back Door of the Circus with George Brinton Beal*. Springfield, MA: McLoughlin Bros., Inc., 1938.

Hammarstrom, David Lewis. *Behind the Big Top*. South Brunswick, NJ: A.S. Barnes, 1980.

———. *Big Top Boss: John Ringling North and the Circus*. Urbana: University of Illinois Press, 1992.

McKennon, Joe. *Circus Lingo*. Sarasota, FL: Carnival Publishers of Sarasota, 1980.

North, Henry Ringling and Alden Hatch. *The Circus Kings: Our Ringling Family Story*. Garden City, NY: Doubleday, 1960.

Parkinson, Tom. "A 1973 Interview with Art Concello." *Bandwagon* 45, no. 5 (September–October 2001).

Pilgrim, Alastair. *The Fundamentals of Flying Trapeze*. United Kingdom: Red Hands Pub., 2012.

Taylor, Robert Lewis. *Center Ring: The People of the Circus*. Garden City, NY: Doubleday, 1956.

Index

About the Author

Maureen Brunsdale was born and raised in North Dakota. She grew up on the family farm north of Fargo, where her curiosity was both stoked and given free rein. After attending St. Olaf College, Maureen obtained master's degrees at the University of Iowa and the University of South Dakota. Eventually (and kind of by accident), she landed what she calls "the best job on campus" in Special Collections at Illinois State University's Milner Library. There, she oversees four collections—none more unique, colorful, and engaging than the one focusing on the circus and its allied arts. Her passion for learning shines through the prism of the circus, whose people, customs, practices, and history are every bit as endearing as those she encountered on the farm!

CPSIA information can be obtained
at www.ICGtesting.com
Printed in the USA
BVHW041942150623
666020BV00001B/11

9 781538 172100